# Buddhism in Contemporary World

# Buddhism in Contemporary World

Dr. I.N. Singh

PRASHANT PUBLISHING HOUSE
DELHI-110094

*Published by :*
**Prashant Publishing House**
C-34, 28 Foota Road, Gali-3,
West Karwal Nagar, Delhi-110094
Phone : 011-22963970, Mob. : 9810396373
e-mail.: prashantpublishinghouse@gmail.com

**Buddhism in Contemporary World**

*First Published 2018*

**ISBN** 978-81-937193-1-2



---

**PRINTED IN INDIA**
Published by Mr. R.K. Jha M/s Prashant Publishing House and Published at H.S. Offset House Press, Delhi.

# Contents

# Preface

Buddhism has adapted to rapid economic, social, cultural and political transformations in the modern, post-modern and globalized world. Since its inception in India in the sixth century BC, Buddhism spread, first throughout Asia, and then globally in the nineteenth and twentieth centuries.

The history of Buddhism in India, which lasted about 1500 years, can be divided into 500 year periods, during which distinctive forms of Buddhism emerged. This is an idealized and schematic picture, but it is convenient, and it can be matched up with where Buddhism spread during these periods and what forms of Buddhism became dominant there. Buddhist doctrine and practice in the earliest period were agreed upon in a series of Councils, sometimes reckoned to be three, or four.

Buddhism has shown a remarkable flexibility and an ability to co-exist with a variety of social structures as it spread not only to farming and herding societies, but also to highly complex Asian and Western urban centers.

Buddhism appeals very much to the modern world because it is reasonable and scientifically based. Buddha said, "Do not believe in anything that I say just out of respect for me, but test it for yourself, analyze it, as if you were buying gold." Modern-day people like such a non-dogmatic approach.

There are many dialogues between scientists and Buddhist leaders, such as His Holiness the Dalai Lama. Together they are discussing and investigating what is reality. Buddha said that all problems come from not understanding reality, from being confused in this regard. If we were aware of who we are and how the world and we exist, we would not create problems out of our confusion. Buddhism has an extremely open attitude in examining what is true. For example, His Holiness the Dalai Lama has said that if scientists can prove that something Buddha or his followers taught is incorrect or just superstition, he would be happy and willing to drop it from Buddhism. Such an approach is very attractive to Western people.

In the West, the popularity of Buddhism was inspired by the academic study of Asian religions, the romanticism of Orientalism, the Beat-generation of the 1950s, the hippies of the 1960s and the contemporary New Age-movement – as well as by Asian migration to the West. Buddhists work, not only for world peace, but also for increased social engagement, ecological awareness and gender equality.

This is a reference book. All the matter is just compiled and edited in nature, taken from the various sources which are in public domain.

The book deals with Buddhism in view of what ails the modern world today. The threat of global nuclear destruction is a real possibility. What a mess the human race has landed itself in! The progress of science and technology has brought many comforts and luxuries to mankind, but at the same time, it has also endangered the human species because of nuclear war weapons, if used, there will be no escape from the destruction far and wide.

*—Editor*

# 1

# Introduction

It seems to be very appropriate and even necessary at the outset to draw a well-defined line of demarcation between what is understood as Hinayana Buddhism and what is known as Mahayana Buddhism. Most people imagine that there is only one school of Buddhism and that one school is no other than the Buddhism they have learned from the Buddhist books written or compiled or translated by Western Orientalists--Orientalists who are in many respects prejudiced against the doctrine which they propose to study most impartially. Owing to these unhappy circumstances, the outsiders are either generally ignorant or altogether misinformed of the true character of Buddhism. For what is understood by the Western people as Buddhism is no more than-one of its main divisions, which only partially expresses the spirit of its founder.

I said here "divisions," but it may be more proper to say "stages of development." For Buddhism, like so many other religions, has gone through several stages of development before it has attained the present state of perfection among the Oriental nations. And it will be evident to you that if we catch only a glimpse of an object and try to judge the whole from this transient impression, we place ourselves in a most awkward position, and shall be at a loss how to extricate ourselves from it. Therefore, let me try in the beginning to take a comprehensive view of the subject we here propose to expound.

Properly speaking, Hinayana Buddhism is a phase of Mahayana Buddhism. The former is preparatory for the latter.

It is not final, but merely a stepping stone which leads the walker to the hall of perfect truth. Hinayanism is therefore more or less pessimistic, ascetic, ethical (to be distinguished from religious), and monastical. It fails to give a complete satisfaction to a man's religious yearnings. It does not fully interpret the spirit of Buddha.

The Buddhism now, prevailing in Ceylon, Burma, and Siam may be considered to be betraying in a certain way a Hinayana tendency. The Buddhism of present Japan, on the other hand, is Mahayanistic. It is more comprehensive, more religious, more humanistic, and more satisfying to the innermost needs of the religious consciousness. It cannot be said to be absolutely free from superstition, error, prejudice, etc., for it is a constantly growing, ever-living faith which knows no ossification or fossilization. Some pious people are apt to consider their religious belief to be absolutely fixed and unchanging since the dawn of human consciousness; but they have forgotten, in my opinion, the fact that the human mind is still keeping on unfolding itself, that it has not yet exhausted all its possibilities, that it is constantly coming to a clearer consciousness as to its own nature, origin, and destiny. But what I firmly believe is that in the Buddhism of Japan today are epitomized all the essential results reached through the unfolding of the religious consciousness during the past twenty or thirty centuries of Oriental culture.

In a word, what has been known in the West as the teaching of Buddha does not represent it in its true, unadulterated colour, for it is Hinayanistic in tendency; that is, it is exclusive and not comprehensive, narrow and limited, and not all absorbing and assimilating. What I propose to expound in this lecture tonight is the Mahayana Buddhism, so called by Buddhist scholars of the East.

Let me point out in this connection what is most characteristic of Buddhism as distinguished from any other religion. I refer to a predominant tendency of Buddhism toward intellectuality, and it seems to me that the reason why Buddhism is always ready to stand before the tribunal of science and let her pass a judgment upon its merits or demerits is due to this intellectual tenor. It goes without saying that the intellect does not constitute the most essential element of religion, but we must not forget that a religious system too much given up to sentimentalism (understanding it in its purely psychological sense) is generally prone to accede to unwarranted mysticism, ignoring altogether the legitimate claim of the intellect. Buddhism is fortunately saved from this grievous blunder, and always endeavours not to give a free rein to the wantonness of imagination and the irrationality of affection. Love without enlightenment excludes, discriminates, and contradicts itself. Love is not love unless it is purified in the mill of spiritual insight and intellectual discrimination.

What are, then, the fundamental teachings of Buddhism? I deem it best to consider it from two standpoints, ethical and philosophical, or practical and speculative, or affective and intellectual. The philosophical or speculative is preparative for the ethical or practical, for religion is not a system of metaphysics which plays with verbalism and delights in sophistry, but its aim is pre-eminently practical and spiritual. It must bear fruit in this our everyday life.

To begin with the metaphysical side of Buddhism:

(1) We Buddhists believe that as far as phenomenality goes, things that exist are all separate and discrete, they are subject to the law of individuation and therefore to that of limitation also. All particular things exist in time and space and move according to the law of cause and effect, not only physically but morally. Buddhism does not, though sometimes understood by Western people to do so, advocate the doctrine of emptiness or annihilation. It most assuredly recognizes the multitudinousness and reality of phenomena. This world as it is, is real, not void. This life as we live it, is true, and not a dream.

(2) We Buddhists believe that all these particular things surrounding us come from one ultimate source which is all-powerful, all-knowing, and all-loving. The world is the expression or manifestation of this reason or spirit or life, whatever you may designate it. However diverse, therefore, things are, they all partake of the nature of the ultimate

being. Not only sentient beings, but non-sentient beings, reflect the glory of the Original Reason. Not only man but even the lower animals and inorganic substances manifest the divinity of their source. To use the Christian term, God, it 1 is visible and audible not only in one of its highest manifestations, whom Christians call Jesus Christ, but also in the meanest and most insignificant piece of stone lying in a deserted field. God's splendour is seen not only in the Biblical lilies, but also in the mud and mire from which they grow. The melody of divine reason is heard not only in the singing of a bird or in the composition of an inspired musician, but also in the "slums of life" as Emerson phrases it.

(3) This recognition of the oneness of things naturally leads to our third belief, that the one is the many and the many is the one. God does not dwell in the heavens. It does not direct its affairs in a closed office situated somewhere outside this world. It did not create heaven and earth out of nothingness. According to Buddhism, it is a serious error to seek God outside this life, outside this universe. It is living right among ourselves and directing the course of things according to its innate destiny. Though Buddhists refuse to have God walk out of us, they do not identify it with the totality of existence, they are not willing to cast their lot with pantheists so called. God is immanent, surely enough, but it is greater than the totality of things. For the world may pass away, the universe may be shaken out of its foundation, but God will remain and will create a new system out of the former ruins. The ashes of existence will never be scattered to the winds, but they will gather themselves in the ever designing hand of God and build themselves up to a new order of things, in which it is ever shining with its serene radiance.

To sum up the first part of this discourse, what may be called the metaphysical phase of Buddhism is to recognize (1) the reality of the phenomenal world, (2) the existence of one ultimate reason, and (3) the immanence of this reason in the universe.

Now to come to the practical side of Buddhism: The aim of Buddhism, to state it briefly, is to dispel the clouds of ignorance and to make shine the sun of enlightenment. We are selfish because we are ignorant as to the nature of self. We are addicted to the gratification of the passions, because we are ignorant as to the destiny of humanity. We are quarrelsome and want to make ourselves powerful and predominant at the expense of our fellow-beings, because we are ignorant of the ultimate reason of the universe. Buddhists do not recognize any original sin, but acknowledge the existence of ignorance, and insist on its total removal as the surest means of salvation. Let us, therefore, all be enlightened as to the statement made before. Let us know that we are all one in the reason of the universe, that the phenomenal world is real only to the extent it manifests reason, that egoism has no absolute sway in this life, for it destroys itself when it tries to preserve itself through its arrogant assertion, and that perfect peace is only attained when I recognize myself in you and you in me. Let us all be enlightened as to these things, and our ignorance and egoism are forever departed; the wall that divides is destroyed, and there is nothing which prevents us from loving Our enemies; and the source of divine love is open in our hearts, the eternal current of sympathy has now found its unobstructed path. This is the reason why Buddhism is called the religion of enlightenment.

Now that we stand on this eminence of religious sanctity, we know what Buddhist practical faith is. It is threefold: W to cease from wrong-doing, (2) to promote goodness, and (3) to enlighten the ignorant. Buddhist ethics is the simplest thing to Practise in the world. It has nothing mysterious, nothing superstitious, nothing idolatrous, nothing supernatural. Stop doing anything wrong, which is against the reason of things; do whatever is good, which advances the course of reason in this life; and finally help those who are still behind and weary of life to realize enlightenment: and here is Buddhism in a nutshell. It has nothing to do with prayer and worship and singing and what not. Our simple everyday life of love and sympathy is all that is needed to be a good Buddhist. I was once asked whether there was such a thing as religious life particularly. To which my answer was simple enough: "Attend to Your daily business, do all you can for the promotion of goodness in this world, and out of fullness of heart help your fellow-beings to gain the path of enlightenment. Outside of this there cannot be anything to be specially called a religious life."

In the latter part of the T'ang Dynasty in China, there was a famous poet-statesman who is known in Japanese as Hak-Rak-Ten. He learned that there resided in his district a Buddhist monk greatly noted for his saintly life and scholarly learning. The governor went to see him, intending to discuss some deeply religious topics. As soon as he was ushered into the pretence of the monk, he inquired what was thought by the saint to be the most fundamental teaching of Buddhism. The monk immediately replied that it is the teaching of all enlightened ones to cease doing anything evil, to promote goodness, and to purify one's own heart.

Hak-Rak-Ten was nonplused to receive such a commonplace instruction from the mouth of such a scholarly personage professing the faith of Buddha; for he secretly expected to have something highly metaphysical and profoundly speculative, which would naturally lead them to further philosophizing and contentless abstraction. The poet-statesman therefore retorted: "This is what every child of three summers is familiar with. I desire on the other hand what is most abstruse, most essential, most vital in Buddhism." The monk, however, coldly replied: "Every child of three summers may know what I said now, but even a silvery-haired man of eighty winters finds it difficult to put the Buddhist instruction into the practice of everyday life."

And it is said that thereupon the Governor reverentially bowed and went home wiser. What is philosophical in Buddhism is no more than a preliminary step toward what is practical in it. Every religion, if it deserves the name, must be essentially practical and conducive to the promotion of the general welfare and to the realization of Reason. Though intellectualism is one of the most characteristic features of Buddhism, making it so distinct from any other religious system, it never forgets the fact that our religious consciousness ever demands something concrete, that which is visible to our senses, that which is observable in our everyday life. Religion does not necessarily consist in talking on such subjects as the continuation after death of individual personality, original sin committed by some mythical personages, the last judgment to be given by an unknown quantity, a special historical revelation which takes place in a congested brain, and what not. At least, practical Buddhism does not trouble itself with solving these problems through speculation or imagination or sophistry. Let those theologians who delight in abstraction and supernaturalism discuss them to their hearts' content, for that is their profession. We, plain ordinary Buddhists, will keep on removing selfishness, seeking the light that is everywhere, practising lovingkindness that does not contradict or discriminate. Says an ancient sage, "The Way is near, and thou seekest it afar." Why, then, shall we ever attempt to walk away from the path which extends right in front of us, so wide and well paved?

## HISTORY OF BUDDHISM IN INDIA

Buddhism is a Dharmic religion originating in ancient India. A brief history of major events regarding the history of Buddhism in India is given below.

### Siddhartha Gautama

Siddhartha Gautama was the historical founder of Buddhism. Siddhartha Gautama was born as a Kshatriya prince in ancient India.

After asceticism and meditation, Siddhartha Gautama discovered the Buddhist Middle Way—a path of moderation away from the extremes of self-indulgence and self-mortification. Siddhartha Gautama attained enlightenment sitting under a pipal tree, now known as the Bodhi tree in Bodh Gaya. Gautama, from then on, was known as "The Perfectly Self-Awakened One", the Samyaksambuddha.

Buddha found patronage in the ruler of Magadha, emperor Bimbisara. The emperor accepted Buddhism as personal faith and allowed the establishment of many Buddhist "Viharas". This eventually led to the renaming of the entire reigon as Bihar. At the Deer Park near Varanasi in northern India, Buddha set in motion the Wheel of Dharma by delivering his first sermon to the group of five companions with whom he had previously sought enlightenment. They, together with the Buddha, formed the first saegha, the company of Buddhist monks, and hence, the first formation of Triple Gem (Buddha, Dharma and Sangha) was completed.

## BUDDHIST MOVEMENTS

Many movements emerged during the next 400 years following Buddha's passing: first the schools of Nikaya Buddhism, of which only Theravada remains today, and then the formation of Mahayana, a pan-Buddhist movement based on the acceptance of new scriptures.

### Ashoka

Emperor Ashoka the Great (304 BC–232 BC) was the ruler of the Maurya Empire in present-day eastern India from 273 BC to 232 BC. Ashoka reigned over most of India after a series of military campaigns. Emperor Ashoka's kingdom streched from South Asia and beyond, from present-day Afghanistan and parts of Persia in the west, to Bengal and Assam in the east, and as far south as Mysore.

According to legend, emperor Ashoka was overwhelmed by guilt after the conquest of Kalinga, following which he accepted Buddhism as personal faith with the help of his Brahmin mentors Radhasvami and Manjushri. Ashoka established monuments marking several significant sites in the life of Shakyamuni Buddha, and according to Buddhist tradition was closely involved in the preservation and transmission of Buddhism. He used his position to propagate the relatively new philosophy to new heights, as far as ancient Rome and Egypt.

### Dharma Masters

Indian shramanas propogated Buddhism in reigons, including China, Vietnam and Central Asia.

The Indian dhyana master Buddhabhadra was the founding abbot and patriarch of the Shaolin Temple. Buddhist monk and esoteric master from North India (6th Century CE), Bodhiruci is regarded as the patriarch of the Ti-Lun school. Bodhidharma (c. 6th century CE) was the Buddhist monk traditionally credited as the founder of Chan (Zen) Buddhism in China.

In 580, an Indian monk named Vinitaruci travelled to Vietnam after completing his studies with Sengcan, the third patriarch of Chinese Zen. This, then, would be the first appearance of Vietnamese Zen, or Thien Buddhism.

The Yogacara texts were composed in the period of Buddhism known to practitioners as The Third Turning of the Wheel. The Yogacara studies texts form a survey of all of The Three Turnings of the Wheel of Dharma.

Originating around a set of scriptures and treatises composed by such early Indian masters as the brothers Vasubandhu and Asanga (who was said to be inspired by the legendary Maitreya-natha), this school held a prominent position in the Indian scholastic tradition for several centuries. It was also transmitted to Tibet by Dharmarakshita who intiated Atisha into the Yogachara lineage, where its teachings became an integral part of much of Tibetan Buddhism up to modern times, and to East Asia, where it was studied with intensity for several centuries.

Padmasambhava, in Sanskrit meaning *"lotus-born"*, is said to have brought Tantric Buddhism to Tibet in the 8th century. In Bhutan and Tibet he is better known as "Guru Rinpoche" ("Precious Master") where followers of the Nyingma school regard him as the second Buddha.

## Decline of Buddhism in India

Buddhism declined in India following the loss of patronage due to the fall of sympathetic kingdoms such as Magadha, Kosala, Guptas, Palas, Harshavardhana and the Kushan Empire. Foreign invasions such as the White Huns and Timur further contributed to the decline of Buddhism.

Hinduism traditionally does not evangelize. Buddhism suffered immensely during the Muslim conquest in the Indian subcontinent with muslim rulers such as Muhammad bin Qasim, Muhammad of Ghor, Qutb-ud-Din and Aurangzeb destroying temples and shrines and seeking conversion of Buddhists to Islam. Hinduism is also known to have competed ideologically with Buddhism, notably under Adi Shankaracharya and the Bhakti movement.

## Anagarika Dharmapala and his Followers

Buddhist revival began in India in 1891, when the Sri Lankan Buddhist leader Anagarika Dharmapala founded the Maha Bodhi Society. Its activities expanded to involve the promotion of Buddhism in India. In June 1892, a meeting of Buddhists was organized at Darjeeling. Dharmapala spoke to the Tibetian Buddhists and presented a relic of the Buddha to be sent to the Dalai Lama.

Dharmapala built many viharas and temples in India, including the one at Sarnath, the place of Buddha's first sermon. He died in 1933, the same year he was ordained a bhikkhu..

## Tibetian Buddhism

Following Dalai Lama's departure from Tibet, Indian Prime Minister Jawaharlal Nehru offered to permit him and his followers to establish a "government-in-exile" in Dharamsala.

Tibetan exiles have settled in the town, numbering several thousand. Most of these exiles live in Upper Dharamsala, or McLeod Ganj, where they established monasteries, temples and schools. The town is sometimes known as "Little Lhasa", after the Tibetan capital city, and has become one of the centres of Buddhism in the world. Lama Gyatso is also known to express solidarity with Hinduism, another Dharmic faith with origins in India. Lama Gyatso has also appeared in Hindu religious ocassions such as the Kumbh.

# GAUTAMA BUDDHA

Siddhartha Gautama was a spiritual teacher from ancient India and the historical founder of Buddhism. He is universally recognized by Buddhists as the Supreme Buddha of our age. The time of his birth and death are uncertain; most modern historians date his lifetime from 563 BCE to 483 BCE, though some have suggested a date about a century later than this..

Gautama, also known as Sakyamuni or Shakyamuni ("sage of the Shakyas"), is the key figure in Buddhism, and accounts of his life, discourses, and monastic rules were summarized after his death and memorized by the saegha. Passed down by oral tradition, the *Tripimaka*, the collection of discourses attributed to Gautama, was committed to writing about 400 years later.

## Buddha's Life

As few of the details of the Buddha's life can be independently verified, it is difficult to gauge the historical accuracy of these accounts. The main sources of information on Siddhartha Gautama's life are the earliest available Buddhist texts. The following is a summary of those narratives.

## Conception and Birth

According to tradition, Siddhartha was born more than 200 years before the reign of the Maurya king Aœoka (273–232 BCE).

Siddhartha was born in Lumbini in modern day Nepal. His father was Suddhodana, the chief of the Shakya nation, one of several ancient tribes on the growing state of Kosala; Gautama was the family name. His mother was Queen Maya, King Sudhodhana's wife, who was a Koliyan princess. On the night Siddhartha was conceived, Queen Maya dreamt that a white elephant entered her right side, and ten lunar months later Siddhartha was born from her right side. As was the Shakya tradition, when his mother Queen Maya fell pregnant, she returned to her father's kingdom to give birth, but after leaving Kapilavastu, she gave birth along the way at Lumbini in a garden beneath a sala tree.

The day of the Buddha's birth is widely celebrated in Buddhist countries as Vesak. Various sources hold that the Buddha's mother died at his birth, a few days or seven days later. The infant was given the name Siddhartha (Pali: Siddhatta), meaning "he who achieves his aim". During the birth celebrations, the hermit seer Asita journeyed from his mountain abode and announced that this baby would either become a great king (chakravartin) or a great holy man. This occurred after Siddhartha placed his feet in Asita's hair and Asita examined the birthmarks. Suddhodarna held a naming ceremony on the fifth day, and invited scholars to read the future. All gave a dual prediction that the baby would either become a great king or a great holy man. Kondanna, the youngest, and later to be the first arahant, was the only one who unequivocally predicted that Siddhartha would become a Buddha.

While later tradition and legend characterized Suddhodana as a hereditary monarch, the descendant of the Solar Dynasty of Ikcvaku (Pali: Okkaka), many scholars believe that Uuddhodana was the elected chief of a tribal confederacy.

## Early Life and Marriage

Siddhartha, destined to a luxurious life as a prince, had three palaces (one for each season) especially built for him. His father, King Suddhodana, wishing for Siddhartha to be a great king, shielded his son from religious teachings or knowledge of human suffering. Siddhartha was brought up by his maternal aunt Maha Pajapati, Maya's younger sister.

As the boy reached the age of 16, his father arranged his marriage to Yauodhara (Pali: Yasodhara), a cousin of the same age. In time, she gave birth to a son, Rahula. Siddhartha spent 29 years as a Prince in Kapilavastu, a place now situated in Nepal. Although his father ensured that Siddhartha was provided with everything he could want or need, Siddhartha felt that material wealth was not the ultimate goal of life.

## The Great Departure

At the age of 29, however, the young prince left his palace for a short excursion. While venturing outside of his palace, and despite his father's effort to remove the sick, aged and suffering, Siddhartha was said to have seen an old crippled man. Disturbed by this, and the fact that all people would eventually grow old, the prince went on further trips where he encountered, variously, a crippled man, a diseased man, a decaying corpse, and an ascetic. These four scenes are referred to as the four sights, or the four heavenly messengers (Pali:*devaduta*). Deeply depressed by these sights, he sought to overcome old age, illness, and death by living the life of an ascetic. Siddhartha soon left his palace, his possessions, and his entire family at age 29, to take up the lonely life of a wandering monk.

Abandoning his inheritance, he is then said to have dedicated his life to learning how to overcome suffering. He meditated with two hermits, and, although he achieved high levels of meditative consciousness, he was still not satisfied with his path.

Siddhartha then chose the robes of a mendicant monk and headed to Magadha in what is today Bihar in India. He began his training in the ascetic life and practicing vigorous techniques of physical and mental austerity. Gautama proved quite adept at these practices, and surpassed even his teachers.

However, he found no answer to his questions regarding freedom from sufferings. Leaving behind his caring teachers, he and a small group of close companions set out to take their austerities even further. Gautama tried to find enlightenment through complete deprivation of worldly goods, including food, and became a complete fasting ascetic. After nearly starving himself to death (some sources claim that he nearly drowned), Gautama began to reconsider his path. Then, he remembered a moment in childhood in which he had been watching his father start the season's plowing, and he had fallen into a naturally concentrated and focused state that was blissful and refreshing.

## The Great Enlightenment

After asceticism and concentrating on meditation or Anapana-sati (awareness of breathing in and out), Gautama is said to have discovered what Buddhists call the Middle Way—a path of moderation away from the extremes of self-indulgence and self-mortification. He accepted a little rice pudding from a village girl named Sujata. Then, sitting under a pipal tree, now known as the Bodhi tree in Bodh Gaya, he vowed never to arise until he had found the Truth. At the age of 35, he attained Enlightenment; according to some traditions, this occurred approximately in May, and according to others in December. Gautama, from then on, was known as the Buddha or "Awakened One". Oftentimes, he is referred to in Buddhism as Shakyamuni Buddha or "The Awakened One of the Skakya Clan."

At this point, he is believed to have stated that he had realized complete awakening and insight into the nature and cause of human suffering which was ignorance, along with steps necessary to eliminate it. These truths were then categorized into the Four Noble Truths; the state of supreme liberation—possible for any being—was called Nirvana. He then came to possess the Nine Characteristics, which are said to belong to every Buddha.

According to one of the stories in the *Ayacana Sutta,* a scripture found in the Pali and other canons, immediately after his Enlightenment, the Buddha was wondering whether or not he should teach the *Dharma* to human beings. He was concerned that, as human beings were overpowered by greed, hatred and delusion, they would not be able to see the true *dharma,* which was subtle, deep and hard to understand. However, a divine spirit, Brahma Sahampati, interceded and asked that he teach the *dharma* to the world, as "there will be those who will understand the *Dharma*". With his great compassion to all beings in the universe, the Buddha agreed to become a teacher.

At the Deer Park near Varanasi (Benares) in northern India, he set in motion the Wheel of Dharma by delivering his first sermon to the group of five companions with whom he had previously sought enlightenment. They, together with the Buddha, formed the first saegha, the company of Buddhist monks, and hence, the first formation of Triple Gem (Buddha, Dharma and Sangha) was completed.

According to tradition, the Buddha emphasized ethics and correct understanding. He questioned the average person's notions of divinity and salvation. He stated that there is no intermediary between mankind and the divine; distant gods are subjected to karma themselves in decaying heavens; and the Buddha is solely a guide and teacher for the sentient beings who must tread the path of Nirvana (Pali: Nibbana) themselves to attain the spiritual awakening called *bodhi* and see truth and reality as it is. The Buddhist system of insight, thought, and meditation practice is not believed to have been revealed divinely, but by the understanding of the true nature of the mind, which could be discovered by anybody.

For the remaining 45 years of his life, the Buddha is said to have travelled in the Gangetic Plain of Northeastern India and Southern Nepal, teaching his doctrine and discipline to an extremely diverse range of people— from nobles to outcaste street sweepers, including many adherents of rival philosophies and religions. The Buddha founded the community of Buddhist monks and nuns (the *Sangha*) to continue the dispensation after his Parinirvana (Pali: Parinibbana) or "complete Nirvana", and made thousands of converts. His religion was open to all races and classes and had no caste structure. On the other hand, Buddhist texts record that he was reluctant to ordain women as nuns: he eventually accepted them on the grounds that their capacity for enlightenment was equal to that of men, but he gave them certain additional rules (Vinaya) to follow.

## The Great Passing

According to the Mahaparinibbana Sutta of the Pali canon, at the age of 80, the Buddha announced that he would soon enter Parinirvana or the final deathless state abandoning the earthly body. After this, the Buddha ate his last meal, which, according to different translations, was either a mushroom delicacy or soft pork, which he had received as an offering from a blacksmith named Cunda. Falling violently ill, Buddha instructed his attendant Ananda to convince Cunda that the meal eaten at his place had nothing to do with his passing and that his meal would be a source of the greatest merit as it provided the much-needed energy for the Buddha.

Ananda protested Buddha's decision to enter Parinirvana in the abandoned jungles of Kuuinara (Pali: Kusinara) of the Mallas. Buddha, however, reminded Ananda how Kushinara was a land once ruled by a righteous king that resounded with joy:

" Kusavati, Ananda, resounded unceasingly day and night with ten sounds — the trumpeting of elephants, the neighing of horses, the rattling of chariots, the beating of drums and tabours, music and song, cheers, the clapping of hands, and cries of "Eat, drink, and be merry!" Buddha then asked all the attendant Bhikshus to clarify any doubts or questions they had.

They had none. He then finally entered Parinirvana. The Buddha's final words were, "All composite things pass away. Strive for your own salvation with diligence." The Buddha's body was cremated and the relics were placed in monuments or stupas, some of which are believed to have survived until the present. For example, The Temple of the Tooth or "Dalada Maligawa" in Sri Lanka is the place where the right tooth relic of Buddha is kept at present.

According to the Pali historical chronicles of Sri Lanka, the Dipavamsa and Mahavamsa, the coronation of Ashoka (Pali: Asoka) is 218 years after the death of Buddha. According to one Mahayana record in Chinese, the coronation of Auoka is 116 years after the death of Buddha. Therefore, the time of Buddha's passing is either 486 BCE according to Theravada record or 383 BCE according to Mahayana record. However, the actual date traditionally accepted as the date of the Buddha's death in Theravada countries is 544 or 543 BCE, because the reign of Auoka was traditionally reckoned to be about 60 years earlier than current estimates (based on Auoka's own inscriptions, and therefore among the soundest dates in early Indian history).

## Physical Characteristics

Buddha is perhaps one of the few sages for whom we have mention of his rather impressive physical characteristics. He was at least six feet tall and had a strong enough body to be noticed by one of the kings and was asked to join his army as a general. He is also believed by Buddhists to have "the 32 Signs of the Great Man".

Although the Buddha was not represented in human form until around the 1st century CE, his physical characteristics are described in one of the central texts of the traditional Pali canon, the Digha Nikaya. They help define the global aspect of the historical Buddha, his physical appearance is described by Prince Siddhartha's wife to his son Rahula upon Buddha's return in the scripture of the "Lion of Men".

## Buddha as Viewed by other Religions

### Hinduism

Buddhism is a dharmic religion. The systems of Buddhism and Hinduism, some say, must not be considered to be either contradictory to one another or completely self contained. Coomaraswamy wrote:

> *"The more superficially one studies Buddhism, the more it seems to differ from Brahmanism in which it originated; the more profound our study, the more difficult it becomes to distinguish Buddhism from Brahmanism, or to say in what respects, if any, Buddhism is really unorthodox."*

Buddhist scholar Rahula Vipola wrote that the Buddha was trying to shed the true meaning of the Vedas. Buddha is said to be a knower of the Veda (vedajna) or of the Vedanta (vedantajna) *and (Sutta Nipata, 463).*

Hinduism and Buddhism share many common features including Sanskrit, yoga, karma and dharma.

### Taoism, Confucianism and Shintoism

The arrival of Buddhism caused Taoism to renew and restructure itself and address existential questions raised by Buddhism. Buddhism was seen as a kind of foreign Taoism and its scriptures were translated into Chinese with Taoist vocabulary. Chan (Seon, Thien, or Zen) Buddhism in particular holds many beliefs in common with philosophical Taoism. Some early Chinese Taoist-Buddhists thought Buddha to be a reincarnation of Lao Tzu born in the land of barbarians. Buddhism shares many commonalities with Neo-Confucianism, which is Confucianism with more religious elements. In fact, the ritual of ancestor worship normally practiced by Confucianists, has been adapted to Chinese Buddhist beliefs.

In the Japanese religion of Shinto, the long coexistence of Buddhism and Shintoism resulted in the merging of Shintoism and Buddhism. Gods in Shintoism were given a position similar to the Hindu gods in Buddhism. Moreover, because one of Mahayana Buddha's (Dainichi Nyorai) symbols was the sun, many equated Amaterasu, the Sun Goddess, as the previous reincarnation (bodhisattva) of Dainichi Nyorai. However, the Tokugawa Shogunate era saw a revival movement within Shinto. Some Shinto scholars started to argue that Buddhas were previous incarnations of Shinto gods, thus turning the position of Shintoism and Buddhism upside down. Shinto and Buddhism were officially separated after the Meiji Restoration.

## Islam

"If you desire to see the most noble of mankind, look at the king in beggar's clothing; it is he whose sanctity is great among men."—*Abdul Atahiya, Arab Poet.*

The Buddhist monastic class flowed into what came to be called Islamic monasticism — Sufism — which has given many poets and scientists to both Islam and the world. The Qalandariyah Sufi Order, a Muslim mystical movement, attracted many Buddhist monks. This order arose in 9th century as a result of the Malamatiyya, and became established in Khorasan (Eastern Persia) as early in the 11th century.

Ascetic practices within the Sufi philosophy are associated with Buddhism. The notion of purification (cleaning one's soul from all evil things and trying to reach Nirvana and to become immortal in Nirvana) plays an important role in Buddhism. The same idea shows itself in the belief of *vuslat* (communion with God) in Sufi philosophy. "The mission of the Buddha was quite unique in its character, and therefore it stands quite apart from the many other religions of the world. His mission was to bring the birds of idealism flying in the air nearer to the earth, because the food for their bodies belonged to the earth." —*Hazrat Inayat Khan.*

The Indian scholar Maulana Abul Kalam Azad proposed in a commentary on the *Qur'an* that Siddhartha Gautama is the prophet of Islam *Dhu'l-Kifl* referred to in Sura 21 and Sura 38 of the Qur'an together with the Biblical characters Ishmael, Idris (Enoch), and Elisha. Azad suggested that the *Kifl* in *Dhu'l-Kifl* (Ar: "possessor of a double portion") is an Arabic pronunciation of Kapilavastu, where the Buddha spent his early life. Azad did not, however, provide direct historical evidence to support his speculation. According to other ancient Muslim scholars *Dhu'l-Kifl* was either a righteous man and not a prophet, or he was the prophet called Ezekiel in the Bible.

## THE DEVELOPMENT OF BUDDHISM

The Process through which Buddhism developed into an organized religion also a clear manifestation of how a religious community came into being. What is the nature of religion? It can be defined in a great number of ways. Even in Marx's writings, religion is conceived differently under different circumstances. He said, "religion is the opiate of the people," which is interpreted in terms of the use of religion as a way of hypnotising the masses. This statement came not from Marx but Feuerbach. It means that the purveyors of religion who claimed that it could bring comfort to humankind were not being honest. Lenin conceived of "religion as the workers' groaning sound," which is interpreted as relating to the agony of the proletariat. Brezhnev said, "Religion has a countless number of definitions.... It may be interpreted as a form of relationship that helps to realize the existence of the mystical superhuman power, for humans believe that they can depend on this power." Brezhnev's definition seems to be more relevant and practical, but is there such a mystical power? How do we adjust to the existence of such a power? Why do people find it necessary to believe in such a power? Is belief in a mystical superhuman power superstitious? This raises some philosophical problems, viz., the problems of religion vis-a-vis superstition and belief.

Is religion a superstition? This question can be debated for a long time and no one knows when it will end, but devout believers most certainly will reject the pronouncement that "religion is superstition." Why? It is because believers frequently rely upon certain ideal principles to interpret what often is called the "mystical superhuman power" in the form of ultimate "truth, goodness, and beauty" (zhen, shan, mei), or else they often look upon the ideals of "truth, goodness, and beauty" as a form of "mystical superhuman power." They sincerely believe it to be true and try very hard to apply these ideals in their social life. Probably the belief in, and dependence upon, this ultimate "truth, goodness and beauty" in the guise of a "mystical superhuman power" is a matter of the human psyche's response to specific social conditions. But believers of the "mystical superhuman power" assume superstition and religion to be two different things. To them, `superstition' can only be a trick played upon those who lack scientific knowledge, i.e. a manifestation of spiritual poverty due to a lack of ideals. Devotees who believe that the "mystical superhuman power" is a manifestation of "truth, goodness, and beauty" may perhaps accept the idea that "religion is synonymous with belief" but certainly will not accept that "religion is superstition." According to them people should have faith: even the agnostics believe in agnosticism.

Religion and belief are undoubtedly related. Religion is based on belief, but whether belief is based on religion, in the classical sense, is a different matter. As a matter of illustration we can say that "we believe in the scientific explanation of atheism" or even accept that "we believe in Confucian philosophy." Nonetheless, there is no doubt that atheism is not a religion, but a scientific doctrine. Even Confucianism may be said to have embodied certain religious elements, although it is not a religion. Therefore, we should distinguish not only between `religion' and `belief,' but also between `religion' and `religious thought.' Otherwise, almost any kind of philosophical discourse could be regarded as a religion, and if that be the case, it would be as good as abnegating the existence of religion.

Based on our understanding of the human psyche, we may postulate that human beings really need a certain kind of belief. The question is whether there is the need for a religious belief. If we could divide religion into two categories--one a scientific belief--and another a non-scientific belief - religion may be said, generally, to belong to the latter category.

What follows immediately will be questions like whether human spiritual life requires a certain kind of self-satisfaction obtained from a non-scientific discipline, or whether social life looks upon religious belief itself as a psychological need. This is too gigantic a problem to be discussed here. We can only postulate that for a non-scientific belief to become an organized religion, it must offer some kind of theoretical bases or support. Also, these arguments must be able to reflect the spirit of the time. If there were no religious teachings to be used as a theoretical system, non-scientific beliefs could become an established religion. Besides, as an established religion, especially one that had coloured the history of the social masses, there must be a perduring church organization, a religious canon, a community of devotees, and a history of religion. In Chinese history, there were thousands of the so-called "religious sects," but not all of them could be regarded strictly as "religious organizations." In fact, a number of them could only be looked upon as "superstitious cults." If that be the case, what then may be thought to be an organized religion? We shall analyze the growth of Buddhism first before illuminating the really meaningful form of religious organization.

An organized religion must have a canon with a philosophical base of its own. The religious teachings should not be nonsensical, but must contain a well-organized system of ideas for the advancement of humankind. The reason why Indian Buddhism has become an influential world religion is that it provides an impressive system of thought which is capable of enlightening the human mind. If Buddhism merely confined itself to a haphazard way of thinking, as is represented in the Taiping Jing, it would have been difficult to become an established religion in China.

Thus, from the end of the Han dynasty, through the Three Kingdoms, till after the Western and Eastern Jin, there emerged Daoists like Ge Hong, Lu Xiujing, Kou Qianzhi, Tao Hongjing and others who, in an attempt to fulfill the requirement of the time, not only integrated some of the Daoist and Confucian ideas but also absorbed some of the Buddhist elements to enrich Buddhism.

A really meaningful and influential religious community must have a formal or more serious form of church organization. Even though the ideas of `immortality' and `the sanctification of the bodies' were subsequently incorporated into the Daoist religion, the saints relied heavily on personal devotion without developing a distinctive church, and so they failed to develop a religion. It was not until the end of the Han dynasty that Buddhism became an established religion with a permanent membership of disciples, together with a body of clergy and church leaders. However, the regimes of the Three Kingdoms and the Western Jin banned this organization, subjecting it to dissolution until the Eastern Jin when Du Zhigong and others revived it and once again set it on course.

An organized religion must also have a more permanent set of religious teaching and canon. Although Buddhism had its own precepts and canon when it was first instituted at the end of the Eastern Han, they were rather simple and impermanent in nature. From the Eastern Han onward, Buddhism gradually became more firmly established under the impact of Buddhism and with the tireless efforts of Lu Xiujing, Kou Qianzhi and others.

An organized religion must have its own canon and scriptures for the guidance of its believers. Although there were a number of Daoist books, like the Laozi (Lao Tzu) and the Zhuangzi, before the Wei and the Jin dynasties, these books came to be accepted as scriptures only after being popularized by the devotees. All these books were written by Daoist philosophers of the early Qin, and they had hardly any connection with Daoist religion.

It was due to the believers' attempt to look for historical evidences that they decided to upgrade them as scriptures. Taiping Jing, for example, was written before the inception of the Daoist religion. Hence, it served only as a groundwork for the development of Buddhism.

However, by the time of the Eastern Jin and the Northern and Southern dynasties, when Buddhism was firmly rooted and a church was organized, a large quantity of scriptures expounding the Daoist canon began to appear (Ge Hong's Pao Pozi, This period saw the appearance of three distinctive categories of scriptures: Sanhuangjing (the Three Emperors Scripture), Shangqingjing (the High Pure Scripture), and Lingbaojing, (the Spirit Protected Scripture). All these scriptures subsequently combined to form the `three caves' (sandong) of the Dizhangjing, namely: the cave of the real (dongzhen), the cave of the gods (dongshen), and the cave of the occult (dongxuan).

An established religion must have a spirit being, or shenling, as a specific object of worship and a history of its own. When Buddhism was first instituted it had inherited part of the saints' tradition. The Daoist disciples claimed that it was imparted to them by the immortals, mostly with Laozi (Lao Tzu)'s assistance. Until the Northern and the Southern dynasties, Daoist disciples created the "rank of the real being" based on the conception of the social hierarchy prevailing at the time.

Tao Hongjing's Zhenlin Yueweitu (Real Spirit's Occupational Status Chart) divided the immortals into seven classes, the highest of which was occupied by the first three: the Primal Lord of Heaven (Yuanshi Tianzun), the Daoist Lord on High (Gaoshang Daojun), and the First Divine Daoist Lord (Yuanhuang Daojun). From then on, these three deities became the most honored in the objects of worship in the Daoist temples (daoguan). Since a religion always finds it necessary to undermine the existence of other competing religions, it has to create a history of its own in order to raise its own status. Thus, being an indigenous Chinese religion, Buddhism had to tackle the entry of alien Buddhism. Besides emphasizing the differences between `Chinese' and `non-Chinese' (huayi zhi bian) to undermine Buddhism, Daoists also spread the story of "Laozi (Lao Tzu) huahu" and elevated Laozi (Lao Tzu)'s position to that of Buddha Sakyamuni's teacher. Consequently, both Buddhism and Buddhism remained in conflict for a long time.

However, it was not until the Eastern Jin and the Northern and Southern dynasties that Buddhism finally became an established religion. The various stages of its development may be summarized as follows.

First, from the Eastern Jin onward, the Daoists began to revive their religion by reorganizing the Daoist community which had become scattered and unstable. At the same time, in order to overcome the inadequacy of Daoist teaching and theoretical formulations, Ge Hong and others had provided a body of Daoist canon and precepts.

Thereafter, as an attempt to consolidate the founding of the Daoist church, a set of religious teaching was formulated; and in order to propagate Daoist teaching the required scriptures were made available. Lastly, so as to set the religion on a proper footing, a compendium of fairy tales and legendary stories was kept alive. The various phases involved in the development of Buddhism may thus be said to be characteristic of the circumstances under which a religious body came into existence. One of our aims of studying the history of religion is to use it as a source for illuminating the various phases of its development so as to enable us to assess, more accurately, the role it played in society.

## DALIT BUDDHIST MOVEMENT

A Buddhist revivalist movement among Dalit Indians was initiated in 1890s by Dalit leaders such as Iyothee Thass, Brahmananda Reddy, and Dharmananda Kosambi. Sri Lankan Buddhist monks played big role for Dalit Buddhist movement in India.. In, 1956 B. R. Ambedkar converted to Buddhism along with followers, giving a major impetus to the Dalit Buddhist movement in India.

### Others

Dharmananda Damodar Kosambi, a Goan, was another important Buddhist thinker of India.

S. N. Goenka, a meditation teacher trained in Burma is an active Buddhist leader in India. Goenka plans to build a stupa. The most significant part of this structure is that it will be more than twice as large as the presently largest dome structure in the world, namely the Gol Gumbaz at Bijapur in India. The stones are to be placed to form a load bearing dome structure without supporting pillars inside the hall.

### British Involvement

British Buddhists have played a role in revival of Buddhism in India through the work of the Karuna Trust, a London-based Buddhist charity set up by members of the Western Buddhist

Order and part of the FWBO. The Karuna Trust's work is inspired by Dr. Ambedkar and seeks to work towards his vision of liberty, equality, fraternity and justice. Karuna's work is also inspired by Sangharakshita, the founder of the Western Buddhist Order, who met Dr. Ambedkar in India. Sangharakshita deeply moved by the situation facing Dalit people, and addressed followers of Dr. Ambedkar at mass public meetings after the latter's death. The Karuna Trust was set up in 1980 by some of Sangharakshita's disciples to address the great material suffering and poverty experienced by millions of Dalit people across India. Through educational and training projects in India and Bangladesh, Karuna supports and enable of some of the world's most disadvantaged people, who are marginalised. Friends of the Western Buddhist Order (FWBO) is a Buddhist movement that was founded in the UK by Sangharakshita (formerly Dennis Lingwood) in 1967, followed by the Western Buddhist Order in 1968. In 1978 Indian wing of the FWBO founded, known as the Trailokya Bauddha Mahasangha Sahayaka Gana.

## Japanese Involvement

A Japanese organization called the Ogawa Trust maintains Nagarjuna Hospital at Mansar, an English language school for poor students, an orphanage, cooperative home industries for women, and various other kinds of aid. The Ogawa Trust has also helped in the building of an ornate Buddhist temple at Kampti, a town near Nagpur. An emerging religious organization called Soka Gakkai International has a chapter in India called Bharat Soka Gakkai. The group was first recognized by the Indian Government in 1986. However, the world-wide organization has been often been called a cult by it's critics; It's current leader, Daisaku Ikeda, has also been called a cult figure.

## Taiwanese Involvement

Taiwanese Buddhists have contributed to the growth of Buddhism in India in multiple ways, one of which is in the ordination of Theravadin nuns. Taiwan, with one of the most active groups of nuns in the world, has begun to facilitate the ordination of women in India. In February 1998 a full ordination ceremony was held at Bodh Gaya by Taiwan's Fo Guang Shan Monastery. 132 applicants arrived to receive ordination as nuns and undertook a nine day period of training and questioning. Of these candidates 66 were from South Asia, and of these at least twenty-eight were from Maharashtra.

## STAGES IN THE HISTORY OF BUDDHISM

The history of Buddhism in India, which lasted about 1500 years, can be divided into 500 year periods, during which distinctive forms of Buddhism emerged. This is an idealized and schematic picture, but it is convenient, and it can be matched up with where Buddhism spread during these periods and what forms of Buddhism became dominant there. Buddhist doctrine and practice in the earliest period were agreed upon in a series of Councils, sometimes reckoned to be three, or four.

1. The First Council was held shortly after the Buddha's death, at Rajagriha (capital of the Kingdom of Magadha). Issues about the conduct of the *Sangha*, the monastic community, in the absence of the Buddha appear to have been settled.
2. The Second Council was held about a century after the Buddha's death, at Vaisali (under Magadhan control). Sometimes this is considered the First Council, or is confused with the previous one. It began to agree on the content of the Buddhist Canon and on the monastic discipline, the *vinaya*.
3. The Third Council was called by the Emperor Ashoka and held at Pataliputra. The content of the Pali *Tripitaka*, "Three Baskets," is supposed to have been settled at this Council, or thereabouts in this period, consisting of the *Sutra-pitaka* [*Sutta* in Pali], the sermons of the Buddha, the *Vinaya-pitaka*, the monastic discipline, and the *Abhidharma-pitaka* [*dharma* is *dhamma* in Pali], the philosophical development of Buddhist doctrine. Buddhism was introduced into Sri Lanka (Ceylon) as the result of Ashoka's own efforts, and the Canon in Pali was preserved there.

4. The Fourth Council was called under the Emperor Kanishka I and held at Jalandhara (or Purushpura, Peshawar, Kanishka's capital). This is not attested in Pali sources, and so one often hears that there were only three Councils. The Council is supposed to have supervised the translation of the *Tripitaka* into Sanskrit. The Canon apparently had not only existed in Pali, but in other Prakrits, which were all consulted for a standard Sanskrit version. It appears to be the Sanskrit texts that were subsequently spread to China. The sutras of the Mahayana may have existed only in Sanskrit from the beginning.

Theravada ("Teaching of the Elders") Buddhism (called "Hinayana," the "Lesser Vehicle," by the Mahayana): In India, 5th century BC to 1st century AD.

- Distinctive doctrines:
  1. The Buddha (Siddhartha Gautama, Shakyamuni) is gone, and individual practitioners must work out their salvation on their own.
  2. The Buddha was unique, and individual practitioners cannot become Buddhas, only *arhats* ("saints"). There will be a fûture Buddha, Maitreya, but not for thousands of years.
  3. *Nirvana* (liberation) and *samsara* (the place of death and rebirth) are definitely different. *Samsara* is a place of suffering to be left behind. *Nirvana* is a liberation that is free of death and rebirth but is beyond description and rational understanding.

Mahayana ("Great Vehicle") Buddhism: In India, 1st century AD to 6th century.

- Distinctive doctrines:
  1. The Gautama Buddha is *not* gone, and individual practitioners are *not* on their own. Instead, the Buddha taught the dharma out of compassion, and his compassion would prevent him from being unavailable to practitioners now. Indeed, to emulate the compassion of the Buddha, practitioners become

*bodhisattvas*, who vow to carry all beings with them into salvation. Bodhisattvas are also available, like the Buddhas, to help people work out their salvation. Maitreya is presently a bodhisattva, but the most important bodhisattva is probably Avalokiteshvara, who developed into the Chinese goddess of Mercy, *Guanyin* (*Kwan-in* in Wade-Giles, *Kannon* in Japan).

2. The Buddha was *not* unique, and individual practitioners who have become bodhisattvas *can* become Buddhas. There are already multiple Buddhas besides Shakyamuni. Most important are Mahavairocana and Amitabha. Amitabha is famous for his Western Paradise, or Pure Land, where he has Vowed to cause anyone who calls on him for help to be born, so they will be free of the world of suffering to work out their ultimate liberation. In Japan Amitabha is known as *Amida* and Mahavairocana as *Dainichi*. Most of the famous Buddha statues in Japan are *not* Shakyamuni: the great outdoor bronze Buddha at Kamakura is Amida, and the Buddha enshrined in the *Todaiji* ("Great Eastern") Temple in Nara (the largest wooden building in the world), is another Buddha named Locana.
3. *Nirvana* and *samsara* are *no longer* definitely different. The "Fourfold Negation" is applied to the relationship between the two. *Samsara* and *Nirvana* are thus neither the same, nor different, nor both the same and different, nor neither the same nor different. This allows some room for maneuver, which may have made Buddhism more palatable in China, where Confucianism never did approve either of the world-denying metaphysics or the monasticism of Buddhism. Distinctively Chinese schools of Buddhism developed, like T'ien-t'ai (*Tendai* in Japan) and Ch'an (*Seon* [*Son*] in Korea, *Thien* in Vietnam, *Zen* in Japan), for whom samsara and Nirvana were virtually identical, so that enlightenment and Nirvana *transformed* the

world rather than eliminated it. The paradoxical metaphysics of Buddhism could be assimilated to the similar paradoxical doctrines of the native Chinese philosophical school of Taoism.

- Places where Mahayana spread: Mahayana Buddhism is presently practiced in China, Korea, Vietnam, and Japan. Buddhism was propagated in China by missionaries from India, like Kumarajiva (344-413), who arrived in China in 401, and Buddhabhadra (359-429), who arrived in 408, and by Chinese pilgrims who travelled to India, like Fa-Hsien (Faxian[3]), who travelled to India between 399 and 414, and Hsuan-tsang (Xuanzang[3], 600-664), who went to India between 629 and 645. Most of these figures concern a China of the Northern and Southern Empires (266-589), when the country was fragmented, and when barbarians, perhaps more susceptible to a foreign doctrine, ruled the North. These journeys were difficult, either by sea around Malaya, where many ships were attacked by pirates or sunk by storms, or by land through Central Asia, on the "Silk Road" caravan route, through deserts and over some of the highest mountains in the world. The highest peaks of the Pamirs and related mountain chains, called *Bam-e Donya* in Persian, "the Roof of the World," are all over 24,000 feet [note]. One story of a Buddhist missionary crossing the Pamirs, Kumarayana, father of Kumarajiva, is that he carried a Buddha image during the day — and the Buddha image carried him during the night! Kumarajiva, Fa-Hsien, and Hsuan-tsang all brought Buddhist texts from India to China and translated them. The Buddhist canon as it arrived in China was in Sanskrit, and it included many special Mahayana Sutras that are not in the Pali Canon (though many are now suspected of being Chinese forgeries). The stories of Fa-Hsien and Hsuan-tsang's travels are important parts of Chinese literature, and Fa-Hsien's account of India during the reign of Chandra Gupta II (375-415) is an important document for the history of India.

- Vajrayana ("Thunderbolt Vehicle") Buddhism: In India, 6th to 11th century.
- Distinctive doctrines: Vajrayana Buddhism is *Tantric* Buddhism, often called "esoteric" Buddhism. Although it is sometimes also translated as "diamond" (i.e. "hard"), the *vajra* (*kongo* in Japanese) was originally the thunderbolt of Indra; and in Vajrayana it symbolizes the magical power of Tantrism. Tantric magic could be worked through *man.d.alas*, sacred diagrams, *mantras*, sacred formulas for recitation (the most famous one being, "Om, mane padme hum"— "The jewel is in the lotus"), and *mudras*, sacred gestures. This Tantric magic could be merely thaumaturgical ("wonder working") or could be regarded as means of achieving liberation in addition to or apart from meditative or meritorious practices. Just as Hindu Tantrism expresses its magical power through goddesses like Kali, Vajrayana emphasizes female figures. Vajrayana comes to balance male Bodhisattvas with female Bodhisattvas as attendants of the various Buddhas. And while Buddhas tend to be regarded as male in all branches of Buddhism, Tibetan Buddhism supplies female figures corresponding to each Buddha, like the "savioresses" Green Tara, White Tara, and Mamaki, who actually vow to always be reborn as women in the process of leading all beings to salvation. Vajrayana symbolism always balances male and female: the Vajra Mandala (or the "jewel" above) corresponds to the Womb (or Matrix) Mandala (the "lotus"). The extent to which Vajrayana *practiced* real sexual union, been the physical male "vajra" and the physical female womb, as part of its Tantrism is unclear and disputed. Often "right-handed" Tantrism is distinguished from "left-handed" Tantrism, in which the former practiced the union of male and female, in symbolic, iconographic form, while the latter practiced it literally. While the "right-handed" forms are mainly what remain in Tibet and in Japanese Shingon today, there is little doubt that real "left-handed" practices existed in the past and survive to an extent in the present, and Tibetan art sometimes

still portrays the more violent and disturbing aspects of Tantric practice — rape, bestiality, etc.

- Places where Vajrayana spread: Vajrayana Buddhism most importantly spread to Tibet and then Mongolia. In Tibet it assumed distinctive forms that are usually called *Lamaism*, since the monks are called Lamas. The present Dalai Lama, who was the priestly ruler of Tibet until he fled the Communist Chinese in 1959, is from a line that is reputed to be successive incarnations of the Bodhisattva Avalokiteshvara. Vajrayana Buddhism also entered China, Japan, etc., as special "esoteric" schools, like the Japanese *Shingon* school. The great temple at Borobudur, outside Jakarta on the island of Java, dates from this period (c.800), and embodies Vajrayana Mandala forms; but in Indonesia Buddhism soon thereafter gave way to Islam.

The end of Buddhism in India. Buddhism may have died out in India in the 11th century because: 1) It had become almost indistinguishable from the Tantric forms of Hinduism. Sophisticated Buddhist doctrine did not appeal to most people, and the actual practices and iconography of Vajrayana could easily be assimilated into Hinduism. And, 2) Islam arrived in earnest in India with the Afghan prince Mahmud of Ghazna, who defeated a coalition of Hindu princes in 1008 and soon annexed the Punjab. As Buddhism was persecuted, conversions to Islam increased, and Buddhism declined. By the time the British arrived, about 25% of India was Moslem. That ultimately led to the partition of the country into India and Pakistan. The Gautama Buddha himself has ended up being regarded as the 9th Incarnation (*Avatar*) of the great Hindu God Vishnu, although the unflattering take on it is that he deliberately taught a false doctrine (i.e. Buddhism) in order to deceive and destroy demons.

## The Final Dharma Age

Another way of dividing the history of Buddhism emerged in the Buddhist tradition as a way of dealing with the prediction of the Buddha himself that the *Dharma* would only last 500 years. This became a matter of concern in China, where Buddhism did not even become established until nearly 1000 years after the time of the Buddha. Indeed, there was uncertainty about when the time of the Buddha had been, but soon enough it was obvious that far more than 500 years had passed. The doctrine that was formulated in response to this we find in K'uei-chi (Tz'u-en, 632-682), founder of the Fa-hsien school early in the T'ang Dynasty, in his *I-lin-chang*, "The Grove of Meanings." There we find a division into three periods based on the existence of Buddhist teaching, Buddhist practice, and Buddhist "proof," i.e. results — supernatural powers and Nirvana:

- The Age of the True Dharma (Sanskrit *Saddharma*, Japanese *shobo*). In the first 500 years of Buddhism (sometimes put at 1000 years, however), the teaching, the practice, and the proof of Buddhism are all evident and effective. This becomes the Buddhist equivalent of the "age of the Apostles" in Christianity or of the "companions of the Prophet" in Islam — when the best exemplars of the religion lived, people whose achievements are now largely beyond the reach of believers (as most Protestants do not believe that any modern Christians can perform miracles on the scale of the Apostles). It becomes, naturally, particularly associated with Buddhism in India, the first step in the *Sangoku*, or "three nations," ideology that later developed in Japan.
- The Age of the Counterfeit Dharma (Sanskrit *Saddharma-pratirupaka*, Japanese *zoho*). In the 1000 years following the True Dharma, the teaching and the practice of Buddhism are evident but the proof fails. While uncertainty about the length of the True Dharma Age could postpone a reckoning, Buddhism in China — which now becomes particularly associated with the second Age — eventually had to face the fact that the full force of the Dharma, as defined by the Buddha himself, was spent. This would seem to remove the point of Buddhist belief and practice altogether, but it was also something whose full implications most Buddhists were unwilling to accept. One result was the popularity of devotionalistic forms of

Buddhism, which substitute intermediate goals before final *Nirvana*. In Pure Land practice, the Vow of the Buddha Amitabha enables devotees to be reborn in a Pure Land, where they will be free of suffering, let alone the Hells, and can work out their salvation without distractions (like hunger or sex). Pure Land Buddhism, indeed, became the most popular form of Buddhism in China and Japan. Another approach, which we see in the T'ien-tai (Japanese *Tendai*) and Ch'an (*Zen*) Schools, was to redefine the "proof," so that avoiding rebirth was no longer the goal of Buddhist practice. Instead, life in the world of*samsara* can become the equivalent of *Nirvana*. This gives to Buddhism itself a very different character, unlike the world-denying tendencies of India and more conformable to the sensibilities of both Confucianism and Taoism. This goes along with discussions about whether it was really necessary to keep Buddhist Precepts. Nevertheless, we do have a continuation of traditional monasticism, and of course not everyone agrees with the new tendencies in thinking.

- The Age of the Final Dharma (Sanskrit *Saddharma-vipralopa*, Japanese *mappo*). If the Counterfeit Dharma posed a disturbing challenge for Buddhism, the Final Dharma was even worse. At that point the real practice and proof of Buddhism are both supposed to no longer be possible. Only the teaching remains. While K'uei-chi didn't yet quite have to worry about that, by the time we get to the Kamakura Period (1186-1336) in Japanese history, it becomes widely accepted that the Final Dharma, *Mappo*, is upon them. This is expected to last no less than 10,000 years. After that, Buddhism will simply be forgotten, and ages will pass, perhaps a million years, before the arrival of the Future Buddha, Maitreya. By this time, of course, Buddhism was already vanishing in India itself. Some Japanese expected this, or were aware of it, others didn't believe it. But it was the kind of thing to reinforce the sense of the fading of the Dharma. The response was a period of religious creativity, in which a number of Chinese schools were adopted and reworked (Tendai, Zen, Jodo), and some original Japanese schools (Jodo Shin, Nichiren) emerged. Japanese monks ceased taking full monastic vows, clerical marriage became tolerated, sometimes sanctioned (in Jodo Shin), later even expected, and Japanese monks could easily gain reputations as formidable drinkers, despite the Precept against intoxicants. To Buddhists elsewhere, this kind of thing often makes it seem that Japanese monks are no longer proper Buddhists.

While many Buddhists now no longer worry about the problem of the fading Dharma, there is no denying the statement of the Buddha, or the role that dealing with this has played in the history of Buddhism.

## DECLINE OF BUDDHISM IN INDIA

The Decline of Buddhism in India, in the land of its birth occurred for a variety of reasons, and happened even as it continued to flourish beyond the frontiers of India. Buddhism was established in the area of ancient Magadha and Kosala by Gautama Buddha in the 6th century BCE, in what is now modern Uttar Pradesh and Bihar. Buddhism, over the next Over 1500 years became the region's dominant belief system, spreading across Indian sub-continent. After the death of Gautama Buddha, Buddhism saw rapid expanzion in its first century, especially in northern and central India.

The Mauryan Emperor Ashoka (304-232 BCE) and later monarchs encouraged the expansion of Buddhism into Asia through religious ambassadors. Chinese scholars traveling through the region between the 5th and 8th centuries CE, such as Faxian, Xuanzang, I-ching, Hui-sheng, and Sung-Yun, began to speak of a decline of the Buddhist *sangha*, especially in the wake of the White Hun invasion. A continuing decline occured after the fall of the Pala dynasty in the 12th century CE, continuiung with the later destruction of monasteries by Muslim conquerors. Buddhism was virtually extinct by the end of the 19th century. In recent times, Buddhism has seen a revival in India due to the influence of Anagarika Dharmapala, Dr. B. R. Ambedkar and Tenzin Gyatso.

## Buddhism under Various Governments

## The Sungas

Following the Mauryans, Pusyamitra Sunga is linked in legend with the persecution of Buddhists and a resurgence of a Hinduism that forced Buddhism outwards to Kashmir, Gandhara and Bactria.. There is some doubt as to whether he did or did not persecute Buddhists actively. A Buddhist tradition holds him as having taken taking steps to check the spread of Buddhism as "the number one enemy of the sons of the Sakya's and a most cruel persecutor of the religion". The *Divyavadana* ascribes to him the razing of *stupas* and *viharas* built by Ashoka, the placing of a bounty of 100 dinaras upon the heads of Buddhist monks (*Shramanas*) and describes him as one who wanted to undo the work of Ashoka. This account has however been described as "exaggerated".

Historian Romila Thapar writes that the Asokavadana legend is, in all probability, a "Buddhist version of Pusyamitra's attack of the Mauryas", and reflects the fact that, with the declining influence of Buddhism in the Imperial court, Buddhist monuments and institutions would receive less attention.

Some historians have rejected the accuracy of the Buddhist texts that record Pushyamitra's persecution of Buddhists. The first accounts appear two centuries after Pushyamitra's reign in *Asokavadana* and the *Divyavadana*. Koenraad Elst posits that historical facts confirm that Pushyamitra allowed and patronized the construction of monasteries and Buddhist universities in his domains, as well as the still-existent stupa of Sanchi.

While Sir John Marshall states that it is possible that the original brick stupa built by Ashoka was destroyed by Pusyamitra and then restored by his successor Agnimitra. Arhaelogical evidence is scarce and uncertain.Following Ashoka's sponsorship of Buddhism, it is possible that Buddhist institutions fell on harder times under the Sungas but no evidence of active persecution has been noted. Etienne Lamotte observes: *"To judge from the documents, Pushyamitra must be acquitted through lack of proof."*

The Sungas were patrons of Hinduism and their lack of royal patronage was also a setback to Buddhism, resulting in the splintering of Buddhism into many forces. Some of them were: the *Saravastivadins*, *Mahasargikas*, *Sthaviravadha*, and *Yogacara*. This resulted in a diversity of opinions and interpretations that led to a conflict between warring schools shortly after the fall of the Mauryans. Later Sunga kings were seen as more amenable to Buddhism and as having contributed to the building of the stupa at Bharhut.

Hinduism traditionally does not evangelize. Hinduism competed in spirtual and political realm with Buddhism. Buddhism also flourished in the realms of the Bactrian kings.

## Guptas

Buddhism and saw a brief revival under the Guptas. By the 4th to 5th century Buddhism was already in decline in northern India, even as it was achieving multiple successes in Central Asia and along the Silk Road as far as China. It continued to prosper in Gandhara under the Shahi kingdom.

## White Huns

Central Asian and North Western Indian Buddhism weakened in the 6th century following the White Hun invasion who followed their own religions such as Tengri, Nestorian Christianity, and Manichean. Their King Mihirakula who ruled from 515 BC suppressed Buddhism destroying monasteries as far as modern-day Allahabad before his son reversed the policy.

## Harsha

In the North and west the collapse of Harshavardana's kingdom gave rise to many small kingdoms. This led to the rise of the martial Rajputs clans across the gangetic plains and marked the end of Buddhist ruling clans along with a sharp decline in royal patronage until a revival under the Pala Empire in the Bengal region. Subsequently the replacement of Buddhist royal lines with Hindu royals and the rise of martial Rajput dynasties further pressured Buddhism.

## Muhammad Bin Qasim

In AD 711, Muhammad bin Quasim attacked the southern shores of Sindh. Muhammad Bin Quasim is linked with Islamic persecution of Buddhists. Quasim destroyed a Buddhist holy site and built a mosque in it's place. It was claimed that the Buddhists helped bin Qasim in conquering parts of India. Al-Baladhuri recorded that two "Samanis" went to Qasim to negiotiate for peace, however he also recorded that it was the inhabitants of Nirum who sent the priests to Qasim. Muhammad bin Qasim also demolished temples and monasteries, e.g. he built at Nirun a mosque on the site of the temple of Budh.

## Mahmud of Ghazni

By the 10th century Mahmud of Ghazni defeated the Hindu-Shahis effectively removing Hindu influence and ending Buddhist self-governance across Central Asia and the Punjab region. He demolished both stupas and temples during his numerous campaigns across north-western India but left those within his domains and Afghanistan alone even as al-Biruni recorded Buddha as the prophet "Burxan". Mahmud of Ghazni is said to have been an iconoclast. Hindu and Buddhist statues, shrines and temples were looted and destroyed and many Buddhists had to take refuge in Tibet.

## Pala's

In the east under the Palas in Bengal, Mahayana Buddhism flourished and spread to Bhutan and Sikkim. The Palas created many temples and a distinctive school of Buddhist art. Mahayana Buddhism flourished under the Palas, between the 8th and the 12th century before it collapsed at the hands of the attacking Sena dynasty.

## Muhammad of Ghor

Muhammad attacked the north-western regions of the Indian subcontinent many times. Gujarat later fell to Muhammad of

Ghor's armies in 1197. Muhammad of Ghor's armies destroyed many Buddhist structures, including the great Buddhist university of Nalanda. In 1200 Muhammad Khilji, one of Qutb-ud-Din's generals destroyed monasteries fortified by the Sena armies, such as the one at Vikramshila. Many monuments of ancient Indian civilization were destroyed by the invading armies, including Buddhist sanctuaries near Benares. Buddhist monks who escaped the massacre fled to Nepal, Tibet and South India.

## The Mongols

In 1215 Genghis Khan conquered Afghanistan and devastated the Muslim world. In 1227 after his death his conquest was divided and Chagatai established the Chagatai Khanate where his son Arghun made Buddhism the state religion during which time he came down harshly on Islam and demolished mosques to build many stupas.

He was succeeded by his brother, and then his son Ghazan who converted to Islam and in 1295 who changed the state religion and after his reign and the splitting of the Chagatai Khanate little mention of Buddhism or the stupas built by the Mongols can be found in Afghanistan and Central Asia can be found in Afghanistan and central Asia.

## Timur (Tamarlane)

Timur was a 14th-century warlord of Turco-Mongol descent, conqueror of much of Western and central Asia, and founder of the Timurid Empire.

Timur destroyed Buddhist establishments and raided areas in which Buddhism had flourished.

## Mughals

Mughal rule also contributed to the decline of Buddhism. They are reported to have destroyed many Hindu temples and Buddhist shrines alike or converted many sacred Hindu places into Muslim shrines and mosques. Mughal rulers like Aurangzeb destroyed Buddhist temples and monasteries and replaced them with Islamic mosques.

# 2

# The Ethics of Buddhism

It is well-known that Buddhism is the most ethical of "religions". An important part of the Noble Eightfold Path relates to the development of ethical conduct; for many a layperson Buddhist practice consists mainly in the "keeping of the precepts"; many Bhikkhus see in the Vinaya rules the essence of the religious life; and even many of the paramitas expected of those aspiring to Buddhahood are ethical in nature. Yet to present the teaching of the Buddha as being solely and exclusively concerned with ethics could serve as a detraction from the real objective of the Buddha-Dhamma, which is to serve as a path or vehicle leading to Enlightenment. While conforming to the norms of Buddhist ethics is essential for this purpose this alone will not guarantee the elimination of ignorance (avijja), which is the real meaning of Enlightenment. The tendency of some exponents of the Dhamma to represent Buddhism as just another ethical system is misleading, especially when put before a newcomer to the Dhamma who may not be able to distinguish between Buddhist ethics and the precepts of other ethical teachers, and may conclude that Buddhism has nothing new to offer.

All religions inculcate some basic ethics, whether relating to individual or to social conduct. Indeed the advocacy of an ethical system does not need a religious framework, and some: of the great ethical teachers of the world (e.g. Socrates or Confucius) did not feel the need for one. The religion-surrogates of the modern world, like Humanism, rationalism, or Communism, have all evolved their own norms of ethics, however inadequate we may consider them to be. Wherein, then, lies the uniqueness of Buddhist ethics? This question could be answered in many ways, but here we shall look at it from the standpoint of three criteria.

First of all there are the ethical rules themselves. When we consider what actions are considered "good" and what are deemed to be "bad", it might appear that there is a great deal of agreement between the different ethical Systems. Such actions like killing, theft, sexual misconduct, and falsehood seem to be condemned universally. The differences emerge when we examine the question more closely, e.g. when we investigate the rationale for these rules, whether they are absolute or are relative to some other end, and so on. The rule against killing could be taken as an example. Many ethical systems proscribe only the killing of humans (i.e. murder), but Buddhism applies the rule to all sentient existence. Furthermore even in the case of humans, exceptions are sometimes allowed, e.g. for "holy" or "just" war. Buddhism admits of no such exemptions. In Buddhism the ethical quality of actions depends on the mental factors associated with their commission or even contemplation, and on the impact they have on the well-being of others. If action is committed with greed, aversion or delusion it is unwholesome (akusala), but the degree of moral reprehensibility (and karmic consequence) depends on a whole host of factors. Even an "accidental" killing could have adverse consequences if it was caused through negligence and unmindfulness, which is a kind of "Delusion" (moha). What has been said of the rule regarding killing, may also be extended to the other ethical precepts as well. Furthermore Buddhist ethics does not stop at the Five Precepts (panca siila), which provides only the very minimum for the proper conduct of lay persons.

The second criterion that could be adduced for the evaluation of ethical Systems relates to the motivation for adhering to the ethical rules of the system, religious or secular. In Buddhism the goal of ethical conduct is self-control, self-understanding, and self-development. It is an essential prerequisite for the training of the mind, the elimination of ignorance and the attainment of Enlightenment. Theistic religions usually require the adherence to their ethical precepts as a means to the union with God, whether in an abstract metaphysical sense or more directly as entry into a kingdom ruled by God, or even the enjoyment of pleasures in a heavenly paradise. In such a system the most important rule, precept or commandment is not usually an ethical one, but belief in, love of, submission and obedience to, and veneration of God. This is thus placed at the head of the Judeo-Christian decalogue, with the ethical rules coming subsequently. When we look at "secular" ethics, such as those embodied in legal systems, the objective is usually the avoidance of social conflict, the regularization of property rights, and the like. Of course, some secular laws (e.g. those relating to the so-called "victimless crimes") are more directly "moral" in nature, but these too usually are indirect social objectives. The pursuit of Buddhist ethics too leads to social harmony, but this harmony is achieved through individual perfection, rather than through the compulsory observance of legalistic rules. But because of the non-compulsive nature of Buddhist ethics, they are not intended to replace the laws of society, but neither are those of other ethical systems erected on religious and philosophical foundations.

The third aspect of the question relates to the way in which "good" and "bad" conduct results in appropriate consequences. This is the question of the "policing of the rules". Here two approaches may be distinguished. One is where some kind of trial and punishment (or reward) is instituted individually for each person. The supreme judicial authority could be God to the theist; or simply the normal judicial processes of society in the case of the secularist and the materialist. The second approach relies on the workings of an impersonal law (like the Law of Karma in its Buddhist and Hindu-Jam forms). The legal model of trial-and-punishment is best suited to the enforcement of the laws of society, such as are necessary for the preservation of the authority of the State and the well-being of society. When this model is used to evaluate personal moral conduct and behaviour, as in the theory of divine judgement, several curious features arise. One that could be mentioned is the doctrine of the "forgiveness of sins". According to this doctrine the exercise of divine grace could wipe out "sins" and negate the principle that actions bring their own reward. In such a system the ultimate factor which determines the destiny of an individual is not the scrupulous observance of the ethical rules of the system, but the element of blind faith in its dogmas.

In Buddhism the operation of the law of kamma (karma) is all-pervasive and universal. Its exact modus operandi is not detailed, and may not be immediately obvious. Unlike in some other versions of the karmic hypothesis, in Buddhism there is no mechanical equivalence between action and result (vipaka). As mentioned above the karmic quality of an act depends on a whole host of circumstances. In the accumulation of kammas, good and bad, the fruiting of some may be postponed or delayed while that of others could be immediate. What is certain is that the law of kamma makes divine authority, divine grace, etc. redundant.

Thus in spite of superficial similarities, Buddhist ethics differs from other ethical systems when analysed in detail. In the Noble Eightfold Path the elements corresponding to morality and ethics are Right Speech, Right Action and Right Livelihood. These three together constitute siila. The cultivation of siila normally proceeds alongside progress in the other two great constituents of the Path, namely mental training (bhavana) and wisdom-insight (panna). Because of the mutually supportive nature of the three components of morality, mental development and wisdom, it is difficult to argue about the relative importance of these three components. Nonetheless it has long been the generally accepted view that panna is both the threshold as well as the culmination of Buddhist practice, with the other two components of sla and bhavana being the chief means to the realization of this great objective.

The distinction between ends and means is very important in the understanding of the true place of ethics in Buddhism. For the ordinary person (putujjana) ethical conduct may appear to be an end in itself, but for the adept (sekha) it is a means to the realization of a greater end. Because of the Buddha's custom of proclaiming the Dhamma according the varied capacities of his listeners, there are diverse references to the importance of siila in the Buddha's discourses which at first sight might appear to be inconsistent or even contradictory. This apparent inconsistency, however, disappears when the actual context is considered. By way of illustration we can consider two places in the Pali Cannon of Buddhism which seem to attach different degrees of importance to morality (siila) in the Buddha's system.

"The first of these comes from the Brahmajala Sutta. This is the first discourse in the Sutta Pitaka (the section dealing with Buddhist doctrines), and this exalted position accorded to it reflects its importance to the early Buddhists, perhaps to the Buddha himself. This discourse was occasioned by a report brought to the Buddha of derisive commuents made on him, his Doctrine and the Sangha by a wandering teacher called Suppiya, and the equally unfounded praise bestowed on him by Brahmadatta a follower of Suppiya. This had led to conflict between teacher and pupil, and disquiet amongst the followers of the Buddha. The Buddha commences the discourse by advising his followers to consider all statements made about him, whether favourable or unfavourable, in an objective manner, with equanimity and even-handedness, and then to reject what was wrong, whether it be unfounded blame or unfounded praise, and to point out these errors in a calm and reasoned manner.

The Buddha anticipated that much of the praise heaped on him would be for the wrong reasons: "It is in respect only of trifling things (appamattaka.m) or matters of little value (oramattaka.m), or mere morality (siilamattaka.m) that an unconverted man (putujjana) when praising the Buddha would speak". What is interesting from our point of view is that the Buddha considers the mere keeping of ethical rules to be a matter not worthy of any real praise. In this sutta the Buddha groups ethical rules into three categories. The first of these (the cula siila) contains the basic ethical precepts (like the "killing of living things") which are usually included amongst the Five Precepts laid down for the guidance of lay persons. The other two categories (the majjhima and maha siilas) contain, ethical rules of lesser importance or those specially laid down for monks. As against these "moralities", none of which is deserving of real praise, the Buddha describes those things that are deserving of real praise. These are the "things profound difficult to realize, hard to understand, tranquillising, sweet, not to be grasped by mere logic, subtle, comprehensible only to the wise". More specifically they turn out to be the realization of Right View (samma di.t.ti), and the refutation of wrong views, in which connection the Buddha outlines the famous list of sixty-two schools of thought, ranging from theism to materialism, which then as now, were the main contenders with the Dhamma. Even though the Brahmajala was mainly concerned with what was praiseworthy in a Buddha, it does provide a clear statement of the principle that wisdom-insight (panna) ranks above siila and bhavana in the accomplishments necessary for the realization of the Buddhist goal of Nibbana.

The second extract from the Dhama which we shall consider seems to paint a slightly different picture. This is probably the best known stanza in the Dhamapada, itself the best-known of the Buddhist books. This Stanza (No.183) with its usual translation is as follows:

*Sabbapapassa akara.na.m, kusalassa upasamapda,*

*sacittapariyodapana.m eta.m Buddhana sasana.m*

*Not to do any evil, to do good,*

*To purify one's mind, this is the teaching of the Buddhas.]*

The ethical import of this Stanza is obvious. It seems to claim that the Buddha's teaching is threefold: avoid unethical conduct, cultivate good deeds, and train one's mind. There is no question of the ethical purport of the first two postulates. "Training the mind" could also be interpreted as an ethical postulate, especially when we consider the Buddhist view that evil thoughts generated by an unguarded mind are karmically effective.

The last phrase of this Stanza is usually taken to mean that the three ethical postulates constitute the whole (or at least the most important part) of the Dhamma. However it could be taken to mean that these ethical principles are part of the teachings of the Buddha, and not necessarily the part that constitutes the

Buddha's unique discovery. In the Commentary to the Dhammapada it is stated that this and the two following Stanzas constituted the admonition (ovadagata) delivered by the previous legendary Buddhas to bhikkhus on the uposatha days.

In the explanation of the meaning of the terms in this Stanza, the Commentator says that "to do good" really means the "generation and development of skillful acts from ordination until the realization of the path of Arahat-hood", while "purifying the mind" means the elimination of the five "hindrances" which are obstacles to the realization of jhanic states during meditation.

All this is in keeping with the general purpose of these stanzas, which was to serve as exhortations to Bhikkhus on the uposatha day, and not to serve as a summary of the Buddha-Dhamma.

The uniqueness of Buddhist ethics lies in its many outstanding qualities. It is all-embracing and comprehensive without being impractical or impossible to follow. It is free from taboos relating to diet, dress, behaviour etc. which very often pass as ethical principles. It serves the needs of the worldling as well as those of the recluse. It is useful to the rich and to the poor; to the powerful as well as to the powerless. To conform to Buddhist ethics one need not have to be a "buddhist"; and it serves as a norm to measure the ethical standard of other teachings. But Buddhist ethics is only the threshold for those who wish to pursue the Buddha's path to Enlightenment and the end of all ill.

## BUDDHIST ETHICS AND SOCIAL CRITICISM

Buddhism arose in India during a period of intense intellectual and social ferment. It was a period during which the authority of the Vedas had been placed in doubt, the concept of god as a supreme being and creator was in question, the hereditary restrictions on caste mobility were under attack, and the efficacy of Brahminical rituals was being challenged. The authors of the Upanishads had opened the door for various heterodox currents to emerge in society, and amongst the most significant of these were the Lokayatas who polemicized against religious charlatans, and the Nyayavadis whose rational epistemology created the foundation for intense philosophical debate and encouraged the investigation of the real world based on reason and logic, freed from the burden of superstition and irrational adherence to burdensome rituals. Various ideological sects competed for the attention and acceptance of the ruling elites and the public. The most important amongst these were the Jains and the Buddhists. Although each of the various sects made original and interesting contributions to philosophy, it was the early Buddhists who attempted to provide a unified philosophical system where ethical conduct and social criticism lay at the very core of their ideological system.

Although today, Buddhism is viewed as a religion by many of its followers, the early Buddhists sects were either strongly atheistic or agnostic. The atheists believed that rather than "God having created man in his own image" it was man who had created "God" in his image. In their view, the liberation of humanity was contingent upon humanity shedding the delusion that "God" existed.

Other parables from surviving Buddhist texts indicate agnosticism. For instance, there is a suggestion that Buddhist followers ought not to waste their time on unsolvable metaphysical questions such as "does god exist". The search to identify the "one true god" or to speculate on the nature of god was seen as an exercise in futility.

But the most frequently cited argument against god by the Buddhists was that if an omnipotent and omniscient being such as "God" truly existed, and who was also all good, there could not be the kind of dukkha (suffering) that was so widespread in the real world.

These shlokas (verses) from the Bhuridatta Jataka illustrates this point:

> *If the creator of the entire world they call "God" be the lord of every being, why does he order such misfortune, and not create concord?*

If the creator of the entire world they call "God" be the lord of every being, why let prevail deceit, lies and ignorance, why create such inequity and injustice?

If the creator of the entire world they call "God" be the lord of every being, then an evil master is he, knowing what's right did let wrong prevail!

Unlike religions that ascribed earthly miseries to human sinfulness that brought upon the wrath of a vengeful god who needed to be feared, Buddhism saw the root of human suffering in ignorance that could only be ended through the acquisition of wisdom. Rather than expect some supernatural entity to end human suffering, the Buddhists argued that it was in human hands to end their sorrows through conduct and action driven by knowledge and correct understanding of human nature and the physical world. Hence, the aspiration for knowledge (jigyasa) was seen as the answer to blind faith. Although the Buddhists were not alone in developing this view, the elaboration of this point of view became pivotal to early Buddhist philosophy.

Central to Buddhist philosophy was an understanding of human nature and what caused dukkha-i.e. human suffering. They saw human personality as constituting five attributes, i.e. body, feeling, perception, disposition and consciousness, and used this framework to develop their understanding of human suffering. Citing examples of conditions that led to human suffering, such as aging, sickness and death, or association with the unpleasant, (or separation from the pleasant), or the inability to get what one wished-they concluded that suffering was a condition of stress and conflict inherent within human existence and interaction with the world. They also connected suffering to the very impermanence of things. They observed how people lamented over the loss of a loved one, or experienced sorrow when something or someone that had once given them happiness became separated from them.

They noted that even human pleasures were not immune from suffering because they didn't last forever, and the loss of pleasure inevitably left people feeling deprived. Seeing as how clinging to things (that were necessarily impermanent) was one of the primary causes of dukkha, they cautioned against excessive attachment. At the same time, they recognized a recurring and more general type of existential unease and anxiety (anicchha) that arises from the very transience of life, and our inability to control or comprehend all worldly phenomenon, which they characterized as viparinama-dukkha.

But the Buddhists did not see dukkha only emanating from the difficulties of an individual. They also saw suffering emerge on a much larger scale from hostile social conditions such as poverty, war, and social oppression which they described as dukkha-dukkha.

As a formula (char-mulya) for addressing these different types of suffering, the Buddhists advocated a four-fold scheme of (a) recognizing the problem i.e. suffering (dukkha); (b) identifying the cause of the suffering-such as craving stemming from ignorance (samudaya); (c) establishing the goal of ending the problem (nirodha)-i.e. the cessation of suffering (nirvana); (d) conducting life in a manner that was consistent with the cessation of suffering-following the right path or engaging in the right practice (marga).

Followers were thus goaded into developing both a sense of personal ethics and a social conscience:

> *"He who has understanding and great wisdom does not think of harming himself or another, nor of harming both alike. He rather thinks of his own welfare, of that of others, of that of both, and of the welfare of the whole world. In that way one shows understanding and great wisdom." Anguttara Nikaya-(Gradual Sayings)*
>
> *"By protecting oneself (e.g., morally), one protects others; by protecting others, one protects oneself." Samyukta Nikaya (Kindred Sayings)*

Human actions (kamma, kaama, or karma) in the Buddhist framework were to be judged based on both the intention or motive (chetanaa) and the consequences (vipaaka) of the action. Altruistic actions which helped in the establishment and promotion of a just society were encouraged in the dharmaniyama (moral duty code).

{The discourses, or suttas in the Digha Nikaya, illustrate how there was deep concern with the creation of social conditions favourable to the cultivation of Buddhist values and the expansion of social equity and justice. These views undoubtedly influenced the creation of a "welfare state" during the reign of emperor, Ashoka (B.C. 274-236)}

In their theories of causality Buddhists challenged the view that human destiny was unaffected by the ethics or morality of human actions. They countered the doctrine of amoral causation (akriyavaada) whose adherents argued that there was no merit in doing good and no demerit for doing evil. (An extreme expression of such thinking was seen in philosophers who denied all morality and saw no crime in the killing of any person.)

Realizing that such a world-view could lead to the rejection of moral distinctions and personal responsibility for ones actions, they argued strenuously against such beliefs. They also argued against the theory of Makkali Ghosha (or Ghoshala) who believed that human fate was predetermined, and therefore denied that human actions had any bearing on the results of things (ahetuvaada) and maintained that human intention and effort were essentially powerless in changing human destiny, and therefore advocated fatalism (niyati).

They also countered philosophers from the school of "absolute skepticism" who doubted everything and never committed themselves to any specific position in doctrinal debates. Philosophers from this school such as Sanjaya Belarthaputra (who was known as a theorist of endless equivocation or an equivocationist (amraavikkhepavaadin)) were criticized in the Brahmajaala Sutta (or Sutra) as "eel-wrigglers" who were incapable of taking a definitive stance on the vital philosophical questions of the day. Such skepticism was seen as emanating from both the fear of being in error and the lack of knowledge (or inability) to provide reasonable answers to question put forward for discussion. Such all-pervading doubt coupled with a cynical skepticism (vichikicchaa) was viewed as a serious mental hindrance, a fetter in the path to wisdom.

Other theories that contradicted the notion that human actions mattered were theories of accidentalism (ahetu-apachayavaada), theistic determinism (ishvaranimmaanavaada) and past-action determinism (purvaketavaada or purvekatahetu). All of these were opposed by the Buddhists. Accidentalism was an indeterminist theory which held that whatever was experienced was uncaused and unconditioned by human intervention. Theistic determinism was a determinist theory, which held that whatever was experienced was due to God's will or by plan of a "Supreme-Being". Past-action determinism was also a determinist theory, but it held the belief that whatever was experienced, whether pleasurable or painful or indifferent was entirely due to ones past actions (from a previous life), and ones present actions had no relevance.

The danger in each of these theories was highlighted in these words: "Thus for those who fall back on these three erroneous views as essential dogma, there is neither the will to do what is ought to be done, or not to do what is ought not to be done, nor necessity to do this deed or abstain from that deed. No moral improvement or intellectual culture can be expected from them."

Some of the theories in circulation at that time built on a germ of truth but generalized to the point of absurdity. For instance the accidentalists were correct only to the extent that certain things did indeed appear to happen by random chance or accident. But they failed to recognize that sometimes what may have seemed to be accidental was more due to inadequate understanding or improper or incomplete perception, and that other activities had a clearly discernible cause. To deal with the extreme generalizations of such theorists, they introduced a middle standpoint for their epistemology and ethics.

They thus rejected the theory admitting that everything exists (sabba atthii ti) and in permanence-i.e. the extreme of eternalism (sassatavaada), and its opposite which advocated that nothing actually exists (sabba natthii ti) i.e. nihilism (the denial of all reality in real-world phenomenon) or the extreme of annihilationalism (ucchedavaada). Related to their critique of the eternalist and nihilist philosophies was their rejection of both hedonism and self-mortification (attakilamathaanuyoga) which they viewed as painful, fruitless, unprofitable and ignoble.

Buddhist texts also expressed suspicion about claims by heretical teachers of being constantly "all-knowing" and "all-seeing" and in possession of "all-embracing knowledge-and-vision." Such claims were countered with arguments relating to the actual behaviour of such charlatans in different situations. For instance, they wondered why such "all-knowing" and "all-seeing" spiritual teachers lost their way in an unfamiliar place or why they were unable to escape from trouble while countering a fierce animal such as dog, elephant, horse or bull. Moreover, if they were really omniscient, they wouldn't need to ask for people's names, clans, or the name of a village or market town or make enquiries about anything. That they did such things indicated that their knowledge was evidently limited just like that of any average worldly person (puthujjana).

Unlike religions that were based on revealed truth or the sanctity of every word in a holy textbook, the Buddhist belief system prescribed reasoning based on investigation as the means of determining ones dhamma, (or dharma as in Hindu practise). In a parable in the Kaalaama Sutta, followers of Budhism are advised not to accept any moral codes on the following ten grounds: (1) Vedic authority (anussava), (2) tradition (paramparaa), (3) hearsay or report (itikiraa), (4) textual authority (pittakasampadaa), (5) apparent agreebility of the view (sama o no garu), (6) authority of the holder of the view (takkahetu), (7) apparent logicality of the view (nayahetu), (8) the fact that the view is an accepted standpoint (aakaaraparivitakka), (9) inadequate reflection on reasons (bhabbaruupataa), or (10) the fact that the view agrees with one's own.

In this manner, the Buddhism developed a very sophisticated philosophical system in which social ethics were integrated with rational investigation of human nature, social organization and the physical world. Buddhist ideas and concepts left a powerful impression on other Indian philosophical and religious belief systems, and over time, many commonalities developed amongst the competing ideologies.

However, there were also certain problems with the Buddhist world view which prevented its complete acceptance by intellectuals committed to the scientific method. For instance, although the Buddhists rejected the theory of past action determinism, they did posit the existence of a soul which survived a person's death and carried with it the merits and demerits of a person's past lives. Presumably this concept was essential to the Buddhist goal of encouraging right conduct but it was rejected by those who considered the soul as inseparable from the body and did not believe that the soul survived death. Those who rejected the concept of transmigration of the soul naturally couldn't accept the idea that human destiny had anything to do with merits and demerits accumulated in previous incarnations of the "soul". In their view, morality and ethics were entirely social constructs and had to be dealt with accordingly. The realists (such as the Nyayavadis) who shared the Buddhist concern for morals and ethics in society argued that while morals and ethics ought to be encouraged, they could only be enforced through societal laws and judicial codes.

Another problem facing the Buddhists was that in many ways, their views were too advanced for their times. Society had not yet developed to the point where education was universal, and knowledge of the real world sufficient to prevent superstitions and irrational beliefs from being completely abandoned by the masses. In an era where society had only limited control over nature, it was inevitable that sections of society would continue with beliefs in deities and supernatural phenomenon in the hope that they may be spared from natural disasters or that their crops might withstand attacks from pests and disease. Thus although the Buddhists had a very important and salutatory effect on Indian society, the most advanced Buddhist concepts could be understood and practised by only a minority in society.

Over time, the spirit of inquiry and rational investigation that had spurred the early Buddhist scholars towards dialectical thinking and critical social analysis became more and more replaced by narrow and literalist interpretations of the earlier texts. For instance, advice against accepting something that appeared "logical" without personal verification was taken to mean that logic could be rejected. Advice against wasting ones time on unsolvable metaphysical questions was also taken too literally and many Buddhist scholars remained aloof from the metaphysical debates pursued by other philosophical schools such as those of the Jains and the Nyaya Vaisheshikas. What they didn't anticipate was that some of these debates might lead to useful advances in mathematics or deeper understanding of human thought processes and new insights on human memory and psychology. These led to valuable advances in the interpretation of moods and emotions-thus benefiting Indian art, literature and music.

In addition, later Buddhist monks lapsed into some of the very things that had been attacked by the early Buddhists such as indulgence in unnecessary and elaborate rituals, belief in supra-natural phenomenon, and alienation of the priests from the masses. Activities such as meditation which were encouraged as a means to gaining wisdom became ends in themselves, and were turned into idealistic fetishes. Although Buddhist monks dutifully delivered sermons on right conduct and right action, they often failed to engage in relevant and timely social criticism-and did not always connect the textual suggestions to concrete practice. Intra-Buddhist disputes developed around less significant details, even as some of the most important ideas that had initially shaped the philosophy were pushed into the background. As a result Buddhism as it was practised came to be associated with idealism and inaction. Whereas the early Buddhists saw no merit in worshipping god or its images, later Buddhism developed a pantheon of deities not very different from other Indian religions. Thus even as Buddhism had spread almost throughout Asia by the 5th-6th C AD, it gradually began to lose its distinct edge and liberating influence on much of Indian society. Within the Indian subcontinent, strains of Buddhism survived in Sri Lanka, Bengal, Bhutan, Sikkim, parts of Bihar and Nepal, and parts of Sindh, Punjab, Kashmir and Afghanistan. In parts of Orissa and adjoining regions (such as Chhattisgarh and Telengana), Tantric (and other) influences reshaped the practice of Buddhism. Yet, Buddhism continued to have an impact outside India and developed pockets of influence as far West as Syria, as well as in much of Central Asia (including what is now Uzbekistan, Tajikistan, Kyrgyzia, Kazakhstan) and Tibet. In the East, its influence was felt on virtually every nation including Burma, Thailand, Malaya and Indonesia, Laos, Cambodia, Vietnam, China, Korea and Japan.

As noted earlier, the vast literature of Buddhism (like much of Hindu or Jain literature) was not a literature of revelation and authority. Its essays on social ethics and moral responsibilities, its treatises on philosophy and science, its art and poetry were but pointers to a path to wisdom. This gave Buddhism both flexibility and adaptability. Owing to its non-hegemonic character and humanist appeal, Buddhism was adopted without coercion or force.

It was also successfully fused with Hinduism in many parts of South East Asia just as elements of it had been integrated into Hindu practices in India. In China, it was integrated with Taoism and Confucian principles; in Japan with Shinto beliefs. For several centuries, within India and outside, several people followed multiple faiths and identified as both Buddhists and Hindus, or as both Buddhists and Tantrics, (or Buddhists and Taoists) and so on. During the Gupta period (and in other reigns), philosophers from various schools of thought received royal patronage and temple grants were conferred for the construction of Buddhist and Hindu monuments alike. It is also important to recognize that the form of Buddhism that was embraced in each nation was often quite different. For instance, in Western and Central Asia, it was not the philosophical or intellectual aspects of Buddhism that were popularized, but rather, its personal moral codes. Buddhist prosletysers imbued their stories of the Buddha with examples of miraculous healing and super-natural compassion so as to win more followers.

While such tendencies were also to be seen as Buddhism travelled within India or outwards, in Burma, Sri Lanka and Thailand, Buddhism developed organizational structures that appear to have been much more resilient. It was perhaps realized that the development of Buddhist virtue would require leadership and constant interaction with the community.

In these nations, Buddhism did not degenerate into the extremes of mysticism or retreatism that became commonplace in certain parts of India (such as in the foothills of the Western Himalayas). Burmese and Thai monks maintained a practical and benevolent connection with the community, and thus retained a measure of respect within the community. This also appears to be the case in Japan.

In Korea, the emphasis on gaining wisdom was taken very seriously, and Buddhist monks took the lead in promoting mass literacy. This propelled the growth of technologies associated with the production of paper, writing instruments, inks, and furniture. And unlike in India, (where due to Upanishadic influences, "inner" wisdom came to be favoured over outer wisdom), Buddhist concern for disseminating the writings of the Buddha had significant positive secular impact. In Korean (and other Eastern) Buddhism, there was the correct realization that a Buddhist mindset, or that a Buddhist society could not be constructed overnight. There was thus the emphasis on the (helical) upgradation of individuals and society towards greater "Buddhahood". This philosophical element was perhaps signficant in that it prevented the sort of philosophical stagnation that occurred in India, where followers too often sought immediate succuor, and thus not only became divorced from reality, but also lost sight of the strategic potential of the philosophy.

In addition, it ought to be noted that Buddhism in India also had to contend with strongly anarchic and ultra-democratic tendencies. Precisely because its philosophical structure emphasized the relative and changing nature of truth, different tendencies under the Buddhist mantle competed for leadership through argument and debate.

Initially, this led to important advances in democratic practices within the Sanghas. But over time, it also led to clashes of egoes, hair-splitting and deadlock. While some Buddhist sects compromised and fused with other tendencies (even alien tendencies), others remained fiercely autonomous. To survive, Buddhism had to confront both the tendency to be co-opted, as well as the tendency to atomize.

However, the catastrophic demise of Buddhism in India was triggered by the onslaught of Islam which first obliterated the remnants of Buddhism in Central Asia, and then later in Afghanistan and India. By and large, Buddhism survived only in those countries that escaped invasions by Islamic conquerors. As a gentle faith that encouraged its followers to abjure violence, it was perhaps unable to protect itself from iconoclasts and proselytizers who intended to enforce a new religio-political order. Accustomed to centuries of peaceful co-existence, India's Buddhists had not anticipated the need to develop viable strategies for self-defence that could have combated the violence of India's Islamic conquerors who virtually obliterated Buddhism from the land of its birth.

Yet, it also appears that (in large part) later Buddhism had deviated considerably from the rational principles outlined in the early texts. Monasteries often became isolated from mainstream society, and monks who focused exclusively on meditative practices and idealistic or esoteric philosophical speculation contributed little to social progress. Some have even argued that the monastic orders had degenerated into sheer parasitism and were becoming a heavy social drain. Consequently, value judgements on the demise of Buddhism and the rise of Islam in India need to be made with a measure of caution. Nevertheless, it must be acknowledged that the ascent of Islam was concomitant with the eclipse of Buddhism, and since the influence of Buddhism was greatly dependant on the existence of the monastic orders, the destruction of monasteries and their conversion to mosques and institutions of Quranic learning simply lead to mass conversions to Islam.

In the long term, this could have had the effect of stunting India's future intellectual development, since the destruction of important institutions of Buddhist learning also led to a notable decline in the opportunity (and social sanction) to study secular subjects such as logic and epistemology (which were also taught at Buddhist universities-such as Bhagalpur).

It might also be observed that the destruction of Buddhist centres of learning coincided with the destruction of extremely valuable textual materials-which could have been potentially rediscovered, and revived or reinterpreted by future generations of Indians so as to achieve a society that was more thoughtful and learned. Islamic texts did not offer anything comparable in terms of causality or epistemology. Nor did they offer the psychological, sociological, or moral insights that had been developed under the ambit of Buddhism. Nor was there any comparable stress on seeking knowledge or constantly updating ones understanding of nature and human society.

One can, therefore, only speculate as to the full consequences of this profound sociolgical and cultural loss (and discontinuity).

But East of India, Buddhism did survive, and in countries such Korea, Thailand and Burma, it continued to enjoy a loyal popular following. Philosophical innovations also took place, and as noted earlier, Buddhist scholars in China, Korea and Japan offered their own commentaries and somewhat individual interpretations of Buddhist concepts and formulations outlined in later (5-7th C.) Indian texts. And although the sacking of monasteries and centres of learning (such as Nalanda and Vikramshila in Bihar) led to records of the original Buddhist texts being permanently destroyed, it has been possible to reconstruct some of them from translations that survived outside India such as in Thailand and Tibet. Notwithstanding the virtual erasure of Buddhism in India, it is possible to infer from these reconstructed texts and other archaeological records (and surviving monuments and artifacts) that Buddhism had a very powerful impact in shaping the destiny of India, and in triggering a social and cultural renaissance that would take Indian and other Asian civilizations to a higher level of social, cultural and material development.

## SUTTA PITAKA

The Sutta Pitaka is the second of the three divisions of the Tipitaka or Pali Canon, the great Pali collection of Buddhist writings, the scriptures of Theravada Buddhism. The Sutta Pitaka contains more than 10,000 suttas (teachings) attributed to the Buddha or his close companions.

## Origins

The scriptures tell how the First Council held shortly after the Buddha's death collected together the discipline (vinaya), and the dhamma in five collections. Tradition holds that little was added to the Canon after this. Scholars are more sceptical, but differ in their degrees of scepticism. Dr. Richard Gombrich, Academic Director of the Oxford Centre for Buddhist Studies, former Boden Professor of Sanskrit at Oxford University and former President of the Pali Text Society, thinks most of the first four nikayas goes back to the Buddha, in content but not in form. The late Professor Hirakawa Akira (surname first in accordance with Japanese practice) says that the First Council collected only short prose passages or verses expressing important doctrines, and that these were expanded into full length suttas over the next century. L. S. Cousins, former lecturer in the Department of Comparative Religion at Manchester University and former President of the Pali Text Society, holds that in early times sutta was a pattern of teaching rather than a body of literature.

Dr. Gregory Schopen, Lecturer in Sanskrit, Tibetan, and Buddhist Studies at the University of Texas at Austin, says that it is not until the fifth to sixth centuries C.E. that we can know anything definite about the contents of the Pali Canon.

## Digha Nikaya

This includes *The Greater Discourse on the Foundations of Mindfulness*, *The Fruits of the Contemplative Life*, and *The Buddha's Last Days*. There are 34 long suttas in this nikaya.

## Majjhima Nikaya

This includes *Shorter Exposition of Kamma*, *Mindfulness of Breathing*, and *Mindfulness of the Body*. There are 152 medium-length suttas in this nikaya.

## Samyutta Nikaya

There are, according to one reckoning, 2,889 shorter suttas clustered together by subject.

## Anguttara Nikaya

These teachings are arranged numerically. It includes, according to the commentary's reckoning, 9,557 short suttas grouped by number, from ones to elevens.

## Khuddaka Nikaya

This is a heterogeneous mix of sermons, doctrines, and poetry attributed to the Buddha and his disciples. The well-known Dhammapada is in this section.

# MAHAYANA

Mahayana is one of two major branches of Buddhism, the other being Theravada. Mahayana originated in the Indian subcontinent of what is today northern Pakistan and spread to China during the first century CE where it was Sinicized and then spread throughout East Asia in its Sinicized form. The main countries in which it is practiced today are China, Japan, Korea and Vietnam.

From Mahayana developed the esoteric Vajrayana found mainly in Tibet and Mongolia, but also in adjacent areas of China, and even Buddihism in India Buddhism in Russia. The Vajarana school claims to encompass all previous schools. The most complete Mahayana Canon today is written in the Chinese language. In East Asia, Mahayana scriptures and terminology are traditionally written in Chinese characters and based upon classical Chinese.

Two mainstream subsets of Mahayana Buddhism today are Amidism or Pure Land. Mahayana is an inclusive faith characterized by the adoption of new texts, in addition to the traditional Pali canon, and a shift in the understanding of Buddhism.

It goes beyond the traditional nontheist Theravada ideal of the release of suffering and personal enlightenment, to instead elevate the Buddha to a God-like status and to create a pantheon of quasi-divine Bodhisattvas that devote themselves to personal excellence, ultimate knowledge and the salvation of humanity and all other sentient beings (animals, ghosts, etc.). In Mahayana, the Buddha became an idealized man-god and the Bodhisattva came to represent the universal ideal of excellence.

The fundamental principles of Mahayana doctrine were based around the possibility of universal salvation for all beings (hence "great vehicle") and the existence of Buddhas and Bodhisattva embodying transcendent Buddha-nature-the eternal Buddha Essence present but hidden in all beings-who strive to achieve such a goal. Mahayana also simplified the expression of faith for the common lay people by allowing salvation to be alternatively obtained through the grace of the Buddha Amitabha by having faith and devoting oneself in prayer to Amitabha. This devotional lifestyle of Buddhism is most strongly emphasized by the Pure Land schools and has greatly contributed to the success of Mahayana in East Asia, where spiritual elements traditionally relied upon prayer and mysticism.

## Doctrine

Mahayana, in contrast to the Theravada school of Buddhism, can be characterized by:

- Universalism, in that everyone will become a buddha;
- Enlightened wisdom as the main focus of realization;
- Compassion through the transferal of merit;
- Salvation-as opposed to liberation-supported by a rich cosmography, including celestial realms and powers, with a spectrum of bodhisattvas, both human and seemingly godlike, who can assist followers.

"Philosophical", Mahayana tends to focus on the first three characteristics (universalism, enlightened wisdom, compassion) without showing much interest in supernatural constructions, while "devotional" Mahayana focuses mainly on salvation towards other-worldly realms.

## Universalism

Mahayana traditions generally consider that buddhahood is not final. This is based on a subtle doctrinal distinction between the Mahayana and the early Buddhist schools concerning the issues of *nirvana-with-remainder* and *nirvana-without-remainder*. The early schools considered that nirvana-without-remainder always follows nirvana-with-remainder (Buddhas first achieve enlightenment and then, at 'death', mahaparinirvana) and that nirvana-without-remainder is final; whereas the Mahayana traditions consider that nirvana-without-remainder is always followed by nirvana-with-remainder – the state of Sravakabuddhahood is not final, and is eventually succeeded by the state of buddhahood, or total enlightenment.

This distinction is most evident regarding doctrinal concerns about the capability of a buddha after nirvana (which is identified by the early schools as being nirvana-without-remainder). Most importantly, amongst the early schools, a samyaksambuddha is not able to directly point the way to nirvana after death. This is a major distinction between the early schools and the Mahayana, who conversely state that once a samyaksambuddha arises, he or she continues to directly and actively point the way to nirvana until there are no beings left in samsara. Because the views of early schools and Mahayana differ in this respect, this is exactly why the Mahayana do not talk about a bodhisattva postponing nirvana, and exactly why the early schools do. For example, the early schools held that Maitreya will not attain nirvana while Gautama Buddha's teachings still exist. While the Mahayana schools hold that Maitreya will be the next buddha manifest in this world and will introduce the dharma when it no longer exists, he is not postponing his nirvana to do so, and when he dies (or enters mahaparinirvana), he will likewise continue to teach the dharma for all time. Moreover, Mahayana argues that although it is true that for this world-system, Maitreya will be the next buddha to manifest, there are an infinite number of world-systems, many of which have currently active Buddhas or Buddhas-to-be manifesting.

So, based on the doctrinal distinctions between the early schools and the Mahayana concerning the meaning of nirvana-without-remainder, we see two distinct views concerning the path of the bodhisattva, with the early schools stating that bodhisattvas postpone their own nirvana, whereas the Mahayana schools state that bodhisattvas attempt to reach nirvana as soon as possible, just as sravakas do, but with the motive to continue to effortlessly benefit all beings for all time due to the distinction of views regarding the ability of a buddha after mahaparinirvana.

Because the Mahayana traditions assert that eventually everyone will achieve samyaksambuddhahood or total enlightenment, the Mahayana is labelled universalist, whereas because the Nikaya traditions assert that there are three routes to nirvana, which are distinct, they are considered not to be universalist.

## Enlightened Wisdom

According to Mahayana, traditional Buddhism tends to focus on an ascetic, individual approach to the attainment of nirvana: suppression of desire, removal from the world, solitude. Its followers are sravakas and pratyekabuddhas.

The primary focus of Mahayana is bodhicitta, the vow to strive for buddhahood or awakened mind (bodhicitta) both for oneself and for the benefit of all other sentient beings. Being a high-level bodhisattva involves possessing a mind of great compassion conjoined with insight into reality, realizing emptiness (shunyata, zz), and/or the tathagatagarbha (buddhic essence of all things). With this mind the practitioner will realize the final goal of full enlightenment, or buddhahood: an omniscient, blissful mind completely free from suffering and its causes, that is able to work tirelessly for the benefit of all living beings. Six virtues or perfections (paramitas) are listed for the bodhisattva: generosity, patience, meditation, morality, energy and wisdom.

Many "philosophical" schools and sutras of Mahayana Buddhism have focused on the nature of enlightenment and nirvana itself, from the Madhyamika and its rival, Yogacara, to the Tathagatagarbha teachings and Zen.

## Compassion

Compassion, or Karuna, is the other key concept of Mahayana, and is considered the indispensable complement to enlightened wisdom. Compassion is important in all schools of Buddhism, but is particularly emphasized in Mahayana. It relies on the idea that excess acquired merit can be transmitted to others.

The bodhisattvas are the main actors of compassion, Avalokitesvara (known in East Asia as Kuan Yin) being foremost among them. Although having reached enlightenment, bodhisattvas usually make a vow to postpone entering into nirvana until all other beings have also been saved. They devote themselves to helping others reach enlightenment.

The Mahayana idea also that salvation is universal allowed for one to focus less on the release of personal sufferring and more on humanity's salvation, and is consequently described to be more compassionate and caring for the welfare of others than other traditions of Buddhism. A comparison between Hinayana (earlier Buddhist traditions) and Mahayana made by the 10th century Tibetan author Je Gampopa in *The Jewel Ornament of Liberation* follows: 'Clinging to the well-being of mere peace' signifies the lower capacity [Hinayana] attitude wherein the longing to transcend suffering is focused on oneself alone. This precludes the cherishing of others and hence there is little development of altruism. [...] When loving kindness and compassion become part of one, there is so much care for other conscious beings that one could not bear to liberate oneself alone. [...] Master Manjushriikiirti has said: 'A Mahayana follower should not be without loving kindness and compassion for even a single moment', and 'It is not anger and hatred but loving kindness and compassion that vouchsafe the welfare of others'.

## Salvation

"Devotional" Mahayana developed a rich cosmography, with various supernatural Buddhas and bodhisattvas residing in paradisiacal realms. The concept of trinity, or trikaya, supports these constructions, making the Buddha himself into a transcendental god-like figure.

Under various conditions, these realms could be attained by devotees after their death so that when reborn they could strive towards buddhahood in the best possible conditions. Depending on the sect, this salvation to "paradise" can be obtained by faith, imaging, or sometimes even by the simple invocation of the Buddha's name. This approach to salvation is at the origin of the mass appeal of devotional Buddhism, especially represented by the Pure Land.

This rich cosmography also allowed Mahayana to be quite syncretic and accommodating of other faiths or deities. Various origins have been suggested to explain its emergence, such as "popular Hindu devotional cults (*bhakti*), and Persian and Greco-Roman theologies, which filtered into India from the northwest" (Tom Lowenstein, "The vision of the Buddha").

## Mahayana Scriptures

The Mahayana scriptures were written probably around the 1st century BCE. Some of them, such as the Perfection of Wisdom sutras, are presented as actual sermons of the Buddha that had been hidden. By some accounts, these sermons were passed on by oral tradition, as with other sutras; other accounts state that they were hidden and then revealed several centuries later by some mythological route. In addition to sutras, some Mahayana texts are essentially commentaries.

Among the earliest major Mahayana scriptures attested to historically are the Perfection of Wisdom (Prajna-Paramita) sutras, the Avatamsaka Sutra, the Lotus Sutra, the Vimalakirti Sutra, and the Nirvana Sutra.

The Mahayana sometimes divide Shakyamuni Buddha's teachings into three general categories, known as "turnings of the wheel of dharma (truth)": the Hinayana, the Prajna Paramita, and the Tathagatagarbha teachings.

The Mahayana canon further expanded after Buddhism was transmitted to other countries such as China and Tibet, where the existing texts were translated. New texts, such as the Platform Sutra and the Sutra of Perfect Enlightenment were explicitly not of Indian origin, but were widely accepted as valid scriptures on their own merits. Other later writings included the Linji Lu, a commentary by Chan master Linji Yixuan. In the course of the development of Korean Buddhism and Japanese Buddhism, further important commentaries were composed. These included, for example, in Korea, some of the writings of Jinul, and in Japan, works such as Dogen's Shobogenzo.

## Origins

Mahayana as a distinct movement began around the 1st century BCE in the area around the Kushan Empire (now part of Pakistan) before it was transmitted in a highly evolved form to China in the second century CE. Mahayana's exact origin is unknown, however, a number of common elements and background are suggested by various scholars and theologians.

The Abhidharma in the modern Theravada Pali canon and a Sarvastivada Abhidharma composed in Sanskrit that survives in both the Chinese and Tibetan traditions, has no common order of composition. This indicates that overall, Buddhism became increasingly fragmented and that this might have led to a widening distance between laity and sangha, who were increasingly preoccupied with theological speculation.

The Mahayana movement, on the other hand, was ecumenical, reflecting a wide range of theology from both the Sthaviravada and Mahasanghika sects. (Paul Williams, "Mahayana Buddhism", 1989). Moreover, those who believe that Mahayana sutras were invented during this period speculate that the process of reshuffling sutras in terms of relevance to various Abbhidharma eventually led to editing itself. This process slowly eroded the taboo regarding the composition of new sutras.

Another important element is the lay practice of stupa devotion, which was actively encouraged by Ashoka. According to Akira Hirakawa (A History of Indian Buddhism: From Sakyamuni to Early Mahayana), stupas — which were initially mere monuments to Gautama Buddha — increasingly became the place of devotion and of spreading Buddhism to the masses, the majority of whom were illiterate Hindus. On the inside wall of the stupa, pictures were drawn or sculpted depicting the life of Buddha and his previous lives as a bodhisattva. This has given rise to devotion to the trancendent omnipresent and always-present Buddha and the bodhisattvas, distinct from the purely monastic sangha.

## Epigraphical Evidence

One of the first known mentions of the Buddha using the word Bhagavat or Bhagavan ("Supreme Lord") is a dedication on a relic vase inserted in a stupa in Gandhara, written in kharoshthi by an Indo-Greek meridarch (civil governor of a province) named Theodorus in the 1st century BCE: "Theudorena meridarkhena pratithavida ime sarira sakamunisa bhagavato bahu-jana-stitiye": "The meridarch Theodorus has enshrined relics of Lord Shakyamuni, for the welfare of the mass of the people."

The earliest stone inscriptions containing recognizably Mahayana formulations and a mention of the Buddha Amitabha were found in the Indian subcontinent in Mathura and dated to around 180 CE. Remains of a statue of a Buddha bear the Brahmi inscription: *"Made in the year 28 of the reign of king Huvishka,... for the Buddha Amitabha"* (Mathura Museum).

Such inscriptions in Indian proper (Mathura) are rather late and few (the next known one is dated to the end of the 3rd century), in comparison to the multiplicity of Mahayana writings transiting from Central Asia to China at that time, and the involvement of Central Asian Buddhist monks, suggesting the focus of Mahayana development was probably in the northwest.

## Scriptures

The first known Mahayana texts are translations made into Chinese by the Kushan monk Lokaksema in the Chinese capital of Luoyang, between 178 and 189 CE. Lokaksema's work includes the translation of the Pratyutpanna Sutra, containing the first known mentions of the Buddha Amitabha and his Pure Land, said to be at the origin of Pure Land practice in China, and the first known translations of the Prajnaparamita Sutra, a founding text of Mahayana Buddhism.

## The 4th Buddhist Council

The formal rise of Mahayana Buddhism has been dated to around the middle of the 2nd century CE, when the Kushan emperor Kanishka convened the 4th Buddhist Council in Gandhara, which confirmed the formal scission of Mahayana

Buddhism ('YXN) from the traditional Nikaya schools of Buddhism. This was also the time and place of a rich cultural interaction between Buddhism and Hellenistic culture, which influenced the early representations of Buddhas, in what is known as Greco-Buddhist art.

## Expansion (1st c.CE–10th c.CE)

From the 1st century CE and within the space of a few centuries, Mahayana was to flourish and spread in from India to South-East Asia, and towards the north to Central Asia, China, Korea and Japan. Mahayana disappeared from India during the 11th century, and consequently lost its influence in South-East Asia where it was replaced by Theravada Buddhism from Sri Lanka. Mahayana remains, however, the most followed of the Buddhist doctrines to this day in Eastern Asia and the world.

## THERAVAADA BUDDHIST ECONOMIC ETHICS

The economic ethics of Theravaada Buddhism, especially attitudes toward wealth, poverty, charity, and labor cannot be understood without understanding something about Buddhist soteriologies (i.e., theories of how a person achieves enlightenment). The earliest Buddhist soteriology was summarized in the Four Noble Truths: (1) suffering exists; (2) the cause of suffering is craving (attachment); (3) there is a way out of this suffering; and (4) this way is the Eightfold Path. This Eightfold Path consisted of three types of activity: (1) moral conduct; (2) mental discipline; and (3) wisdom. Moral conduct in turn included three of the eight components of the Path: (a) right conduct; (b) right speech; and (c) right livelihood, each of which involved various prescriptions for behaviour, attitudes, and mental dispositions.

Early Buddhist soteriologies must also be understood by examining the major concepts of karma, *anaatman*, nirvana/sa.msaara and *pratiitya-samutpaada* (dependent coorigination) to see how they helped define such soteriologies. Karma, for example was understood to apply to all actions including moral ones and implied that a person's present situation was the result of past acts, thoughts, and feelings in this life and previous ones.

It also taught that the effects of a person's actions carry on beyond the present life into future lives. Therefore, meritorious acts in the present life will result in rewards in future lives. Karma thus can be conceived of as a Buddhist basis for justice in the sense that through it each individual received what he or she deserved in life based upon past actions. This of course included the economic realm with the implication that one's economic position (i.e., wealth) was the result of one's actions in this or previous lives-with good ethical actions leading to a better position in terms of wealth and bad ethical actions leading to a worse position. In this way, karma offered a rational explanation for social, economic, and political inequalities while also implying that economic justice *already* was achieved, i.e., persons economically have what they deserve, at least to start off. Karma thus contributed to a strong sense of morality as conditioning one's existence and to a stress on individual responsibility rather than social forces as the cause of one's present situation.

In addition to karma, the Buddhist concepts of nirvana and sa.msaara were also central to understanding Buddhist soteriologies and had important implications for views toward poverty and wealth. In early Theravaada Buddhism, for example, nirvana and sa.msaara were viewed as far apart-nirvana being the "unborn" and "unbecome"-and defined in terms of what sa.msaara was not. The soteriological goal was to escape sa.msaara through escaping craving, and to do this through practicing the Eightfold Path. Only when a person had escaped sa.msaara could they attain nirvana, whether nirvana was conceived of as an ethical state or also as a metaphysical one. The implication for early Theravaada Buddhist believers was that to attain nirvana right ethical behaviour was a key. Another implication was that since sa.msaara had little value, economic activities (which generally were associated with the realm of sa.msaara) could never have genuine religious significance.

The concept of *pratiitya-samutpaada* was a third major concept that helped determine Buddhist soteriology. It did so by pointing to the interdependence of all things and actions. In ethical terms, this implied that although the individual was ultimately responsible for his own karma, since all sentient beings are connected and since compassion is a virtue, helping one's fellow sentient beings also had value, including help of a material nature. Thus there was a strong moral basis for giving and not withholding material or spiritual assistance to others.

Finally, the concept of *anaatman* implied that since no eternal unchanging *aatman* (self) existed, there was no reason to withhold giving to others, or to hoard wealth, since there was no "I" that needed to be protected or defended more than others. Yet, the idea of *anaatman* also held a potential paradox. That is, if there was no self, then what individual or personal moral obligation could exist? Could ethics even be possible if there was no self? The most common early Theravaada Buddhist answer to this was that whether there was a self or not, karma continued to exist and wrongful moral actions led to negative karma while right actions led to positive karma. Thus the nonexistence of self did not imply that actions and their results, or ethical responsibility, could not exist.

The above discussion highlights the correspondence between the key concepts of Theravaada Buddhism and attitudes toward wealth, poverty, and ethical action. Based upon this, in the earliest Buddhism most kinds of economic behaviour of monks (e.g., labor, agricultural production, and possession or accumulation of wealth outside of one's robe and begging bowl) were proscribed, and monk economic ethics were mainly negative. With the passage of time, however, some Vinayas were relaxed. Individual monks were allowed to keep money, and monasteries were allowed to sell or use for profit goods donated to them, as well as lend out money and collect interest-as long as the profits went to the benefit of the Three Treasures, i.e., the sangha, the Buddha, and the Dharma. Economic activities undertaken by individual monks for personal profit, however, as well as monk labor (whether it involved agriculture or commercial activities), continued to be proscribed.

In contrast to these early monk economic ethics, early economic ethics for the laity appeared clearly different since they allowed the laity to hold wealth and even praised the creation of wealth through diligent work following one's chosen or given occupation. However, lay economic ethics also stressed the avoidance of craving or attachment to such wealth and that it must be shared with the sangha and with family and friends. In addition, early lay economic ethics praised the value of labor and devotion to most secular occupations (with some exceptions).

Such a more lenient attitude toward lay accumulation of wealth and labor was not simply the result of monks trying to ensure their own material support from the laity. It was also the result of a clear and consistent logic in the early Buddhist view of reality that what had ultimate value for both monk and laity was the individual attainment of enlightenment. Although best pursued as a monk, such attainment of enlightenment was also possible for lay people. As a result, economic ethics, whether for monk or for laity, ultimately were directed toward furthering this goal of enlightenment. For both, the key to achieving this goal was overcoming craving. As the laity needed to earn their living, accumulating wealth was allowed and even encouraged as long as too much craving was avoided. Since the monks were on a different point in the path toward nirvana and required stricter discipline, it was considered better for them not to accumulate or hold wealth at all. This system required that the laity support the sangha in order to allow individual monks to devote themselves to their own enlightenment, but also so that they could teach the Dharma to the laity and give knowledge and understanding which furthered the process of laity enlightenment. Through giving to the sangha (*daana*), the laity earned merit which would help them receive better karma; by avoiding economic activities in favor of meditation and teaching, monks spread the Dharma and contributed to the overall supreme goal of maximum progress toward enlightenment for all.

Lay economic ethics taught in early Buddhism thus focused upon three areas: (1) accumulating wealth through hard work, diligence and setting certain restrains on one's own consumption; (2) choosing and pursuing the right occupation (i.e., avoiding occupations such as killing animals, trade in weapons, and the like); and (3) sharing wealth honestly acquired with family, friends and the sangha. Such merchant-type values in early

Buddhist lay ethics contrasted sharply with the economic ethics of Brahminism, which reflected the patriarchal clan-based ethics of an agricultural society.

Support for this influence of merchant-class values upon early Buddhist lay ethics can be found in early Buddhist suutras and stories which refer to lay wealth in a way which tends to assume a certain amount of wealth already being held, and in the strong emphasis upon giving and receiving rather than the high value put in Brahmin ethics upon sacrifices. The influence of merchant-class ethics is also apparent in the three main themes of such suutras and stories: (1) diligence and honesty in acquisition of wealth; (2) restrain of one's own consumption in order to accumulate wealth; and (3) reinvestment of this wealth to produce more wealth, merit and happiness for self and others.

The best-known early suutra which exhibits these themes was the *Singaalovaada Sutta* or *Admonition to Singaala*, sometimes referred to as the Buddhist laymen's Vinaya. In it an ethic of diligent accumulation of wealth through hard work, restrained consumption, and reinvestment of profits into one's business is stressed, as in the following passage:

*The wise and moral man*
*Shines like a fire on a hilltop*
*Who does not hurt the flower.*
*Such a man makes his pile*
*As an anthill, gradually.*
*Grown wealthy, he thus*
*Can help his family*
*And firmly bind his friends*
*To himself. He should divide*
*His money in four parts;*
*On one he should live,*
*With two expand his trade,*
*And the fourth he should save*
*Against a rainy day.*

What is particularly interesting about this passage is that it urges that only a fourth of all one's wealth should be consumed for daily living while the other three-fourths should be saved, most of it to be reinvested in one's trade. This reflects a merchant-based mentality which while perhaps not ascetic in the same sense as the so-called Protestant ethic, does put a strong emphasis on saving and reinvestment. The suutra goes on to give specific advice on how to avoid squandering this accumulated wealth by avoiding such things as idleness, bad friends, addiction to intoxicants, roaming the streets at odd hours, frequenting shows, and indulging in gambling.

Other early suutras emphasize strongly the virtue of nonattachment to wealth as the foundation of all morals in society. This can be seen in both the *Cakkavatti-Siihanaada* and *Kuu.tadanta Suttas*, in which the generosity of a righteous king for the destitute becomes the basis for the establishment of virtue and prosperity in lay society. At the same time, a lack of such generosity was presented as the beginning of a steady expansion of vice and evil and a steady decay of society. Suutras such as the *Mahaa-Sudassana Sutta*, moreover, by stressing the impermanence of all wealth and worldly possessions, no matter how great their extent, reinforced the value of nonattachment to wealth.

With the passage of time, the lay virtue of generosity and giving only became more and more predominant. This was reflected in the many stories in the suutras of unbridled generosity leading to good karma and spiritual advancement. At the same time, while suutras pointed out the dangers of wealth in terms of creating craving, poverty was never advocated for the laity, but was viewed as a "suffering in the world for a layman."

Yet even though giving became the supreme lay virtue, there was a subtle difference between the earlier suutras, in which giving to both the poor *and* the sangha was urged, and later suutras, in which giving to the sangha was the main theme. In this way *daana* (giving to the sangha) became the central concept of lay economic ethics. By giving to the sangha, the individual not only furthered his own soteriological quest and karma, but benefited society and contributed to the betterment of others' karma through supporting the educational act of spreading the Dharma.

The concept of *daana* along with the concept of karma also contribute to a certain set of ideas about economic justice in Theravaada Buddhist economic ethics. On the one hand, the notion of karma has been used to argue *in favor* of an idea of justice existing in Theravaada Buddhist economic ethics, as follows:

Such equality before the law of kamma resembles the West's notion of procedural justice... there is equality of opportunity in the sense that the law of kamma treats all evenhandedly in rewarding virtue and punishing vice, and the determining essence of virtue (the attitude of nonattachment) is presumably an equal possibility for all.

Economic inequalities existing in society thus can be viewed as the result of past karmic acts and do not violate a sense of justice but in fact confirm it.

On the other hand, the concept of karma can also be used to argue *against* an idea of justice in Theravaada Buddhism. This is possible through emphasizing an interpretation of karma which implies that the way to nirvana is through a slow accumulation of individual merit effected by religious giving and individual acts of compassion rather than an interest in effecting social justice in the Western sense of an equitable distribution of wealth:

> *... The law of kamma, with its all encompassing explanation of existing inequalities, tends to do away with Buddhist perplexity over the plight of the poor. Buddhist emphasis on the virtue of charity tends to outweigh interest in justice and so ethical reflection is shifted away from evaluation of the existing distribution of wealth.*

What both of the above arguments share is a tendency to regard the issue of economic justice as one involving the need for greater economic equality and redistribution of wealth from the rich to the poor. This of course is only one interpretation of justice. If accepted, however, there is little clear evidence in

Theravaada Buddhism supporting redistribution of wealth, except for the idea of *daana*, which implied redistribution of wealth *to the sangha* and not necessarily to the poor, and the idea of *karu.naa*, which implied more individually-based acts of compassion toward one's fellow sentient beings rather than an overall program for social change.

Support for an idea of economic or social equality in the form of an economically or socially classless society also never seems to have been envisioned in early Theravaada Buddhism, at least for the laity. Instead, clear differences in social, economic, and political levels seem to be assumed, a fact reflected in the lack of a clear prohibition against ownership or use of slaves either by layman or temple (though slave trading was proscribed). In addition while within the early sangha a large degree of economic and to some degree political equality existed, this equality was never extended beyond the sangha to a prescription for society as a whole. Moreover even within the sangha, there was a class structure in the sense of different levels of spiritual development and seniority which were acknowledged and affected how different monks were treated. Thus equality in early Theravaada Buddhism seems to have been primarily a spiritual ideal viewed in terms of equal *potential* for all to achieve spiritual enlightenment. This conclusion is supported by the fact that in contrast to Brahminism, almost all classes of people could and did enter the early Buddhist order of monks.

Early Theravaada Buddhist economic ethics and ideas regarding social and economic inequality were also strongly affected by various viewpoints of the proper relationship between the sangha and the state or king. Although the earliest Buddhism tended to view contact with the king as something to be avoided like a poisonous snake, and kings were labeled among other disasters that might occur to a person, by the time of King A"soka and afterward, Buddhism began to develop a close relationship with the state in most places where it existed, including India and Ceylon, and later Southeast Asia, China, Japan, and Tibet. This relationship was based upon the idea of the Cakravartin king, or the ideal enlightened king who carried out the Dharma in society and supported the sangha, in return for which he received the sangha's spiritual protection and legitimization. The story of King A"soka of course seems to provide a major historical context for this ideal, and the stone edicts left by his rule point to the close and mutually beneficial relationship between him and the Buddhist sangha. These edicts refer to social policies which have been referred to by some scholars as a type of ancient "welfare state" in that various facilities for the poor, sick, and indigent were constructed by the state, in addition to state support for the sangha. Yet a closer reading of these edicts themselves makes clear that A"soka never intended to change the fundamental economic and social structure of his society. Instead, he focused his social activism more upon spreading the Dharma through charitable works for the poor, sick, and imprisoned, religious giving to the sangha, and encouraging meditation and proper treatment of one's father and mother, teacher, relatives, slaves and servants, priests and ascetics, and animals.

From the historical example of A"soka and other instances of sangha/state cooperation, early Theravaada Buddhism developed and evolved its own concept of the ideal relationship between sangha and state which, as two recent scholars have termed it, was a "purposeful political strategy of adjustment and accommodation" toward the state reflecting a "distinctly Buddhist understanding of the possibilities for social change" through "gradual reform with emphasis on religious education." In other words, here was established the typically Buddhist amelioratory approach to social change that would continue to affect both Theravaada and Mahaayaana traditions later on. In this approach, the role of the enlightened king or state was to formulate specific laws for society based upon general ideas and principles given by the Buddha. At the same time, the political role of the sangha was to teach the Dharma to the king and support the state by obeying the laws of the land (and not challenge the given economic distribution and social structure). In this way, while ideas about social and economic justice did seem to exist in early Theravaada Buddhism, they existed in the form of particular ideas about karma, *daana* and the state/sangha relationship which were clearly different than most current Western ideas about justice. Yet, this should not be surprising since current Western ideas are themselves a product of a long evolution of concepts, and although related to their predecessors in Judeo-Christian ethics and Roman law, are still clearly different from them.

In conclusion, wealth and labor had value in early Theravaada Buddhist ethics, but a value ultimately smaller than that given to the pursuit of enlightenment for the monk and gaining merit through *daana* for the laity. Wealth was never an evil in itself, either for laity or monk, but was to be welcomed as the result of past merits, as long as one never became attached to it. Giving was the way to avoid such attachment and for the laity such giving increasingly became giving to the sangha (*daana*), rather than directly to the poor or reinvesting into one's secular business. Moreover, in contrast to the Calvinist with his God of predestination, the Theravaadist layman never was assured of his salvation, and constantly had to work to earn it through the creation of additional merit through additional *daana*. This led to an emphasis on investment in *daana* over investment in one's secular business, with the ultimate consequence for the Theravaada Buddhist that his "proof of salvation" was found "not in accumulating and creating new wealth, but in giving it away in the form of *daana*." As a result, a type of Protestant asceticism emphasizing the accumulation of wealth which was then invested into one's secular business and (according to Weber) contributed to the development of modern capitalism in the West, never was encouraged in the Theravaada tradition once the idea of *daana* became dominant. Some scholars go even further and argue that this very tradition of *daana* is an important reason for the slower development of modern capitalism in countries with a strong Theravaada tradition.

## KARMA IN BUDDHISM

In a discourse (Anguttara Nikaya Nibbedhika Sutta) the Buddha said : "Intention (*cetana*), monks, is kamma, I say. Having willed, one acts through body, speech and mind".

Every time a person acts there is some quality of intention at the base of the mind and it is that quality rather than the outward appearance of the action that determines the effect. For example, a man walking in a forest encounters a deer that runs past him in distress. Subsequently, a man dressed in hunting gear with a gun also passes him asking which direction the deer went.

The man misinforms the hunter sending him in a direction other than that in which the deer went. Although he has told a lie, he has acted out of compassion for the deer which forms the underlying intention behind his action. That volition (*cetana*) behind the action will be a cause for his own future well-being. On the other hand if a person professes piety and virtue but nonetheless acts with greed, anger or hatred (veiled behind an outward display of well-meaning intent) then the fruit of those actions will bear testimony to the fundamental intention that lay behind them and will be a cause for future unhappiness. In this sense the Buddha spoke of wholesome actions (*kusala-kamma*) and unwholesome actions (*akusala-kamma*).

Karma is thus used as an ethical principle, rather than a cosmological explanation for the world. Buddhists believe that the actions of beings determine their own future, and because of this there are no private actions: all actions have a consequence.

The emphasis of karma in Buddhism is on cause, not on effect: Buddhists do not say "it was due to her karma that it happened to her"-indeed the karmic consequences of one's actions are dependent on sufficient conditions.

There is a further distinction between wholesome kamma that leads to more exalted and rarefied forms of samsaric happiness (birth in higher realms), to neutralizing actions (called in Sanskrit and Pali *Kriya*) which lead to enlightenment: (nirvana). Therefore there is samsaric good karma, which leads to more fortunate rebirths (such as the human realm), and then there is liberating karma-which is supremely good. Nonetheless, the Buddha advocated the practise of wholesome actions: "Refrain from unwholesome actions/Perform only wholesome ones/Purify the mind/This is the teaching of the Enlightened Ones." Dhp v.183.

*Ṡamsaric karma* is typically divided into the three: good, neutral, and bad (in accordance with the degree of samsaric happiness or suffering that will mature as a consequence). Likewise, liberating karma is divided into three: according to whether it will mature the being as a uravakabuddha, pratyekabuddha, or a samyaksambuddha.

In Buddhism, the term karma is often used to refer only to *samsaric karma*, as indicated by the twelve nidanas of dependent origination.

The differentiation between "good" karma and "liberating" karma has been used by some scholars to argue that the development of Tantra depended upon Buddhist ideas and philosophies.

Because of the inevitability of consequence, Karma entails the notion of Buddhist rebirth. However, karma is not the sole basis of rebirth. The rebirths of eighth stage (and above) Bodhisattvas in the Mahayana tradition refers to those liberated beings who consciously choose to be reborn in a future life in order to help others still trapped in Samsara.

Some people have problems with the teaching on karma, often of what exactly the Buddha is asking them to believe in when asking them to have conviction in karma.

- First, action really is happening — it's not an illusion.
- Second, you really are responsible for your actions. There's no outside force like the stars or some good or evil being acting through you. When you're conscious, you're the one who decides what to do.
- Third, your actions have results — you're not just writing on the water — and those results can be good or bad depending on the quality of the intention behind the act.

A very good example of the working of karma in real life is recorded by Mr. Yuan Liao-Fan, a sixteenth century high ranking government officer in China. He wrote the Liao-Fan Four Lessons with the hope that it would teach his son, Yuan Tian-Qi, how to understand the true nature of destiny.

## Wrong Understandings of Karma

In Buddhism, Karma is not pre-determinism, fatalism or accidentalism, as all these ideas lead to inaction and destroy motivation and human effort that a human being can change for the better no matter what his or her past was and are designated as "wrong view" in Buddhism.

1. Pubbekatahetuvada: The belief that all happiness and suffering arise from previous karma (Past-action determinism).
2. Issaranimmanahetuvada: The belief that all happiness and suffering are caused by the directives of a Supreme Being (Theistic determinism).
3. Ahetu-apaccayavada: The belief that all happiness and suffering are random, having no cause (Indeterminism or Accidentalism).

"Bhikkhus, adhering to previously done kamma as the essence, there are neither motivation nor effort with what should be done and what should not be done... Not upholding ardently what should be done, nor abandoning what should be abandoned, those ascetics and Brahmins are as if deluded, lacking a control, incapable of having any true teaching. (Buddha)

In Buddhism, Karma is simply there as a guide and an indication of what your present is and how one's future can be made better by self effort, otherwise, fatalism and pre-determinism is the anti-thesis of the notion of perfection or self-conquest-which is the primary aim of Buddhism.

*The Buddha asserts effort and motivation as the crucial factors in deciding the ethical value of these various teachings on kamma.*

# 3

# Buddhist Cosmology

Buddhist cosmology is the description of the shape and evolution of the universe according to the canonical Buddhist scriptures and commentaries.

## INTRODUCTION

The self-consistent Buddhist cosmology which is presented in commentaries and works of Abhidharma in both Theravada and Mahayana traditions, is the end-product of an analysis and reconciliation of cosmological comments found in the Buddhist sutra and vinaya traditions. No single sutra sets out the entire structure of the universe.

However, in several sutras the Buddha describes other worlds and states of being, and other sutras describe the origin and destruction of the universe. The synthesis of these data into a single comprehensive system must have taken place early in the history of Buddhism, as the system described in the Pali Vibhajyavada tradition (represented by today's Theravadins) agrees, despite some trivial inconsistencies of nomenclature, with the Sarvastivada tradition which is preserved by Mahayana Buddhists. The picture of the world presented in Buddhist cosmological descriptions cannot be taken as a literal description of the shape of the universe. It is inconsistent, and cannot be made consistent, with astronomical data that were already known in ancient India. However, it is not intended to be a description of how humans perceive their world; rather, it is the universe as seen through the divyacakcus, the "divine eye" by which a Buddha or an arhat who has cultivated this faculty can perceive all of the other worlds and the beings arising (being born) and passing away (dying) within them, and can tell from what state they have been reborn and into what state they will be reborn. Buddhist cosmology can accordingly be divided into two related kinds: spatial cosmology, which describes the arrangement of the various worlds within the universe, and temporal cosmology, which describes how those worlds come into existence, and how they pass away.

## SHUNYATA

Shunyata is a term, translated as "Emptiness" or "Voidness", which constitutes an aspect of the Buddhist metaphysical critique as well as Buddhist epistemology and phenomenology. Uunyata signifies that everything one encounters in life is empty of soul, permanence, and self-nature. Everything is inter-related, never self-sufficient or independent; nothing has independent reality. Yet uunyata never connotes nihilism, which Buddhist doctrine considers to be a delusion, just as it considers materialism to be a delusion.

In the Mahayana Tathagatagarbha sutras, in contrast, only impermanent, changeful things and states (the realm of samsara) are said to be empty in a negative sense-but not the Buddha or Nirvana, which are stated to be real, eternal and filled with inconceivable, enduring virtues.

### Origin and Development of Uunyata

The theme of uunyata emerged from the Buddhist doctrines of Anatta (Pali, Sanskrit: Anatman—the nonexistence of the self, or Atman) and Paticcasamuppada (Pali, Sanskrit: pratityasamutpada, Interdependent Arising). The Sunna Sutta, part of the Pali Canon, relates that the monk Ananda, the attendant to Gautama Buddha asked, "It is said that the world is empty, the world is empty, lord. In what respect is it said that the world is empty?" The Buddha replied, "Insofar as it is empty of a self or of anything pertaining to a self: Thus it is said, Ananda, that the world is empty." Uunyata is a key theme of the Heart Sutra, which is commonly chanted by Mahayana Buddhists worldwide.

Uunyata was further developed by Nagarjuna and the Madhyamaka school, which is usually counted as an early Mahayana school. Uunyata ("positively" interpreted-see Tathagatagarbha section below) is also an important element of the Tathagatagarbha literature, which played a formative role in the evolution of subsequent Mahayana doctrine and practice. It should be noted that the exact definition and extent of shunyata varies within the different Buddhist schools of philosophy. In the Tibetan Buddhist tradition, detailed dialogs between the perspectives of the various schools are preserved in order to train students.

## Uunyata in Presecular Buddhism, in the Nikayas

Sunnata "Emptiness" (sunnata) in Pali contexts is not the metaphysical Zero (Nonbeing as the principle of Being, Infinite Possibility as distinguished from Indefinite Actuality), but a characteristic of this world, as in S IV.295 96, where it has been explained that when the Almsman returns from a deathlike Contemplation in which consciousness and feeling have been arrested, "three touches touch him," "emptiness (sunnato)," "formlessness (animito)" and "making no plans (appanihito phasso)," and he discriminates (viveka) accordingly; and the meaning of "emptiness" 'is explained at M 1.29, "emancipation of the mind by Emptiness (sunnata ceto vimutti) being consequent upon the realization that `this world is empty of spirit or anything spiritual' (sunnam idam attena va attaniyena) "; sunnata is synonymous with anatta; of which it really only paraphrases and isolates the privative AN. It is no doubt in the same sense that in A 1.72, "the texts are coupled with `emptiness' (suttanta... sunnata patisannuta) "; there is, in fact, nothing more characteristic of Buddhist teaching than its constant resort to negatives (above all in the sense of the word anatta), which even some contemporary hearers found perplexing. The denial of spirituality to contingent things in particular is a denial of any real essence to these things in themselves, and thus forms the basis of the more sweeping sunyavada doctrine which in the Mahayana denies not any "value" but any essence to even the Buddha's appearance and to the promulgation of the Dhamma itself. If such a doctrine disturbs us, it may be found more palatably expressed in the Vajracchedika Sutra thus, "Those who see me in the body (rupena) and think of me in sounds (ghosaih), their way of thinking is false, they do not see me at all.... The Buddha cannot be rightly understood (rjuboddhum) by any means (upayena). Not that "means" are not dispositive to a right understanding, but that if regarded as ends, even the most adequate means are a hindrance. In such a radical iconoclasm as this all traditional teachings are finally agreed. What is true of ethics is also true of the supports of contemplation: as in the well known Parable of the Raft, the means are of no more use when the goal has been reached.

## Sunyata in the Heart Sutra

The Heart Sutra (one of the Mahayana Perfection of Wisdom Sutras) declares that the skandhas, which constitute our mental and physical existence, are empty in their nature or essence, i.e., empty of any such nature or essence. But it also declares that this emptiness is the same as form (which connotes fullness)— i.e., that this is an emptiness which is at the same time not different from the kind of reality which we normally subscribe to events; it is not a nihilistic emptiness that undermines our world, but a "positive" emptiness which defines it.

- "The noble bodhisattva, Avalokitesvara, engaged in the depths of the practice of the perfection of wisdom, looked down from above upon the five skandhas (aggregates), and saw that they were empty in their essential nature."
- "Hear, O Sariputra, emptiness is form; form is just emptiness. Apart from form, emptiness is not; emptiness, form is not. Emptiness *is* that which is form, form *is* that which is emptiness. Just thus are perception, cognition, mental construction, and consciousness."

- "Hear, O Sariputra, all phenomena of existence are marked by emptiness: not arisen, not destroyed, not unclean, not clean not deficient nor fulfilled."

The Heart sutra also states that emptiness is empty, of the self, and is the world of the self of non-self, and while being independent of thing it reflects it directly.

## Uunyata in Nagarjuna

For Nagarjuna, who provided the most important philosophical formulation of uunyata, emptiness as the mark of all phenomena is a natural consequence of dependent origination; indeed, he identifies the two. In his analysis, any enduring essential nature (i.e., fullness) would prevent the process of dependent origination, would prevent any kind of origination at all, for things would simply always have been and always continue to be. That things happen is proof that things lack the kind of nature attributed to them in mainstream Indian metaphysics.

An interesting consequence of this is that this enables Nagarjuna to put forth a bold argument regarding the relation of nirvana and samsara. If all phenomenal events (i.e., the events that constitute Samsara) are empty, then they are empty of any compelling ability to cause suffering. For Nagarjuna, Nirvana is neither something added to Samsara nor any process of taking away from it (i.e., removing the enlightened being from it). In other words, Nirvana is simply Samsara rightly experienced in light of a proper understanding of the emptiness of all things.

## Sunyata in the Tathagatagarbha Sutras

The class of Buddhist scriptures known as the *Tathagatagarbha* sutras presents a seemingly variant understanding of Emptiness, according to which the Buddha and Nirvana, unlike compounded, conditioned phenomena, are not empty of intrinsic existence, but merely empty of the impermanent, the painful and the Self-less. In the "Srimala Sutra" the Buddha is seen as empty of all defilement and ignorance, not of intrinsic Reality. The "Mahayana Mahaparinirvana Sutra" supports such a vision and views Ultimate Emptiness as the Buddhic cognition ("jnana") which perceives both Emptiness and non-Emptiness, wherein "the Empty is the totality of Samsara and the non-Empty is Great Nirvana". The Buddha in the *Mahayana Mahaparinirvana Sutra* further indicates that to view absolutely everything as empty is an unbalanced approach and constitutes a deviation from the middle path of Buddhism: "The wise perceive Emptiness and non-Emptiness, the Eternal and the Impermanent, Suffering and Bliss, the Self and the non-Self.... To perceive the Emptiness of everything and not to perceive non-Emptiness is not termed the Middle Way; to perceive the non-Self of everything and not to perceive the Self is not termed the Middle Way." Moreover, this particular sutra contains a passage in which the Buddha castigates those who view the Tathagatagarbha (which is the indwelling, immortal Buddha-element) in each being as empty, declaring of them that they are effectively committing a form of painful spiritual suicide through their wrongheaded stance: "By having cultivated non-Self in connection with the Tathagatagarbha and having continually cultivated Emptiness, suffering will not be eradicated but one will become like a moth in the flame of a lamp." (Tibetan version of the *Mahayana Mahaparinirvana Sutra*). The attainment of nirvanic Liberation ("moksha"), by contrast, is said to open up a realm of "utter bliss, joy, permanence, stability, [and] eternity", in which the Buddha is "fully peaceful" (Dharmakshema "Southern" version). Perhaps the clearest statement of Tathagatagarbha Buddhism's understanding of Emptiness is found in the Angulimaliya Sutra, where we read the following clarifying explanation:

"... by cultivating extreme emptiness and continually considering things to be empty, one will behold the utter destruction of all phenomena. Though Liberation is not empty, one will see and think it to be empty. Thus, for example, having thought hail-stones to be jewels, one comes to think that real gems are empty [uunya]. Likewise, you too think of phenomena which are not empty [auunya] to be empty [uunya], for viewing phenomena as empty, you dissolve into emptiness (uunya) even those phenomena which are not empty. Some phenomena are empty [of existence] and some phenomena are not empty [of existence]. Just like the hail-stones, the billions of *kleshas* [mental and moral afflictions] are empty [of existence], like the hail-stones, those phenomena appertaining to ignorance are empty [of existence] and swiftly fade away. Like the real beryl gems, the Buddha is eternal. Liberation is like the real beryl gems."

Thus in the distinctive Tathagatagarbha sutras a balance is drawn between the empty, impermanent and coreless realm of samsara and the everlasting, liberative Reality of the Buddha and Nirvana.

## LIST OF BUDDHISTS

A number of noted individuals have been Buddhists.

### Historical Buddhist Thinkers and Founders of Schools

Individuals are grouped by nationality, except in cases where the vast majority of their influence was felt elsewhere. Gautama Buddha and his contemporary disciples ('Buddhists') are listed separately from later Indian Buddhist thinkers, teachers and contemplatives.

### Buddha's Disciples and Early Buddhists

- The Buddha, Siddhartha Gautama
- Disciples of the Buddha
- Family of the Buddha
- Ambapali
- Ananda, Siddhartha's cousin, personal attendant of the Buddha and one of his chief disciples
- Anathapindika
- Angulimala
- Anuruddha
- Assaji
- Ajatasattu
- Bimbisara
- Channa
- Cunda
- Dabba Mallaputta

- Devadatta
- Dhammadinna
- Hatthaka of Alavi
- Janussoni
- Jayasena
- Jivaka Komarabhacca
- Maha Kaccana
- Kaccayana Gotta
- Kankharevata
- Maha Kappina
- Kasi Bharadvaja
- Kevatta
- Khema
- Khujjuttara
- Kisa Gotami
- Kondanna
- Maha Kotthika
- Magandiya
- Mahakauyapa
- Mallika
- Maudgalyayana
- Maya Devi
- Migara
- Nanda
- Maha Pajapati Gotami
- Pasenadi
- Pukkusati
- Punna
- Rahula
- Ratthapala
- Revata
- Samavati
- Sariputta (Pali, *Shariputra* Sanskrit), one of the two chief disciples of the Buddha.

- Suddhodana
- Sundari
- Sunita
- Udena
- Upali, foremost desciple in knowledge of the Vinaya.
- Uppalavanna
- Vacchagotta
- Velukandakiya
- Visakha
- Yasa
- Yashodhara.

## Later Indian Buddhists (after Buddha)

- Aryadeva, foremost disciple of Nagarjuna, continued the philosophical school of Madhyamika
- Asanga, founder of the Yogachara school, widely considered the most important Mahayana philosopher (with Nagarjuna)
- Atisha, holder of the "mind training" teachings, considered an indirect founder of the Geluk school of Tibetan Buddhism
- Bhavaviveka, early expositor of the Svatantrika Madhyamikha
- Buddhaghosa, (Theravadin commentator)
- Buddhapalita, early expositor of the Prasangika Madhyamikha
- Candragomin, renowned grammarian
- Chandrakirti, considered the greatest exponent of Prasangika Madhyamika
- Dharmakirti, famed logician, author of the *Seven Treatises*; student of Dignana's student Ishvarasena; said to have debated famed Hindu scholar Shankara
- Dignaga, famed logician
- Gunaprabha, foremost student of Vasubandhu, known for his work the *Vinayasutra*

- Kamalashila (8th century), author of important texts on meditation
- Luipa, one of the eighty-four tantric mahasiddas
- Nagarjuna, founder of the Madhyamika school, widely considered the most important Mahayana philosopher (with Asanga)
- Nagpopa, one of the eighty-four tantric mahasiddas
- Nadapada, (Tib. *Naropa*), Tilopa's primary disciple, teacher of Marpa the Translator and Khungpo Nyaljor
- Sakyaprabha, prominent expositor of the Vinaya
- Saraha, famed mahasiddha, forefather of the Tibetan Kagyu lineage
- Shantarakshita, abbot of Nalanda, founder of the Yogachara-Madhyamika who helped Padmasambhava establish Buddhism in Tibet
- Shantideva, (8th century) author of the *Bodhisattvacaryavatra*
- Talika, (*Tilopa* in Tibetan), recipient of four separate transmissions from Nagarjuna, Nagpopa, Luipa, and Khandro Kalpa Zangmo; Naropa's teacher
- Vasubandhu, author of the *Abhidharmakosha*
- Vimuktisena, commentator on texts of Asanga's.

## Indo-Greek

- Dharmaraksita (3rd century BCE), Greek Buddhist missionary of Ashoka the Great, and a teacher of Nagasena.
- Mahadharmaraksita (2nd century BCE), Greek Buddhist master during the time of Menander.
- Nagasena (2nd century BCE), Buddhist sage questioned about Buddhism by Milinda, the Indo-Greek king in the *Milinda Panha*.

## Central Asian

- An Shih Kao, a Parthian monk and the first known Buddhist missionary to China, in 148 CE.
- Dharmaraksa, a Yueh-Chih Buddhist monk, the first known translator of the Lotus Sutra into Chinese.

- Jnanagupta (561-592), a monk and tranlator from Gandhara, Pakistan.
- Kumarajiva (c. 401), a Kuchean monk, and one of the most important translators.
- Lokaksema, a Kushan monk, the first translator of Mahayana scriptures into Chinese, around 180 CE.
- Prajna (c. 810). A monk and translator from Kabul, who translated important texts into Chinese and educated the Japanese Kukai in Sanskrit texts.

## Chinese

- Baizhang Huaihai
- Bodhidharma (legendary first patriarch of Zen in China)
- Fazang
- Ba Tuo/Fo Tuo
- Fa Xian (translator and pilgrim)
- Seng Chou
- Joshu (9th century Chinese Zen monk)
- Huangbo Xiyun
- Fu Yu
- Jinaluo
- Fa Ru
- Hui Guang
- Huineng (6th Patriarch of Zen in China)
- Ingen (17th century Chinese Zen monk, founder of the Obaku sect of Zen)
- Pu Ji
- Daoji (Buddhist monk revered as a deity in Taoism)
- Jnanayasas (translator)
- Linji (9th century Chinese monk, founder of the Linji school of Zen)
- Sanghapala (6th century monk (Mon-Khmer?) who translated many texts to Chinese)
- Shen Xiu (Tang Dynasty, the chief of Shao-Lin Temple, made great contribution to Zen)

- Xuanzang (brought Yogacara to China to found Faxiang school, significant pilgrim, translator)
- Yi Jing (pilgrim and translator)
- Yunmen Wenyan (founder of one of the five Chan schools)
- Zhiyi (founder of Tiantai school)
- Zongmi (WG: Tsung-mi; fifth patriarch of Chinese Huayan school)
- Ou-Yang Jin-Wu
- Hong Yi (also calligraphist, painter, master of seal carving).

## Tibetan

- Gampopa, a student of Jetsun Milarepa and founder of the Karma Kagyu lineage of Tibetan Buddhism
- Dolpopa founder of the Jonang school and the Shentong philosophy
- Jamgon Kongtrul Lodro Thaye, the first Jamgon Kongtrul
- Karsey Kongtrul, the second Jamgon Kongtrul
- Khungpo Nyaljor, founder of the Shangpa Kagyu lineage
- Longchenpa one of the greatest Nyingma philosophers
- Marpa (Marpa the Translator, Marpa of Lhobrag), student of Naropa and a founder of the Kagyu lineage of Tibetan Buddhism
- Milarepa, a foremost student of Marpa Lotsawa who is said to have achieved Buddhahood in one lifetime
- Padmasambhava Indian semi-legendary founder of Nyingma school of Tibetan Buddhism
- Sakya Pandita one of the greatest Sakya philosophers
- Taranatha important Jonang scholar
- Tsongkhapa (14th century Tibetan monk, founder of the Geluk school of Tibetan Buddhism, based upon the Kadam tradition)
- Yeshe Tsogyal, important female student of Padmasambhava.

## Japanese

- Dogen Zenji (founder of Soto Zen, based upon the Chinese Caodong tradition)
- Eisai (12th century Japanese monk, travelled to China and returned to found the Japanese Rinzai sect of Zen)
- Ippen, founder of the Japanese Pure Land Ji sect (*Ji-shu*)
- Ikkyu
- Bankei Yotaku (1622-1693), 'Unborn' Zen
- Hakuin Ekaku (1686-1769, Rinzai Zen)
- Honen, founder of the Japanese Pure Land Jodo sect (*Jodo-shu*)
- Kukai (9th century Japanese monk, founder of Shingon)
- Myoe (Japanese monk of the Shingon and Kegon schools, known for his propagation of the Mantra of Light)
- Nichiren (founder of Nichiren Buddhism)
- Nikko (founder of Nichiren Shoshu Buddhism)
- Roben (8th century Japanese monk, invited Simsang to Japan and founded the Kegon tradition, based upon the Korean Hwaeom school)
- Ryokan (18th century Japanese Zen monk and poet)
- Saicho (9th century Japanese monk, founder of Tendai tradition, based upon the Chinese Tiantai school)
- Shinran, founder of the Japanese Pure Land Jodo Shin sect (*Jodo Shinshu*)
- Takuan Soho (Zen teacher, and, according to legend, mentor of the swordsman Miyamoto Musashi).

## Korean

- Gihwa (1376-1433) Korean Seon monk; wrote commentaries on the Diamond Sutra and Sutra of Perfect Enlightenment
- Jinul Korean Seon monk (1158-1210); founder of modern Korean gong'an meditation system
- Simsang (8th century Korean monk, who at the request of Roben helped transmit Hwaeom to Japan, thereby founding the Japanese Kegon tradition)

- Uisang (7th century Korean monk, founder of Hwaeom tradition, based upon the Chinese Huayan school)
- Weonhyo (617-668) Korean monk; prolific commentator on Mahayana sutras
- Wonchuk.

## Thai

- Somdej Toh (Thai monk specializing in magical amulets)
- Phramonkolthepmuni (1885-1959) (Thai monk who founded the Dhammakaya Tradition)
- Khun Yay Maha Ratana Upasika Chandra Khonnokyoong (1909-2000) (Thai nun who headed Wat Phra Dhammakaya).

## Historical Rulers and Political Figures

- Ashoka the Great (304–232 BC), Mauryan Emperor of ancient India, and the first Buddhist ruler to send Buddhist missionaries outside of India throughout the Old World
- Brhadrata, the last ruler of the Mauryan dynasty
- Menander (Pali: Milinda), 2nd century BCE, an Indo-Greek king of northwestern India, who questioned Nagasena about Buddhism in the *Milinda Panha*, and is said to have become an arhat.
- Theodorus (1st century BCE), Indo-Greek governor, author of a Buddhist dedication.
- Kanishka, ruler of the Kushan Empire
- Shotoku (574-622), crown prince and regent of Japan
- Liang Wudi (502-549), emperor during the Chinese Liang Dynasty
- Harshavardhana (606-648), Indian emperor who converted to Buddhism.
- Wu Zetian
- Jayavarman VII (1181-1219), king of Cambodia
- Ming Done, king of Myanmar and facilitator of "5th World Theravada Buddhist Sanga's Council" or Sangayana
- Mongkut, king of Thailand and founder of the Thammayut Nikaya

- Emperor Ming of Han China.
- Tang Dynasty
- Kublai Khan Mongol Ruler.

## SPATIAL COSMOLOGY

Spatial cosmology can also be divided into two branches. The *vertical cosmology* describes the arrangement of worlds in a vertical pattern, some being higher and some lower. The*sahasra cosmology* describes the grouping of these vertical worlds into sets of thousands, millions or billions.

### Vertical Cosmology

In the vertical cosmology, the universe exists of many worlds – one might say "planes" – stacked one upon the next in layers. Each world corresponds to a mental state or a state of being. A world is not, however, a location so much as it is the beings which compose it; it is sustained by their karma and if the beings in a world all die or disappear, the world disappears too. Likewise, a world comes into existence when the first being is born into it. The physical separation is not so important as the difference in mental state; humans and animals, though they partially share the same physical environments, still belong to different worlds because their minds perceive and react to those environments differently.

The vertical cosmology is divided into three realms, or dhatus, each corresponding to a different type of mentality. These three (Tridhatu) are the Arupyadhatu, the Rupadhatu, and the Kamadhatu. This technical division does not correspond to the more informal categorization of the "six realms". In the latter scheme, all of the beings born in the Arupyadhatu and the Rupadhatu may be classified as "gods" or "deities", as can a considerable fraction of the beings born in the Kamadhatu, even though the deities of the Kamadhatu differ more from those of the Arupyadhatu than they do from humans. It is to be understood that deva is an imprecise term referring to any being living in a longer-lived and generally more blissful state than humans. Most of them are not "gods" in the common sense of the term, having little or no concern with the human world and rarely if ever interacting with it; only the lowest deities of the Kamadhatu correspond to the gods described in many polytheistic religions.

The term "brahma" is used both as a name and as a generic term for one of the higher devas. In its broadest sense, it can refer to any of the inhabitants of the Arupyadhatu and the Rupadhatu. In more restricted senses, it can refer to an inhabitant of one of the nine lower worlds of the Rupadhatu, or in its narrowest sense, to the three lowest worlds of the Rupadhatu. A large number of devas use the name "Brahma", e.g. Brahma Sahampati, Brahma Sanatkumara, Baka Brahma, etc. It is not always clear which world they belong to, although it must always be one of the worlds of the Rupadhatu below the Uuddhavasa worlds.

## ARUPYADHATU

The Arupyadhatu (Sanskrit) or Arupaloka (Pali) or "Formless realm" would have no place in a purely physical cosmology, as none of the beings inhabiting it has either shape or location; and correspondingly, the realm has no location either. This realm belongs to those devas who attained and remained in the Four Formless Absorptions of the arupadhyanas in a previous life, and now enjoys the fruits (vipaka) of the good karma of that accomplishment. Bodhisattvas, however, are never born in the Arupyadhatu even when they have attained the arupadhyanas.

There are four types of Arupyadhatu devas, corresponding to the four types of arupadhyanas:

- Naivasamjnanasamjnayatana or Nevasannanasannayatana "Sphere of neither perception nor non-perception". In this sphere the formless beings have gone beyond a mere negation of perception and have attained a liminal state where they do not engage in "perception" but are not wholly unconscious. This was the sphere reached by Udraka Ramaputra, the second of the Buddha's two teachers, who considered it equivalent to enlightenment.

- Akimcanyayatana or Akincannayatana "Sphere of Nothingness" (literally "lacking anything"). In this sphere formless beings dwell contemplating upon the thought that "there is no thing". This is considered a form of perception, though a very subtle one. This was the sphere reached by Araa Kalama, the first of the Buddha's two teachers; he considered it to be equivalent to enlightenment.
- Vijnananantyayatana or Vinnananancayatana "Sphere of Infinite Consciousness". In this sphere formless beings dwell meditating on their consciousness (vijnana) as infinitely pervasive.
- Akauanantyayatana or Akasanancayatana "Sphere of Infinite Space". In this sphere formless beings dwell meditating upon space or extension as infinitely pervasive.

## Rupadhatu

The Rupadhatu or "Form realm" is, as the name implies, the first of the physical realms; its inhabitants all have a location and bodies of a sort, though those bodies are composed of a subtle substance which is of itself invisible to the inhabitants of the Kamadhatu. According to the Janavasabha Sutta, when a brahma (a being from the Brahma-world of the Rupadhatu) wishes to visit a deva of the Trayastrimsha heaven (in the Kamadhatu), he has to assume a "grosser form" in order to be visible to them.

The beings of the Form realm are not subject to the extremes of pleasure and pain, or governed by desires for things pleasing to the senses, as the beings of the Kamadhatu are. The bodies of Form realm beings do not have sexual distinctions.

Like the beings of the Arupyadhatu, the dwellers in the Rupadhatu have minds corresponding to the dhyanas. In their case it is the four lower dhyanas or rupadhyanas. However, although the beings of the Rupadhatu can be divided into four broad grades corresponding to these four dhyanas, each of them is subdivided into further grades, three for each of the four dhyanas and five for the Uuddhavasa devas, for a total of seventeen grades (the Theravada tradition counts one less grade in the highest dhyana for a total of sixteen).

Physically, the Rupadhatu consists of a series of planes stacked on top of each other, each one in a series of steps half the size of the previous one as one descends. In part, this reflects the fact that the devas are also thought of as physically larger on the higher planes. The highest planes are also broader in extent than the ones lower down, as discussed in the section on *Sahasra cosmology*. The height of these planes is expressed in *yojanas*, a measurement of very uncertain length, but sometimes taken to be about 4,000 times the height of a man, and so approximately 4.54 miles or 7.32 kilometers.

## Uuddhavasa Worlds

The Uuddhavasa worlds, or "Pure Abodes", are distinct from the other worlds of the Rupadhatu in that they do not house beings who have been born there through ordinary merit or meditative attainments, but only those Anagamins ("Non-returners") who are already on the path to Arhat-hood and who will attain enlightenment directly from the Uuddhavasa worlds without being reborn in a lower plane (Anagamins can also be born on lower planes). Every Uuddhavasa deva is therefore a protector of Buddhism. Because a Uuddhavasa deva will never be reborn outside the Uuddhavasa worlds, no Bodhisattva is ever born in these worlds, as a Bodhisattva must ultimately be reborn as a human being.

Since these devas rise from lower planes only due to the teaching of a Buddha, they can remain empty for very long periods if no Buddha arises. However, unlike the lower worlds, the Uuddhavasa worlds are never destroyed by natural catastrophe. The Uuddhavasa devas predict the coming of a Buddha and, taking the guise of brahmins, reveal to human beings the signs by which a Buddha can be recognized. They also ensure that a Bodhisattva in his last life will see the four signs that will lead to his renunciation.

The five Uuddhavasa worlds are:

- Akanicmha or Akanimmha – World of devas "equal in rank" (literally: having no one as the youngest). The highest of all the Rupadhatu worlds, it is often used to refer to the highest extreme of the universe. The current Shakra will eventually be born there. The duration of life in Akȧnicmha is 16,000 kalpas (Vibhajyavada tradition). The height of this world is 167,772,160 yojanas above the Earth.

- Sudarshana or Sudassi – The "clear-seeing" devas live in a world similar to and friendly with the Akanicmha world. The height of this world is 83,886,080 yojanas above the Earth.
- Sudnsha or Sudassa – The world of the "beautiful" devas are said to be the place of rebirth for five kinds of anagamins. The height of this world is 41,943,040 yojanas above the Earth.
- Atapa or Atappa – The world of the "untroubled" devas, whose company those of lower realms wish for. The height of this world is 20,971,520 yojanas above the Earth.
- Avnha or Aviha – The world of the "not falling" devas, perhaps the most common destination for reborn Anagamins. Many achieve arhatship directly in this world, but some pass away and are reborn in sequentially higher worlds of the Pure Abodes until they are at last reborn in the Akanicmha world. These are called in Pali Buddhamsotas, "those whose stream goes upward". The duration of life in Aviha is 1,000 kalpas (Vibhajyavada tradition). The height of this world is 10,485,760 yojanas above the Earth.

## Bihatphala Worlds

The mental state of the devas of the Bihatphala worlds corresponds to the fourth dhyana, and is characterized by equanimity (upekca). The Bihatphala worlds form the upper limit to the destruction of the universe by wind at the end of a mahakalpa, that is, they are spared such destruction.

- Asannasatta (Vibhajyavada tradition only) – "Unconscious beings", devas who have attained a high dhyana (similar to that of the Formless Realm), and, wishing to avoid the perils of perception, have achieved a state of non-perception in which they endure for a time. After a while, however, perception arises again and they fall into a lower state.

- Bihatphala or Vehapphala – Devas "having great fruit". Their lifespan is 500 mahakalpas. (Vibhajyavada tradition). Some Anagamins are reborn here. The height of this world is 5,242,880 yojanas above the Earth.
- Punyaprasava – The world of the devas who are the "offspring of merit". The height of this world is 2,621,440 yojanas above the Earth.
- Anabhraka – The world of the "cloudless" devas. The height of this world is 1,310,720 yojanas above the Earth.

## Subhaktsna Worlds

The mental state of the devas of the Subhaktsna worlds corresponds to the third dhyana, and is characterized by a quiet joy (sukha). These devas have bodies that radiate a steady light. The Subhaktsna worlds form the upper limit to the destruction of the universe by water at the end of a mahakalpa, that is, the flood of water does not rise high enough to reach them.

- Subhaktsna or Subhakinna/Subhakinha – The world of devas of "total beauty". Their lifespan is 64 mahakalpas (some sources: 4 mahakalpas) according to the Vibhajyavada tradition. 64 mahakalpas is the interval between destructions of the universe by wind, including the Subhaktsna worlds. The height of this world is 655,360 yojanas above the Earth.
- Apramanasubha or Appamanasubha – The world of devas of "limitless beauty". Their lifespan is 32 mahakalpas (Vibhajyavada tradition). They possess "faith, virtue, learning, munificence and wisdom". The height of this world is 327,680 yojanas above the Earth.
- Parittauubha or Parittasubha – The world of devas of "limited beauty". Their lifespan is 16 mahakalpas. The height of this world is 163,840 yojanas above the Earth.

## Abhasvara Worlds

The mental state of the devas of the Abhasvara worlds

corresponds to the second dhyana, and is characterized by delight (priti) as well as joy (sukha); the Abhasvara devas are said to shout aloud in their joy, crying *aho sukham*. These devas have bodies that emit flashing rays of light like lightning. They are said to have similar bodies (to each other) but diverse perceptions. The Abhasvara worlds form the upper limit to the destruction of the universe by fire at the end of a mahakalpa, that is, the column of fire does not rise high enough to reach them. After the destruction of the world, at the beginning of the vivartakalpa, the worlds are first populated by beings reborn from the Abhasvara worlds.

- Abhasvara or Abhassara – The world of devas "possessing splendor". The lifespan of the Abhasvara devas is 8 mahakalpas (others: 2 mahakalpas). Eight mahakalpas is the interval between destructions of the universal by water, which includes the Abhasvara worlds. The height of this world is 81,920 yojanas above the Earth.
- Apramanabha or Appamanabha – The world of devas of "limitless light", a concept on which they meditate. Their lifespan is 4 mahakalpas. The height of this world is 40,960 yojanas above the Earth.
- Parittabha or Parittabha – The world of devas of "limited light". Their lifespan is 2 mahakalpas. The height of this world is 20,480 yojanas above the Earth.

## Brahma Worlds

The mental state of the devas of the Brahma worlds corresponds to the first dhyana, and is characterized by observation (vitarka) and reflection (vicara) as well as delight (priti) and joy (sukha). The Brahma worlds, together with the other lower worlds of the universe, are destroyed by fire at the end of a mahakalpa.

- Mahabrahma – the world of "Great Brahma", believed by many to be the creator of the world, and having as his titles "Brahma, Great Brahma, the Conqueror, the Unconquered, the All-Seeing, All-Powerful, the Lord, the Maker and Creator, the Ruler, Appointer and Orderer, Father of All That Have Been and Shall Be." According to the Brahmajala Sutta (DN.1), a Mahabrahma is a being from the Abhasvara worlds who falls into a lower world through exhaustion of his merits and is reborn alone in the Brahma-world; forgetting his former existence, he imagines himself to have come into existence without cause. Note that even such a high-ranking deity has no intrinsic knowledge of the worlds above his own. Mahabrahma is 1 $D_2$ yojanas tall. His lifespan variously said to be 1 kalpa (Vibhajyavada tradition) or 1 $D_2$ kalpas long (Sarvastivada tradition), although it would seem that it could be no longer than $D_4$ of a mahakalpa, i.e., all of the mahakalpa except for the Samvartasthayikalpa, because that is the total length of time between the rebuilding of the lower world and its destruction. It is unclear what period of time "kalpa" refers to in this case. The height of this world is 10,240 yojanas above the Earth.

- Brahmapurohita – the "Ministers of Brahma" are beings, also originally from the Abhasvara worlds, that are born as companions to Mahabrahma after he has spent some time alone. Since they arise subsequent to his thought of a desire for companions, he believes himself to be their creator, and they likewise believe him to be their creator and lord. They are 1 yojana in height and their lifespan is variously said to be $D_2$ of a kalpa (Vibhajyavada tradition) or a whole kalpa (Sarvastivada tradition). If they are later reborn in a lower world, and come to recall some part of their last existence, they teach the doctrine of Brahma as creator as a revealed truth. The height of this world is 5,120 yojanas above the Earth.
- Brahmaparicadya or Brahmaparisajja – the "Councillors of Brahma" or the devas "belonging to the assembly of Brahma". They are also called Brahmakayika, but this name can be used for any of the inhabitants of the Brahma-worlds. They are half a yojana in height and their lifespan is variously said to be $D_3$ of a kalpa (Vibhajyavada tradition) or $D_2$ of a kalpa (Sarvastivada tradition). The height of this world is 2,560 yojanas above the Earth.

## Kamadhatu

The beings born in the Kamadhatu differ in degree of happiness, but they are all, other than arhats and Buddhas, under the domination of Mara and are bound by desire, which causes them suffering.

## Heavens

The following four worlds are bounded planes each 80,000 yojanas square, which float in the air above the top of Mount Sumeru. Although all of the worlds inhabited by devas (that is, all the worlds down to the Caturmaharajikakayika world and sometimes including the Asuras) are sometimes called "heavens", in the western sense of the word the term best applies to the four worlds listed below:

- Parinirmita-vaœavartin or Paranimmita-vasavatti – The heaven of devas "with power over (others') creations". These devas do not create pleasing forms that they desire for themselves, but their desires are fulfilled by the acts of other devas who wish for their favour. The ruler of this world is called Vauavartin (Pali: Vasavatti), who has longer life, greater beauty, more power and happiness and more delightful sense-objects than the other devas of his world. This world is also the home of the devaputra (being of divine race) called Mara, who endeavours to keep all beings of the Kamadhatu in the grip of sensual pleasures. Mara is also sometimes called Vauavartin, but in general these two dwellers in this world are kept distinct. The beings of this world are 4,500 feet tall and live for 9,216,000,000 years (Sarvastivada tradition). The height of this world is 1,280 yojanas above the Earth.
- Nirmanarati or Nimmanarati – The world of devas "delighting in their creations". The devas of this world are capable of making any appearance to please themselves. The lord of this world is called Sunirmita (Pali Sunimmita); his wife is the rebirth of Visakha, formerly the chief of the upasikas (female lay devotees) of the Buddha. The beings of this world are 3,750 feet tall and live for

2,304,000,000 years (Sarvastivada tradition). The height of this world is 640 yojanas above the Earth.

- Tucita or Tusita – The world of the "joyful" devas. This world is best known for being the world in which a Bodhisattva lives before being reborn in the world of humans. Until a few thousand years ago, the Bodhisattva of this world was Uvetaketu (Pali: Setaketu), who was reborn as Siddhartha, who would become the Buddha Uakyamuni; since then the Bodhisattva has been Natha (or Nathadeva) who will be reborn as Ajita and will become the Buddha Maitreya (Pali Metteyya). While this Bodhisattva is the foremost of the dwellers in Tucita, the ruler of this world is another deva called Santucita (Pali: Santusita). The beings of this world are 3,000 feet tall and live for 576,000,000 years (Sarvastivada tradition). The height of this world is 320 yojanas above the Earth.
- Yama – Sometimes called the "heaven without fighting", because it is the lowest of the heavens to be physically separated from the tumults of the earthly world. Its ruler is the deva Suyama; according to some, his wife is the rebirth of Sirima, a courtesan of Rajagriha in the Buddha's time who was generous to the monks. The beings of this world are 2,250 feet tall and live for 144,000,000 years (Sarvastivada tradition). The height of this world is 160 yojanas above the Earth.

## Worlds of Sumeru

The world-mountain of Sumeru is an immense, strangely shaped peak which arises in the centre of the world, and around which the Sun and Moon revolve. Its base rests in a vast ocean, and it is surrounded by several rings of lesser mountain ranges and oceans. The three worlds listed below are all located on or around Sumeru: the Trayastrimua devas live on its peak, the Caturmaharajikakayika devas live on its slopes, and the Asuras live in the ocean at its base. Sumeru and its surrounding oceans and mountains are the home not just of these deities, but also vast assemblies of beings of popular mythology who only rarely intrude on the human world.

- Trayastrimsha or Tavatimsa – The world "of the Thirty-three (devas)" is a wide flat space on the top of Mount Sumeru, filled with the gardens and palaces of the devas. Its ruler is Shakra devanam indra, "lord of the devas". Besides the eponymous Thirty-three devas, many other devas and supernatural beings dwell here, including the attendants of the devas and many apsarases (nymphs). The beings of this world are 1,500 feet tall and live for 36,000,000 years (Sarvastivada tradition) or 3/4 of a yojana tall and live for 30,000,000 years (Vibhajyavada tradition). The height of this world is 80 yojanas above the Earth.
- Caturmaharajikakayika or Catummaharajika – The world "of the Four Great Kings" is found on the lower slopes of Mount Sumeru, though some of its inhabitants live in the air around the mountain. Its rulers are the four Great Kings of the name, Viruhaka, Dhritaracmra, Virupakca, and their leader Vaishravana. The devas who guide the Sun and Moon are also considered part of this world, as are the retinues of the four kings, composed of Kumbhanas (dwarfs), Gandharvas (fairies), Nagas (dragons) and Yakcas (goblins). The beings of this world are 750 feet tall and live for 9,000,000 years (Sarvastivada tradition) or 90,000 years (Vibhajyavada tradition). The height of this world is from sea level up to 40 yojanas above the Earth.
- Asura – The world of the Asuras is the space at the foot of Mount Sumeru, much of which is a deep ocean. It is not the Asuras' original home, but the place they found themselves after they were hurled, drunken, from Trayastrimsha where they had formerly lived. The Asuras are always fighting to regain their lost kingdom on the top of Mount Sumeru, but are unable to break the guard of the Four Great Kings. The Asuras are divided into many groups, and have no single ruler, but among their leaders are Vemacitrin (Pali: Vepacitti) and Rahu.

## Earthly Realms

- Manucyaloka – This is the world of humans and human-like beings who live on the surface of the earth. The mountain-rings that engird Sumeru are surrounded by a vast ocean, which fills most of the world. The ocean is in turn surrounded by a circular mountain wall called Cakravaa which marks the horizontal limit of the world. In this ocean there are four continents which are, relatively speaking, small islands in it. Because of the immenseness of the ocean, they cannot be reached from each other by ordinary sailing vessels, although in the past, when the cakravartin kings ruled, communication between the continents was possible by means of the treasure called the cakraratna, which a cakravartin and his retinue could use to fly through the air between the continents. The four continents are:

- o Jambudvipa or Jambudipa is located in the south and is the dwelling of ordinary human beings. It is said to be shaped "like a cart", or rather a blunt-nosed triangle with the point facing south. (This description probably echoes the shape of the coastline of southern India.) It is 10,000 yojanas in extent (Vibhajyavada tradition) or has a perimeter of 6,000 yojanas (Sarvastivada tradition) to which can be added the southern coast of only 3 D $_2$ yojanas' length. The continent takes its name from a giant Jambu tree (Syzygium cumini), 100 yojanas tall, which grows in the middle of the continent. Every continent has one of these giant trees. All Buddhas appear in Jambudvipa. The people here are five to six feet tall and their length of life varies between 80,000 and 10 years.
- o Purvavideha or Pubbavideha is located in the east, and is shaped like a semicircle with the flat side pointing westward (i.e., towards Sumeru). It is 7,000 yojanas in extent (Vibhajyavada tradition) or has a perimeter of 6,350 yojanas of which the flat side is 2,000 yojanas long (Sarvastivada tradition). Its tree is the acacia. The people here are about 12 feet tall and they live for 250 years.
- o Aparagodaniya or Aparagoyana is located in the west, and is shaped like a circle with a circumference of

about 7,500 yojanas (Sarvastivada tradition). The tree of this continent is a giant Kadambu tree. The human inhabitants of this continent do not live in houses but sleep on the ground. They are about 24 feet tall and they live for 500 years.

- o Uttarakuru is located in the north, and is shaped like a square. It has a perimter of 8,000 yojanas, being 2,000 yojanas on each side. This continent's tree is called a kalpavrikca (Pali: kapparukkha) or kalpa-tree, because it lasts for the entire kalpa. The inhabitants of Uttarakuru are said to be extraordinarily wealthy. They do not need to labour for a living, as their food grows by itself, and they have no private property. They have cities built in the air. They are about 48 feet tall and live for 1,000 years, and they are under the protection of Vaishravana.

- Tiryagyoni-loka or Tiracchana-yoni – This world comprises all members of the animal kingdom that are capable of feeling suffering, from the smallest insect to the elephant.
- Pretaloka or Petaloka – The pretas, or "hungry ghosts", are mostly dwellers on earth, though due to their mental state they perceive it very differently from humans. They live for the most part in desert and waste places.

## NARAKAS

Naraka or Niraya is the name given to one of the worlds of greatest suffering, usually translated into English as "hell" or "purgatory". As with the other realms, a being is born into one of these worlds as a result of his karma, and resides there for a finite length of time until his karma has achieved its full result, after which he will be reborn in one of the higher worlds as the result of an earlier karma that had not yet ripened. The mentality of a being in the hells corresponds to states of extreme fear and helpless anguish in humans.

Physically, Naraka is thought of as a series of layers extending below Jambudvipa into the earth. There are several schemes for counting these Narakas and enumerating their torments. One of the more common is that of the Eight Cold Narakas and Eight Hot Narakas.

## Cold Narakas

- Arbuda – the "blister" Naraka
- Nirarbuda – the "burst blister" Naraka
- Amama – the Naraka of shivering
- Hahava – the Naraka of lamentation
- Huhuva – the Naraka of chattering teeth
- Utpala – the "blue lotus" Naraka
- Padma – the "lotus" Naraka
- Mahapadma – the "great lotus" Naraka.

Each lifetime in these Narakas is twenty times the length of the one before it.

## Hot Narakas

- Sanjiva – the "reviving" Naraka. Life in this Naraka is $162*10^{10}$ years long.
- Kalasutra – the "black thread" Naraka. Life in this Naraka is $1296*10^{10}$ years long.
- Samghata – the "crushing" Naraka. Life in this Naraka is $10{,}368*10^{10}$ years long.
- Raurava – the "screaming" Naraka. Life in this Naraka is $82{,}944*10^{10}$ years long.
- Maharaurava – the "great screaming" Naraka. Life in this Naraka is $663{,}552*10^{10}$ years long.
- Tapana – the "heating" Naraka. Life in this Naraka is $5{,}308{,}416*10^{10}$ years long.
- Pratapana – the "great heating" Naraka. Life in this Naraka is $42{,}467{,}328*10^{10}$ years long.
- Avici – the "uninterrupted" Naraka. Life in this Naraka is $339{,}738{,}624*10^{10}$ years long.

## The Foundations of the Earth

All of the structures of the earth, Sumeru and the rest,

extend downward to a depth of 80,000 yojanas below sea level – the same as the height of Sumeru above sea level. Below this is a layer of "golden earth", a substance compact and firm enough to support the weight of Sumeru. It is 320,000 yojanas in depth and so extends to 400,000 yojanas below sea level. The layer of golden earth in turn rests upon a layer of water, which is 8,000,000 yojanas in depth, going down to 8,400,000 yojanas below sea level. Below the layer of water is a "circle of wind", which is 16,000,000 yojanas in depth and also much broader in extent, supporting 1,000 different worlds upon it.

## Sahasra Cosmology

While the vertical cosmology describes the arrangement of the worlds vertically, the sahasra (Sanskrit: "thousand") cosmology describes how they are grouped horizontally. The four heavens of the Kamadhatu, as mentioned, occupy a limited space no bigger than the top of Mount Sumeru. The three Brahma-worlds, however, stretch out as far as the mountain-wall of Cakravaa, filling the entire sky. This whole group of worlds, from Mahabrahma down to the foundations of water, constitutes a single world-system. It corresponds to the extent of the universe that is destroyed by fire at the end of one mahakalpa.

Above Mahabrahma are the Abhasvara worlds. These are not only higher but also wider in extent; they cover 1,000 separate world-systems, each with its own Sumeru, Cakravaa, Sun, Moon, and four continents. This system of 1,000 worlds is called a sahasra-cuika-lokadhatu, or "small chiliocosm". It corresponds to the extent of the universe that is destroyed by water at the end of 8 mahakalpas. Above the Abhasvara worlds are the Subhaktsna worlds, which cover 1,000 chiliocosms, or 1,000,000 world-systems. This larger system is called a dvisahasra-madhyama-lokadhatu, or "medium dichiliocosm". It corresponds to the extent of the universe that is destroyed by wind at the end of 64 mahakalpas.

Likewise, above the Subhaktsna worlds, the Uuddhavasa and Bihatphala worlds cover 1,000 dichiliocosms, or 1,000,000,000 world-systems. This largest grouping is called a trisahasra-mahasahasra-lokadhatu or "great trichiliocosm".

## Temporal Cosmology

Buddhist temporal cosmology describes how the universe comes into being and is dissolved. Like other Indian cosmologies, it assumes an infinite span of time and is cyclical. This does not mean that the same events occur in identical form with each cycle, but merely that, as with the cycles of day and night or summer and winter, certain natural events occur over and over to give some structure to time.

The basic unit of time measurement is the mahakalpa or "Great Eon". The exact length of this time in human years is never defined exactly, but it is meant to be very long, to be measured in billions of years if not longer.

A mahakalpa is divided into four kalpas or "eons", each distinguished from the others by the stage of evolution of the universe during that kalpa. The four kalpas are:

- Vivartakalpa "Eon of evolution" – during this kalpa the universe comes into existence.
- Vivartasthayikalpa "Eon of evolution-duration" – during this kalpa the universe remains in existence in a steady state.
- Samvartakalpa "Eon of dissolution" – during this kalpa the universe dissolves.
- Samvartasthayikalpa "Eon of dissolution-duration" – during this kalpa the universe remains in a state of emptiness.

Each one of these kalpas is divided into twenty antarakalpas each of about the same length. For the Samvartasthayikalpa this division is merely nominal, as nothing changes from one antarakalpa to the next; but for the other three kalpas it marks an interior cycle within the kalpa.

## Vivartakalpa

The Vivartakalpa begins with the arising of the primordial wind, which begins the process of building up the structures of the universe that had been destroyed at the end of the last mahakalpa. As the extent of the destruction can vary, the nature of this evolution can vary as well, but it always takes the form of beings from a higher world being born into a lower world.

The example of a Mahabrahma being the rebirth of a deceased Abhasvara deva is just one instance of this, which continues throughout the Vivartakalpa until all the worlds are filled from the Brahmaloka down to Naraka. During the Vivartakalpa the first humans appear; they are not like present-day humans, but are beings shining in their own light, capable of moving through the air without mechanical aid, living for a very long time, and not requiring sustenance; they are more like a type of lower deity than present-day humans are.

Over time, they acquire a taste for physical nutriment, and as they consume it, their bodies become heavier and more like human bodies; they lose their ability to shine, and begin to acquire differences in their appearance, and their length of life decreases. They differentiate into two sexes and begin to become sexually active. Then greed, theft and violence arise among them, and they establish social distinctions and government and elect a king to rule them, called Mahasammata, "the great appointed one". Some of them begin to hunt and eat the flesh of animals, which have by now come into existence. These developments are described in the Agganna Sutta (DN.27).

## VIVARTASTHAYIKALPA

### First Antarakalpa

The Vivartasthayikalpa begins when the first being is born into Naraka, thus filling the entire universe with beings. During the first antarakalpa of this eon, human lives are declining from a vast but unspecified number of years (but at least several tens of thousands of years) toward the modern lifespan of less than 100 years. At the beginning of the antarakalpa, people are still generally happy. They live under the rule of a universal monarch or "wheel-turning king" (cakravartin), who conquer. The Mahasudassana-sutta (DN.17) tells of the life of a cakravartin king, Mahasudassana (Sanskrit: Mahasudaruana) who lived for 336,000 years. The Cakkavatti-sihanada-sutta (DN.26) tells of a later dynasty of cakravartins, Dahanemi and five of his descendants, who had a lifespan of over 80,000 years. The seventh of this line of cakravartins broke with the traditions of his forefathers, refusing to abdicate his position at a certain age, pass the throne on to his son, and enter the life of a sramana. As a result of his subsequent misrule, poverty increased; as a result of poverty, theft began; as a result of theft, capital punishment was instituted; and as a result of this contempt for life, murders and other crimes became rampant.

The human lifespan now quickly decreased from 80,000 to 100 years, apparently decreasing by about half with each generation (this is perhaps not to be taken literally), while with each generation other crimes and evils increased: lying, adultery, evil speech, greed and hatred, wrong views, incest and other sorts of sexual abnormalities, disrespect for parents and elders. During this period, according to the Mahapadana-sutta (DN.14) three of the four Buddhas of this antarakalpa lived: Krakucchanda Buddha (Pali: Kakusandha), at the time when the lifespan was 40,000 years; Kanakamuni Buddha (Pali: Konagamana) when the lifespan was 30,000 years; and Kauyapa Buddha (Pali: Kassapa) when the lifespan was 20,000 years.

Our present time is taken to be toward the end of the first antarakalpa of this Vivartasthayikalpa, when the lifespan is less than 100 years, after the life of Uakyamuni Buddha (Pali: Sakyamuni), who lived to the age of 80.

The remainder of the antarakalpa is prophesied to be miserable: lifespans will continue to decrease, and all the evil tendencies of the past will reach their ultimate in destructiveness. People will live no longer than ten years, and will marry at five; foods will be poor and tasteless; no form of morality will be acknowledged. The most contemptuous and hateful people will become the rulers. Incest will be rampant. Hatred between people, even members of the same family, will grow until people think of each other as hunters do of their prey.

Eventually a great war will ensue, in which the most hostile and aggressive will arm themselves and go out to kill each other. The less aggressive will hide in forests and other secret places while the war rages. This war marks the end of the first antarakalpa.

## Second Antarakalpa

At the end of the war, the survivors will emerge from their hiding places and repent their evil habits. As they begin to do good, their lifespan increases, and the health and welfare of the human race will also increase with it. After a long time, the descendants of those with a 10-year lifespan will live for 80,000 years, and at that time there will be a cakravartin king named Saekha. During his reign, the current bodhisattva in the Tucita heaven will descend and be reborn under the name of Ajita. He will enter the life of a sramana and will gain perfect enlightenment as a Buddha; and he will then be known by the name of Maitreya (Pali: Metteyya).

After Maitreya's time, the world will again worsen, and the lifespan will gradually decrease from 80,000 years to 10 years again, each antarakalpa being separated from the next by devastating war, with peaks of high civilization and morality in the middle. After the 19th antarakalpa, the lifespan will increase to 80,000 and then not decrease, because the Vivartasthayikalpa will have come to an end.

## Samvartakalpa

The Samvartakalpa begins when beings cease to be born in Naraka. This cessation of birth then proceeds in reverse order up the vertical cosmology, i.e. pretas then cease to be born, then animals, then humans, and so on up to the realms of the deities. When these worlds as far as the Brahmaloka are devoid of inhabitants, a great fire consumes the entire physical structure of the world. It burns all the worlds below the Abhasvara worlds. When they are destroyed, the Samvartasthayikalpa begins.

## Samvartasthayikalpa

There is nothing to say about the Samvartasthayikalpa, since nothing happens in it below the Abhasvara worlds. It ends when the primordial wind begins to blow and build the structure of the worlds up again.

## Other Destructions

The destruction by fire is the normal type of destruction that occurs at the end of the Samvartakalpa. But every eighth mahakalpa, after seven destructions by fire, there is a destruction by water. This is more devastating, as it eliminates not just the Brahma worlds but also the Abhasvara worlds. Every sixty-fourth mahakalpa, after 56 destructions by fire and 7 destructions by water, there is a destruction by wind. This is the most devastating of all, as it also destroys the Subhaktsna worlds. The higher worlds are never destroyed.

# DHARMA (BUDDHISM)

Dharma or Dhamma in Buddhism has two primary meanings:

- the teachings of the Buddha which lead to enlightenment
- the constituent factors of the experienced world.

## Buddha's Teachings

What is called Buddhism in the west has been referred to in India (the teachings' place of origin) and the east generally for many centuries as Buddha-dharma. This term has no sectarian connotations but simply means "Path of Awakening" and thus conforms to a universal understanding of dharma.

The status of dharma is regarded variably by different traditions. Some regard it as an ultimate and transcendent truth which is utterly beyond worldly things, somewhat like the Christian logos. Others, who regard the Buddha as simply an enlightened human being, see dharma as the 84,000 different teachings that the Buddha gave to various types of people based on their needs. The teachings are expedient means of raising doubt in the hearer's own cherished beliefs and view of life; when doubt has opened the door to the truth, the teaching can be put aside.

"Dharma" usually refers inclusively not just to the sayings of the Buddha but to the later traditions of interpretation and addition that the various schools of Buddhism have developed to help explain and expand upon the Buddha's teachings. For others still, they see the dharma as referring to the "truth" or ultimate reality or "the way things are". The dharma is one of the Three Jewels of Buddhism of which practitioners of Buddhism seek refuge in (what one relies on for his/her lasting happiness). The three jewels of Buddhism are the Buddha (mind's perfection of enlightenment), the dharma (teachings and methods), and the Sangha (awakened beings who provide guidance and support).

## Buddha's Dharma Body

The qualities of the Dharma (Law, truth) is the same as the qualities of the Buddha and forms his "truth body" or "Dhamma Kaya": In the Samyutta Nikaya, Vakkali Sutta, Buddha said to his disciple Vakkali that :

"Yo kho Vakkali dhammam passati so mam passati"

*Vakkali, whoever sees Dhamma, sees me [the Buddha]*

Another reference from the Agganna Sutta of the Digha Nikaya, says to his disciple Vasettha:

"Tathagatassa h'etam Vasettha adivacanam Dhamma-kayo iti pi...":

*O Vasettha! The Word of Dhammakaya is indeed the name of the Tathagata.*

## Qualities of Buddha Dharma

The Teaching of the Buddha also has six supreme qualities:

1. Svakkhato: The Dhamma is not a speculative philosophy, but is the Universal Law found through enlightenment and is preached precisely. Therefore it is excellent in the beginning, excellent in the middle (samadhi – concentration) and excellent in the end,
2. Sandimmhiko : The Dhamma can be tested by practice and therefore he who follows it will see the result by himself through his own experience.
3. Akaliko : The Dhamma is able to bestow timeless and immediate results here and now, for which there is no need to wait until the future or next existence.
4. Ehipassiko : The Dhamma welcomes all beings to put it to the test and come see for themselves.

5. Opanayiko : The Dhamma is capable of being entered upon and therefore it is worthy to be followed as a part of one's life.
6. Paccattam veditabbo vinnuhi: The Dhamma can be perfectly realized only by the noble disciples (Ariyas) who have matured and enlightened enough in supreme wisdom.

Knowing these attributes, Buddhists believe that they will attain the greatest peace and happiness through the practice of the Dhamma. Each person is therefore fully responsible for himself to put it in the real practice.

Here the Buddha is compared to an experienced and skilful doctor, and the Dhamma to proper medicine. However efficient the doctor or wonderful the medicine may be, the patients cannot be cured unless they take the medicine properly. So the practice of the Dhamma is the only way to attain the final deliverance of Nibbana.

These teachings ranged from understanding karma (Pali: kamma) (cause and effect) and developing good impressions in one's mind, to reach full enlightenment by recognizing the nature of mind.

## Dharmas in Buddhist Phenomenology

Other uses include dharma, normally spelled with a small "d" (to differentiate), which refers to a*phenomenon* or *constituent factor* of human experience. This was gradually expanded into a classification of constituents of the entire material and mental world. Rejecting the substantial existence of permanent entities which are qualified by possibly changing qualities, Buddhist Abhidharma philosophy, which enumerated seventy-five dharmas, came to propound that these "constituent factors" are the only type of entity that truly exists. This notion is of particular importance for the analysis of human experience: Rather than assuming that mental states inhere in a cognizing subject, or a soul-substance, Buddhist philosophers largely propose that mental states alone exist as "momentary elements of consciousness", and that a subjective perceiver is assumed.

One of the central tenets of Buddhism, is the denial of a separate permanent "I", and is outlined in the three marks of existence. The three signs: 1. Dukkha (Pali: Dukkha)-Suffering, 2. Anitya (Pali: Anicca)-Change/Impermanence, 3. Anatman (Pali: Anatta)-Non-self. At the heart of Buddhism, is the denial of a "self" or "I" (and hence the delusion) as a separate self-existing entity.

Later, Buddhist philosophers like Nagarjuna would question whether the dharmas (momentary elements of consciousness) truly have a separate existence of their own. (ie Do they exist apart from anything else?) Rejecting any inherent reality to the dharmas, he asked (rhetorically):

*uunyecu sarvadharmecu kim anantam kim antavat*

*kim anantam antavac ca nanantam nantavac ca kim*

*kim tad eva kim anyat kim uauvatam kim auauvatam*

*auauvatam uauvatam ca kim va nobhayam apyatah*

*sarvopalambhapaœamah prapancopaœamah shivah*

*na kva cit kasyacit kaœcid dharmo buddhena deœitah.*

When all dharmas are empty, what is endless? What has an end?

What is endless and with an end? What is not endless and not with an end?

What is *it*? What is *other*? What is permanent? What is impermanent?

What is impermanent and permanent? What is neither?

Auspicious is the pacification of phenomenal metastasis, the pacification of all apprehending;

There is no dharma whatsoever taught by the Buddha to whomever, whenever, wherever. —Mulamadhyamakakarika, Nirvanaparikca, 25:22-24

## Dharma as Righteousness

According to S. N. Goenka, teacher of Vipassana Meditation, the original meaning of dhamma is "dhareti ti dhamma', or "that which is contained". Dharma in the Buddhist scriptures has a variety of meanings, including "phenomenon", and "nature" or "characteristic". Dharma also means 'mental contents', and is paired with citta, which means heart/mind. The pairing is paralleled with the pairing of kaya (body) and vedana (feelings or sensations, that which arise within the body but experienced through the mind), in major sutras such as the Mahasatipatthana sutra. Dharma is also used to refer to the teachings of the Buddha, not in the context of the words of one man, even an enlightened man, but as a reflection of natural law which was re-discovered by this man and shared with the world. A person who lives their life with an understanding of this natural law, is a "dhammic" person, which is often translated as "righteous".

## SAMSARA (BUDDHISM)

Samsara, the Sanskrit and Pali term for "continuous movement" or "continuous flowing" refers in Buddhism to the concept of a cycle of birth (jati) and consequent decay and death (jaramarana), in which all beings in the universe participate and which can only be escaped through enlightenment. Samsara is associated with suffering and is generally considered the antithesis of Nirvana or nibbana.

### Samsara in Nikaya Buddhism

Whereas in Hinduism some being is regarded as being subject to Samsara, Buddhism was founded on a rejection (anatta) of such metaphysical substances, and originally accounts for the process of rebirth/reincarnation by appeal to phenomenological or psychological constituents. Later schools of Buddhism such as the Pudgalavada, however, re-introduce the concept of a "person" which transmigrates. The basic idea that there is a cycle of birth and rebirth is, however, not questioned in early Buddhism and its successors, and neither is, generally, the concept that Samsara is a negative condition to be abated through religious practice concluding in the achievement of final Nirvana.

### Samsara in Mahayana Buddhism

According to several strands of the Mahayana Buddhist tradition, the division of Samsara and Nirvana is attacked using an argument that extends some of the basic premises of anatman and of Buddha's attack on orthodox accounts of existence. This is found poetically in the "Perfection of Wisdom" literature and more analytically in the philosophy of Nagarjuna and later writers. It is not entirely clear which aspects of this theoretical move were developed first in the sutras and which in the philosophical tradition.

### Samsara in Tibetan Buddhism

Samsara is uncontrollably recurring rebirth, filled with suffering and problems (according to Kalacakra tantra as explained by Dr. A. Berzin). In this sense, Samsara may be translated "Wheel of Suffering."

## MODERN TEACHERS

### Theravada/Vipassana Teachers

- Ajahn Mun Bhuridatta (1870-1949)
- Venerable Ananda Maitreya (1896-1998)
- Bhikkhu Bodhi (1944-)
- Ajahn Brahm (1951-)
- Buddhadasa Bhikkhu (1906-1993)
- Ajahn Chah (1918-1992)
- Venerable Chanmyay Sayadaw
- Dhiravamsa
- Dipa Ma (1911-1989)
- S. N. Goenka (1924-)
- Joseph Goldstein
- Bhante Henepola Gunaratana (1927-)
- Venerable Ledi Sayadaw (1846-1923)
- Ayya Khema (1923-1997)
- Preah Maha Ghosananda (1929-), Supreme Patriarch of Cambodia
- Mahasi Sayadaw (1904-1982)
- Venerable Mogok Sayadaw (Late)

- Nyanasamvara Suvaddhana (born 1913), the 19th Supreme Patriarch of Thailand
- Phrabhavanaviriyakhun (Luang Phaw Dattajeevo) (b.1941), acting abbot of Wat Phra Dhammakaya,
- Phrarajbhavanavisudh (Luang Phaw Dhammajayo) (b.1944), President of the Dhammakaya Foundation
- Sharon Salzberg
- Acharya Godwin Samararatne
- Ajahn Sumedho
- U Ba Khin (1899-1971)
- Sayadaw U Pandita (1921-)
- Walpola Piyananda
- Venerable Webu Sayadaw (Late)
- Shinzen Young.

## Tibetan Buddhist Teachers

- Tenzin Gyatso, the 14th Dalai Lama
- Chagdud Tulku Rinpoche (1930-2002)
- Chogyam Trungpa (1940-1987)
- Dhardo Rimpoche (1917-1990)
- Dudjom Rinpoche (1904-1987)
- Dzogchen Khenpo Choga Rinpoche (1965-)
- Dzongsar Jamyang Khyentse Rinpoche (1961-)
- Qoigyijabu, (1990-) 11th Panchen Lama (According to the People's Republic of China government)
- Lhundub Sopa, (1923-)
- Jigdal Dachen Sakya, 1929-, head of the Sakya School in the USA
- Kalu Rinpoche (1905-1989)
- Namkhai Norbu Rinpoche (1938-)
- Kelsang Gyatso (1931-)
- Kirti Tsenshab Rinpoche (1926-)
- Kyabje Gehlek Rinpoche (1939-)
- Paltul Rinpoche (1965-)

- Pawo Rinpoche (1912-1991; 1993-)
- Pema Chodron (1936-)
- Rangjung Rigpe Dorje (1924–1981), the 16th Karmapa
- Reginald Ray
- Rob Nairn
- Sonam Rinchen (1933-)
- Tarthang Tulku
- Thinley Norbu Rinpoche
- Thrangu Rinpoche (1933-)
- Trinley Thaye Dorje (1983-), regarded by many as the 17th Karmapa
- Thubten Zopa Rinpoche (1946-)
- Tulku Urgyen Rinpoche, (1920-1996), Dzogchen, Mahamudra and the New Treasures of Chokgyur Lingpa (Chokling Tersar).
- Urgyen Trinley Dorje (1985-), also regarded by many as the 17th Karmapa.

## Zen Teachers

Japanese :

- Kodo Sawaki (1880-1965)
- Dainin Katagiri
- D.T. Suzuki
- Taisen Deshimaru
- Kyozan Joshu Sasaki, Roshi (1907-)
- Kodo Sawaki (1880-1965)
- Taizan Maezumi (1931-1995)
- Soyen Shaku, Roshi (1859-1919)
- Nyogen Senzaki, Roshi (18??-1958)
- Eido Shimano, Roshi
- Shunryu Suzuki, Roshi (1904-1971)
- Haku'un Yasutani, Roshi (1885-1973)
- Harada Shodo, Roshi (1945-).

Chinese :

- Ven. Guang Qin (1892-1986)
- Ven. Hsing Yun (1927-)
- Ven. Hsin Ting (1944-)
- Ven. Hsuan Hua (1918-1995)
- Ven. Hsu Yun (1840-1959)
- Ven. Sheng-yen (1931-)
- Ven. Wei Chueh (1928).

European :

- John Garrie Roshi (1923-1998)
- Taisen Dokusho Villalba, Roshi (1956-)
- Fukai Denko Mesa, (1967-)
- Kosen Thibaut, Roshi (1950-)
- Barbara Kosen Richaudeau, (1951-)
- Ludger Tenryu Tenbreul, (1956).

American :

- Anne Hopkins Aitken, (1911-1994)
- Robert Baker Aitken, Roshi (1917-)
- Tenshin Reb Anderson
- Zentatsu Richard Baker, Roshi
- Joko Beck (1917-)
- John Crook (1930-)
- Zoketsu Norman Fischer
- James Ishmael Ford, Roshi (1948-)
- Tetsugen Bernard Glassman, Roshi
- Paul Haller, Roshi
- Cheri Huber
- Soeng Hyang (Barbara Rhodes)
- Philip Kapleau, Roshi (1912-2004)
- Jiyu Kennett, Roshi (1924-1996)
- Bodhin Kjolhede, Roshi (1948-)
- Jakusho Kwong, Roshi (1935-)
- John Daido Loori, Roshi

- Kobutsu Shindo Malone, Roshi
- Elihu Genmyo Smith (1948-)
- John Tarrant, Roshi (1949-)
- Brad Warner, Sensei.

Korean :

- Seung Sahn, Soen Sa (1927-2004)
- Samu Sunim, (1941).

Vietnamese :

- Thich Thien An (1926-1980)
- Thich Nhat Hanh (1926-).

## Miscellaneous

- Anagarika Dharmapala (1864-1933), (The World's Debt to Buddha)
- Natalie Goldberg
- Daisaku Ikeda
- Ven. Ching Kung (1927-)
- Ven. Cheng Yen (1937-)
- Ram Bahadur Bamjan (1989-)
- Sangharakshita (1925-)
- Jan Willis
- Ven. K. Sri Dhammananda (1919-2006).

## Teachers of Controversial Buddhist or Buddhist-influenced Groups

- Shoko Asahara (1955-)
- Inoue Nissho (1887-1967)
- Li Hongzhi (1952)
- Lu Sheng-yen (1945)
- Suma Ching Hai.

## Modern Scholars and Authors

- Bhimrao Ramji Ambedkar (1891-1956)
- Stephen Batchelor
- Alexander Berzin

- Susan Blackmore
- Thomas Cleary
- Edward Conze (1904-1979)
- Mark Epstein
- Ven. Gnanatiloka
- Nakamura Hajime (1911-1999)
- Christmas Humphreys
- Phra Khantipalo
- Nishida Kitaro (1870-1945)
- Nishitani Keiji (1900-1990)
- Johnny Lovewisdom
- Ven. Narada Maha Thera
- Ven. Tai Xu (1890-1947)
- Manhae (1879-1944)
- Abe Masao (born 1915)
- Henry Steel Olcott (1832-1907)
- Walpola Rahula
- C.A.F. Rhys Davids (1857-1942)
- T.W. Rhys Davids (1843-1922)
- Scott Shaw
- Gary Snyder
- D.T. Suzuki (1870-1966)
- Tanaka Chigaku (1861-1939)
- Robert Thurman
- Ven. Yin Shun (1906-2005).

## Modern Politicians, Activists, and Protestors

- Aung San Suu Kyi
- Tenzin Delek Rinpoche
- Phoolan Devi
- Sulak Sivaraksa
- Thich Quang Duc.

## Celebrity Buddhists

- Adewale Akinnuoye-Agbaje, actor

- Roberto Baggio, Italian footballer
- Andrew Black, poker player
- Orlando Bloom, actor
- Leonard Cohen, poet, singer
- Mark Copani, actor
- Patrick Duffy, actor
- Michael Everson, linguist
- Richard Gere, actor
- Allen Ginsberg, poet
- Philip Glass, composer
- Ron Glass, actor
- Herbie Hancock, musician
- Goldie Hawn, actor
- Christmas Humphreys, judge, scholar
- Charles Johnson, writer
- Maxi Jazz, rapper
- Courtney Love, singer-songwriter, actress
- Gustav Meyrink, writer, translator, banker
- Kathleen Dee-Anne Norris, actor, model
- Victor Pelevin, novelist
- Steven Seagal, actor, martial artist
- Duncan Sheik, singer-songwriter
- Wayne Shorter, musician
- Tina Turner, singer
- Watazumi Doso, shakuhachi flutist
- Faye Wong, singer
- Adam Yauch, rapper (MCA of the Beastie Boys).

# 4

# Wheel of the Dharma in Buddhism

Today is the last teaching of 1994 so it is time to review what you have done during the year. If you discover that your year has been positive, that you have done lots of practices, learned a lot and meditated a lot, now is the time to appreciate yourself and congratulate yourself on being so successful in spiritual terms, and it is also the time to rededicate yourself to practice, study and meditation in the coming year. On the other hand, if you find that you have been irregular in doing practices and coming to classes, and that you have not actually done anything much that you have more-or-less wasted a year of this precious human life now is the time to feel regret and sadness about it. But being sad about it is not enough this sadness must also become a force impelling you to do better. So now is the time to determine that you will change for the better in the coming year.

Bodhicitta is like the supreme gold-making elixir,
For it transforms the unclean body we have taken
Into the priceless jewel of a Buddha-Form.
Therefore firmly seize this Awakening Mind.

We need to practise, and practise all the time. The practice we most need to undertake is the most wholesome practice of all the practice in which we work wholeheartedly to develop bodhicitta, the state of mind that sincerely and fervently wants to achieve full enlightenment for the sake of all beings. Nothing is as wholesome as concentrating on this mind. It is said that if all the Buddhas of the three times were to put their heads together and discuss what would be most beneficial for suffering beings, giving them happiness in the short-term and in the long-term, they would not find anything more magical than the mind of enlightenment, bodhichitta, for it is the panacea of all ills.

This mind of bodhicitta is of crucial importance, for it is this mind which determines whether or not our practice carries us to the state of enlightenment. For instance if a person were to go away to the mountains, find a suitable cave for meditation and completely seal themselves inside the cave with the strong determination not to come out or see anyone, but to dedicate their entire life to concerted practice, if this person did not have bodhicitta, no matter what practice he or she might do inside the sealed cave, nothing much would come of it in terms of achieving enlightenment.

Thus we must realize the importance of this precious mind of enlightenment. Our efforts to achieve the state of enlightenment must be constant and steady, therefore we need the precious mind of enlightenment continuously. Although you are going to have a month-and-a-half's break for the summer holidays, never have a break from generating bodhicitta.

As Jamgon Lama Tsongkapa says, if one has the alchemists' elixir one can transmute base metal into gold; in the same way, if you have this precious mind of enlightenment, this bodhicitta, this jewel of all minds, it will transmute all your small and seemingly insignificant good deeds into a means by which you will reach the state of enlightenment.

The great Indian Buddhist master Shantideva says something very similar: If we have this mind of enlightenment, although at the moment we have a human body that originally came into being from the sperm and egg of our parents and is thus basically undesirable, impure and unattractive in itself, the elixir of the mind of enlightenment will transform this human body of gross, impure human material into the glorious, magnificent, enlightened body of a Buddha.

*If even the thought to relieve*
*Living creatures of merely a headache*
*Is a beneficial intention*
*Endowed with infinite goodness,*
*What need is there to mention*
*The wish to dispel their inconceivable misery,*
*Wishing every single one of them*
*To realize boundless good qualities?*

The Tibetan master Dzogchen Patrul Rinpoche says, I have been to many lamas of all four traditions of Tibetan Buddhism, I have studied the many tenets and views of Buddhist philosophy and practice. None of the lamas or the texts say that there is a mind that is superior to the precious mind of enlightenment. They all have the same view with règard to the supreme significance of this mind.

Normally we understand the esoteric Buddhist practice of tantra as a very powerful and speedy way of achieving enlightenment so powerful and so speedy that through its means certain people are able to achieve the state of enlightenment in one lifetime even though normally it takes millions of eons to travel the path. However without bodhicitta, even the practice of tantra, so powerful and speedy, will not help a person reach the state of enlightenment in one lifetime.

If you really want to know how to engage in extensive merit-gathering practice in a simple way, the secret is bodhicitta. If you manage to develop bodhicitta, then even if you do no more than offer one butter-lamp, one candle, that simple practice of offering one light will gather an enormous amount of merit a universe full of merit so that however much merit is used up the store of merit will never run out. However if you were to engage in extensive offerings without bodhicitta offering ten thousand butter lamps for instance the merits would not be as great as in the first case the merit would only be as great as the number of lamps offered.

During Buddha's own time there was an Indian king called Prasenajit. On many occasions he invited the Buddha and his followers, offering them meals for weeks together. On one of these occasions the Buddha asked the king, To whom should we dedicate the merits? The king requested the Buddha to say the prayers of dedication to whoever had the greatest merits. Assuming that he himself would have the greatest merits because he was offering so much food, the King thought that the Buddha would dedicate the merits to him. However the king didn't have the most merit. Also present was a beggarly monk called Surata who felt so good about the king's generosity in offering food to the Buddha and his followers for weeks and weeks, that he rejoiced sincerely in the king's generosity and thus, through his pure heart, gathered more merits than the king who had incurred a great deal of expense.

*For the one who has perfectly seized this mind*
*With the thought never to turn away*
*From totally liberating*
*The infinite forms of life,*
*From that time hence,*
*Even while asleep or unconcerned,*
*A force of merit equal to the sky*
*Will perpetually ensue.*

For two or three weeks the king didn't get any dedications at the end of the meals he was offering to the Buddha and his many followers. Because it was the custom to say prayers at the end of the meal, and the Buddha and the Sangha didn't dedicate the merits to him, the king felt unhappy and had a very long face. One of his ministers asked him, Lord, is something bothering you? The king answered, Buddha has been here for weeks now. I have been offering food all this time and all this time the beggar Surata has received the dedication. So the minister resorted to a dirty trick. Because the beggar continued to rejoice with a pure heart in the king's generosity, thus unwittingly gathering more merits, the minister decided to have someone chase the beggar so that he would have no chance to feel good about the king's generosity. Because poor Surata had to run for his life, he didn't have time to rejoice, and that day it was found that the king had more merits. Thus that day he got the dedication he wanted!

There is another small anecdote about this poor beggar, Surata. Though he was a beggar in material terms, in spiritual terms he was already quite developed. He is said to have offered one butter lamp with bodhicitta motivation, praying, With this butter lamp may I achieve the state of enlightenment for the sake of all sentient beings, and it is said that the butter lamp was so brilliant that when someone tried to put it out they were unable to do so.

So with the precious mind of enlightenment, even if you burn only one incense stick and offer the fragrance to the holy objects and so on, the merit you will gather will be enormous. If, before you light the incense stick and offer the fragrance, you say to yourself, Today I offer this incense stick to the gurus and the Buddhas may I achieve the state of enlightenment for the sake of all sentient beings, saying it not in a jaded, mechanical way but with full sincerity, you will gather as many merits by burning this one incense stick as there are sentient beings throughout the universe.

*This intention to benefit all beings,*

*Which does not arise in others even for their own sake,*

*Is an extraordinary jewel of the mind,*

*And its birth is an unprecedented wonder.*

Now that I have told you about the need for and importance of bodhicitta, about the magical power of bodhicitta, please dwell in bodhicitta. Remember this: Bodhicitta is the supreme object of meditation, bodhicitta is the supreme object of any practice... Bodhicitta is supreme for it includes the interests of all sentient beings, which is the greatest of all practices. Bodhicitta is called rinchen sem chog, meaning the precious jewel of all minds. It is the core practice the central practice of all bodhisattvas. Ask any bodhisattva, What do you mainly practise? and you will hear nothing other than, I have tried to practise bodhicitta. They will be unanimous in their answer. I could keep on reciting the many teachings about bodhicitta given by the Buddha himself in the Sutras, as well as by Indian masters and scholar practitioners. In his great work Bodhicharyavatara (A Guide to the Bodhisattva's Way of Life) Shantideva says that if someone simply has the good heart to want to relieve another person of a headache, the merit from that good intention cannot be estimated. There is a true story about this. It is the story of Dza.khan Pumo (literally Potter's Daughter, though the person was a man). Dza.khaumlin Pumo had been forbidden by his mother from going to distant islands in the high seas to fetch jewels for his father's trade. Because her husband had lost his life at sea, Dza.khan Pumo's mother didn't want her son to follow in his father's footsteps since she didn't want to lose the only male remaining in the family. In order to stop him, his mother could do nothing more than lie down on the threshold of their house, hoping that out of respect for her he would not jump over her. However he lost his temper and not only walked over his mother's body but also kicked her head.

Dza.khan Pumo sailed for a long time in the company of others. Eventually, as his mother had feared, the boat capsized. They were washed up on the beach of an island and as he walked along the beach trying to find his way, he came upon an iron house and went in. Inside the house he saw a terrible sight: a person whose head was being drilled by a wheel so that brains and blood were oozing out. He was suffering tremendously. Dza.khan Pumo asked him, What is the reason that you have this terrible suffering? He answered, I think it must be because of the dreadful way I behaved towards my mother, walking over her and treating her cruelly. Dza.khan Pumo thought to himself, I am in the same situation, driven by karma to suffer the same consequences of the same actions. The moment he realized that he was there due to the force of karma, a voice from above said, May one who is bound be liberated and one who is free be bound, and he found that the wheel had left the other man's head and was busily drilling into his own. However even while he was suffering the agony of being drilled by the wheel, he was able to feel sympathy for others who might be undergoing the same suffering, thinking to himself, May all other people who are suffering the same consequence through disobedience and walking over their mothers' heads, be free of their suffering: may the sufferings I undergo be sufficient for them too. As soon as he had generated this good-hearted empathy for others, the wheel jumped off his head.

*I bow down to the body of the one*

*In whom the sacred precious mind is born.*

*I seek refuge in that source of joy*

*Who brings to happiness even those who harm him.*

Dza.khan Pumo, this Potter's Daughter, was in fact the historical Buddha Shakyamuni in one of his earlier lives, as a bodhisattva on the way to enlightenment. The reason he was called Potter's Daughter was that before his birth, his mother had many boys but they had all died. Then the parents thought, If we have a boy next time, let's try giving him a girl's name. They did so, and it worked!

One of the ways of generating universal altruism, bodhicitta, is equalizing and exchanging self for others. In equalizing, one recognizes that oneself and others are the same; in exchanging self for others one mentally exchanges one's own position for that of others. This very powerful practice of equalizing and exchanging can be traced back to the experience of the Buddha as the bodhisattva Dza.khan Pumo. If, like Dza.khan Pumo, you have bodhicitta, although you might be temporarily reborn in a bad state of existence due to some unfortunate past action, you won't be there for as long as is usually the case you will pay for your bad karma briefly.

As Shantideva says, if somebody has the kindness and good heart to want to help relieve someone else's headache, and if that kindness and goodness of heart gathers great merit, is there any need to say that if someone generates the good heart wanting to liberate and to work for the ultimate enlightenment of all sentient beings, that person will gather much greater merits?

Today, please meditate on bodhicitta by way of understanding that you yourself and others are the same, and then trying to exchange your cherishing of self for cherishing of others. In other words, your sense of self-cherishing must be displaced by a strong, selfless sense of cherishing others. Let such an attitude develop in your mind. This is one of the ways of generating bodhicitta, universal altruism.

## A HUMAN APPROACH TO WORLD PEACE

When we rise in the morning and listen to the radio or read the newspaper, we are confronted with the same sad news: violence, crime, wars, and disasters. I cannot recall a single day without a report of something terrible happening somewhere. Even in these modern times it is clear that one's precious life is not safe. No former generation has had to experience so much bad news as we face today; this constant awareness of fear and tension should make any sensitive and compassionate person question seriously the progress of our modern world.

It is ironic that the more serious problems emanate from the more industrially advanced societies. Science and technology have worked wonders in many fields, but the basic human problems remain.

There is unprecedented literacy, yet this universal education does not seem to have fostered goodness, but only mental restlessness and discontent instead. There is no doubt about the increase in our material progress and technology, but somehow this is not sufficient as we have not yet succeeded in bringing about peace and happiness or in overcoming suffering.

We can only conclude that there must be something seriously wrong with our progress and development, and if we do not check it in time there could be disastrous consequences for the future of humanity. I am not at all against science and technology — they have contributed immensely to the overall experience of humankind; to our material comfort and well-being and to our greater understanding of the world we live in. But if we give too much emphasis to science and technology we are in danger of losing touch with those aspects of human knowledge and understanding that aspire towards honesty and altruism.

Science and technology, though capable of creating immeasurable material comfort, cannot replace the age-old spiritual and humanitarian values that have largely shaped world civilization, in all its national forms, as we know it today. No one can deny the unprecedented material benefit of science and technology, but our basic human problems remain; we are still faced with the same, if not more, suffering, fear, and tension. Thus it is only logical to try to strike a balance between material development on the one hand and the development of spiritual, human values on the other. In order to bring about this great adjustment, we need to revive our humanitarian values.

I am sure that many people share my concern about the present worldwide moral crisis and will join in my appeal to all humanitarians and religious practitioners who also share this concern to help make our societies more compassionate, just, and equitable. I do not speak as a Buddhist or even as a Tibetan. Nor do I speak as an expert on international politics (though I unavoidably comment on these matters). Rather, I speak simply as a human being, as an upholder of the humanitarian values that are the bedrock not only of Mahayana Buddhism but of all the great world religions. From this perspective I share with you my personal outlook-that:

1. universal humanitarianism is essential to solve global problems;
2. compassion is the pillar of world peace;
3. all world religions are already for world peace in this way, as are all humanitarians of whatever ideology;
4. each individual has a universal responsibility to shape institutions to serve human needs.

## SOLVING HUMAN PROBLEMS THROUGH TRANSFORMING HUMAN ATTITUDES

Of the many problems we face today, some are natural calamities and must be accepted and faced with equanimity.

Others, however, are of our own making, created by misunderstanding, and can be corrected. One such type arises from the conflict of ideologies, political or religious, when people fight each other for petty ends, losing sight of the basic humanity that binds us all together as a single human family. We must remember that the different religions, ideologies, and political systems of the world are meant for human beings to achieve happiness. We must not lose sight of this fundamental goal and at no time should we place means above ends; the supremacy of humanity over matter and ideology must always be maintained.

By far the greatest single danger facing humankind — in fact, all living beings on our planet — is the threat of nuclear destruction. I need not elaborate on this danger, but I would like to appeal to all the leaders of the nuclear powers who literally hold the future of the world in their hands, to the scientists and technicians who continue to create these awesome weapons of destruction, and to all the people at large who are in a position to influence their leaders: I appeal to them to exercise their sanity and begin to work at dismantling and destroying all nuclear weapons. We know that in the event of a nuclear war there will be no victors because there will be no survivors! Is it not frightening just to contemplate such inhuman and heartless destruction? And, is it not logical that we should remove the cause for our own destruction when we know the cause and have both the time and the means to do so? Often we cannot overcome our problems because we either do not know the cause or, if we understand it, do not have the means to remove it. This is not the case with the nuclear threat.

Whether they belong to more evolved species like humans or to simpler ones such as animals, all beings primarily seek peace, comfort, and security. Life is as dear to the mute animal as it is to any human being; even the simplest insect strives for protection from dangers that threaten its life. Just as each one of us wants to live and does not wish to die, so it is with all other creatures in the universe, though their power to effect this is a different matter.

Broadly speaking there are two types of happiness and suffering, mental and physical, and of the two, I believe that mental suffering and happiness are the more acute. Hence, I stress the training of the mind to endure suffering and attain a more lasting state of happiness. However, I also have a more general and concrete idea of happiness: a combination of inner peace, economic development, and, above all, world peace. To achieve such goals I feel it is necessary to develop a sense of universal responsibility, a deep concern for all irrespective of creed, colour, sex, or nationality.

The premise behind this idea of universal responsibility is the simple fact that, in general terms, all others' desires are the same as mine. Every being wants happiness and does not want suffering. If we, as intelligent human beings, do not accept this fact, there will be more and more suffering on this planet. If we adopt a self-centred approach to life and constantly try to use others for our own self-interest, we may gain temporary benefits, but in the long run we will not succeed in achieving even personal happiness, and world peace will be completely out of the question.

In their quest for happiness, humans have used different methods, which all too often have been cruel and repellent. Behaving in ways utterly unbecoming to their status as humans, they inflict suffering upon fellow humans and the other living beings for their own selfish gains. In the end, such short-sighted actions bring suffering to oneself as well as to others. To be born a human being is a rare event in itself, and it is wise to use this opportunity as effectively and skilfully as possible. We must have the proper perspective, that of the universal life process, so that the happiness or glory of one person or group is not sought at the expense of others.

All this calls for a new approach to global problems. The world is becoming smaller and smaller — and more and more interdependent — as a result of rapid technological advances and international trade as well as increasing trans-national relations. We now depend very much on each other. In ancient times problems were mostly family-size, and they were naturally tackled at the family level, but the situation has changed. Today we are so interdependent, so closely interconnected with each other, that without a sense of universal responsibility, a feeling of universal brotherhood and sisterhood, and an understanding and belief that we really are part of one big human family, we cannot hope to overcome the dangers to our very existence — let alone bring about peace and happiness.

One nation's problems can no longer be satisfactorily solved by itself alone; too much depends on the interest, attitude, and cooperation of other nations. A universal humanitarian approach to world problems seems the only sound basis for world peace. What does this mean: We begin from the recognition mentioned previously that all beings cherish happiness and do not want suffering. It then becomes both morally wrong and pragmatically unwise to pursue only one's own happiness oblivious to the feelings and aspirations of all others who surround us as members of the same human family. The wiser course is to think of others also when pursuing our own happiness. This will lead to what I call 'wise self-interest,' which hopefully will transform itself into 'compromised self-interest,' or better still, 'mutual interest.'

Although the increasing interdependence among nations might be expected to generate more sympathetic cooperation, it is difficult to achieve a spirit of genuine cooperation as long as people remain indifferent to the feelings and happiness of others. When people are motivated mostly by greed and jealousy, it is not possible for them to live in harmony. A spiritual approach may not solve all the political problems that have been caused by the existing self-centred approach, but in the long run it will overcome the very basis of the problems that we face today.

On the other hand, if humankind continues to approach its problems considering only temporary expediency, future generations will have to face tremendous difficulties. The global population is increasing, and our resources are being rapidly depleted. Look at the trees, for example. No one knows exactly what adverse effects massive deforestation will have on the climate, the soil, and global ecology as a whole. We are facing problems because people are concentrating only on their short-term, selfish interests, not thinking of the entire human family. They are not thinking of the earth and the long-term effects on universal life as a whole. If we of the present generation do not think about these now, future generations may not be able to cope with them.

## INDIVIDUAL POWER TO SHAPE INSTITUTIONS

Anger plays no small role in current conflicts such as those in the Middle East, Southeast Asia, the North-South problem, and so forth. These conflicts arise from a failure to understand one another's humanness. The answer is not the development and use of greater military force, nor an arms race. Nor is it purely political or purely technological. Basically it is spiritual, in the sense that what is required is a sensitive understanding of our common human situation. Hatred and fighting cannot bring happiness to anyone, even to the winners of battles. Violence always produces misery and thus is essentially counter-productive. It is, therefore, time for world leaders to learn to transcend the differences of race, culture, and ideology and to regard one another through eyes that see the common human situation. To do so would benefit individuals, communities, nations, and the world at large.

The greater part of present world tension seems to stem from the 'Eastern bloc' versus 'Western bloc' conflict that has been going on since World War II. These two blocs tend to describe and view each other in a totally unfavourable light. This continuing, unreasonable struggle is due to a lack of mutual affection and respect for each other as fellow human beings. Those of the Eastern bloc should reduce their hatred towards the Western bloc because the Western bloc is also made up of human beings — men, women, and children. Similarly those of the Western bloc should reduce their hatred towards of the eastern bloc because the Eastern bloc is also human beings. In such a reduction of mutual hatred, the leaders of both blocs have a powerful role to play. But first and foremost, leaders must realize their own and others' humanness. Without this basic realization, very little effective reduction of organized hatred can be achieved.

If, for example, the leader of the United States of America and the leader of the Union of Soviet Socialist Republics suddenly met each other in the middle of a desolate island, I am sure they would respond to each other spontaneously as fellow human beings. But a wall of mutual suspicion and misunderstanding separates them the moment they are identified as the 'President of the USA and the 'Secretary-General of the USSR'. More human contact in the form of informal extended meetings, without any agenda, would improve their mutual understanding; they would learn to relate to each other as human beings and could then try to tackle international problems based on this understanding. No two parties, especially those with a history of antagonism, can negotiate fruitfully in an atmosphere of mutual suspicion and hatred.

I suggest that world leaders meet about once a year in a beautiful place without any business, just to get to know each other as human beings. Then, later, they could meet to discuss mutual and global problems. I am sure many others share my wish that world leaders meet at the conference table in such an atmosphere of mutual respect and understanding of each other's humanness.

To improve person-to-person contact in the world at large, I would like to see greater encouragement of international tourism. Also, mass media, particularly in democratic societies, can make a considerable contribution to world peace by giving greater coverage to human interest items that reflect the ultimate oneness of humanity. With the rise of a few big powers in the international arena, the humanitarian role of international organizations is being bypassed and neglected. I hope that this will be corrected and that all international organizations, especially the United Nations, will be more active and effective in ensuring maximum benefit to humanity and promoting international understanding. It will indeed be tragic if the few powerful members continue to misuse world bodies like the UN for their one-sided interests. The UN must become the instrument of world peace. This world body must be respected by all, for the UN is the only source of hope for small oppressed nations and hence for the planet as a whole.

As all nations are economically dependent upon one another more than ever before, human understanding must go beyond national boundaries and embrace the international community at large. Indeed, unless we can create an atmosphere of genuine cooperation, gained not by threatened or actual use of force but by heartfelt understanding, world problems will only increase. If people in poorer countries are denied the happiness they desire and deserve, they will naturally be dissatisfied and pose problems for the rich. If unwanted social, political, and cultural forms continue to be imposed upon unwilling people, the attainment of world peace is doubtful. However, if we satisfy people at a heart-to-heart level, peace will surely come.

Within each nation, the individual ought to be given the right to happiness, and among nations, there must be equal concern for the welfare of even the smallest nations. I am not suggesting that one system is better than another and all should adopt it. On the contrary, a variety of political systems and ideologies is desirable and accords with the variety of dispositions within the human community. This variety enhances the ceaseless human quest for happiness. Thus each community should be free to evolve its own political and socioeconomic system, based on the principle of self-determination.

The achievement of justice, harmony, and peace depends on many factors. We should think about them in terms of human benefit in the long run rather than the short term. I realize the enormity of the task before us, but I see no other alternative than the one I am proposing — which is based on our common humanity. Nations have no choice but to be concerned about the welfare of others, not so much because of their belief in humanity, but because it is in the mutual and long-term interest of all concerned. An appreciation of this new reality is indicated by the emergence of regional or continental economic organizations such as the European Economic Community, the Association of South East Asian Nations, and so forth. I hope more such trans-national organizations will be formed, particularly in regions where economic development and regional stability seem in short supply.

Under present conditions, there is definitely a growing need for human understanding and a sense of universal responsibility. In order to achieve such ideas, we must generate a good and kind heart, for without this, we can achieve neither universal happiness nor lasting world peace. We cannot create peace on paper. While advocating universal responsibility and universal brotherhood and sisterhood, the facts are that humanity is organized in separate entities in the form of national societies. Thus, in a realistic sense, I feel it is these societies that must act as the building-blocks for world peace.

Attempts have been made in the past to create societies more just and equal. Institutions have been established with noble charters to combat anti-social forces. Unfortunately, such ideas have been cheated by selfishness. More than ever before, we witness today how ethics and noble principles are obscured by the shadow of self-interest, particularly in the political sphere. There is a school of thought that warns us to refrain from politics altogether, as politics has become synonymous with amorality. Politics devoid of ethics does not further human welfare, and life without morality reduces humans to the level of beasts. However, politics is not axiomatically 'dirty.' Rather, the instruments of our political culture have distorted the high ideals and noble concepts meant to further human welfare. Naturally, spiritual people express their concern about religious leaders 'messing' with politics, since they fear the contamination of religion by dirty politics.

I question the popular assumption that religion and ethics have no place in politics and that religious persons should seclude themselves as hermits. Such a view of religion is too one-sided; it lacks a proper perspective on the individual's relation to society and the role of religion in our lives. Ethics is as crucial to a politician as it is to a religious practitioner. Dangerous consequences will follow when politicians and rulers forget moral principles. Whether we believe in God or karma, ethics is the foundation of every religion.

Such human qualities as morality, compassion, decency, wisdom, and so forth have been the foundations of all civilizations. These qualities must be cultivated and sustained through systematic moral education in a conductive social environment so that a more humane world may emerge. The qualities required to create such a world must be inculcated right from the beginning, from childhood. We cannot wait for the next generation to make this change; the present generation must attempt a renewal of basic human values. If there is any hope, it is in the future generations, but not unless we institute major change on a worldwide scale in our present educational system. We need a revolution in our commitment to and practice of universal humanitarian values.

It is not enough to make noisy calls to halt moral degeneration; we must do something about it. Since present-day governments do not shoulder such 'religious' responsibilities, humanitarian and religious leaders must strengthen the existing civic, social, cultural, educational, and religious organizations to revive human and spiritual values. Where necessary, we must create new organizations to achieve these goals. Only in so doing can we hope to create a more stable basis for world peace.

Living in society, we should share the sufferings of our fellow citizens and practice compassion and tolerance not only towards our loved ones but also towards our enemies. This is the test of our moral strength. We must set an example by our own practice, for we cannot hope to convince others of the value of religion by mere words. We must live up to the same high standards of integrity and sacrifice that we ask of others. The ultimate purpose of all religions is to serve and benefit humanity. This is why it is so important that religion always be used to effect the happiness and peace of all beings and not merely to convert others.

Still, in religion there are no national boundaries. A religion can and should be used by any people or person who finds it beneficial. What is important for each seeker is to choose a religion that is most suitable to himself or herself. But, the embracing of a particular religion does not mean the rejection of another religion or one's own community. In fact, it is important that those who embrace a religion should not cut themselves off from their own society; they should continue to live within their own community and in harmony with its members. By escaping from your own community, you cannot benefit others, whereas benefiting others is actually the basic aim of religion.

In this regard there are two things important to keep in mind: self-examination and self-correction. We should constantly check our attitude toward others, examining ourselves carefully, and we should correct ourselves immediately when we find we are in the wrong.

Finally, a few words about material progress. I have heard a great deal of complaint against material progress from Westerners, and yet, paradoxically, it has been the very pride of the Western world. I see nothing wrong with material progress per se, provided people are always given precedence. It is my firm belief that in order to solve human problems in all their dimensions, we must combine and harmonize economic development with spiritual growth. However, we must know its limitations. Although materialistic knowledge in the form of science and technology has contributed enormously to human welfare, it is not capable of creating lasting happiness. In America, for example, where technological development is perhaps more advanced than in any other country, there is still a great deal of mental suffering. This is because materialistic knowledge can only provide a type of happiness that is dependent upon physical conditions. It cannot provide happiness that springs from inner development independent of external factors.

For renewal of human values and attainment of lasting happiness, we need to look to the common humanitarian heritage of all nations the world over. May this essay serve as an urgent reminder lest we forget the human values that unite us all as a single family on this planet.

I have written the above lines
To tell my constant feeling.
Whenever I meet even a 'foreigner,'
I have always the same feeling:
'I am meeting another member of the human family.'
This attitude has deepened
My affection and respect for all beings.
May this natural wish be

My small contribution to world peace.
I pray for a more friendly,
More caring, and more understanding
Human family on this planet.
To all who dislike suffering,
Who cherish lasting happiness—
This is my heartfelt appeal.

## INCENSE OFFERING

Incense offering, or Sang-sol, is a ceremony performed by Tibetans from all walks of life to mark important events in their lives. A widespread national custom, it can be preformed individually or in groups, on occasions such as the Dalai Lama's birthday, marriages, third day of the Tibetan New Year, or preceding other important events.

### Origins

It is not clear whether the Tibetan custom of offering incense originated in India or not, as only two references to such practice can be found in the Indian texts. It is mentioned in the Guhyasamaja Tantra that one should know about the three kinds of fragrance. The other reference is to be found in the story of Bhadri of Magadha, which tells of how she invited the Buddha to her house and made offerings of smoke to him from the roof.

According to the writings of various scholars, it seems that incense offering was carried out in Tibet from the very early times when the teacher Tonpa Sherab, founder of the Bon religion, first came from Zhang Zhung (Afghanistan/Tadzhikistan?) to spread his doctrine in Tibet.

The oldest extant text on incense offering, dates back to the eight century, when the Indian master Padmasambhava came to Tibet and built Samye monastery. This manual, containing detailed instructions on how to preform the ritual, was then hidden by him to await discovery at some appropriate juncture in the future. Several centuries later, two Treasure masters (tertons), one from northern Tibet and another from the south, discovered and revealed it. based on this Treasure (terma) text many Nyingma, Kagyu and Sakya lamas composed the incense offering. Later at the time of the third Dalai Lama, Sonam Gyatso, a lama by the name of Yeshe Wangpo, wrote a text on the incense offering from the Gelugpa point of view. Subsequently, three works were written on the subject by Panchen Lobsang Chogyen (1570-1662) and another by the fifth Dalai Lama.

## OFFERING WATER TO WASH THE FEET-PURIFICATION

Second is water to wash the feet. This is clear water mixed with incense or sandlewood which is made as an offering to all enlightened beings' feet. The symbolic meaning is purification. By cleansing the feet of the enlightened beings, we cleanse all our own negative karma and obscurations.

By making offerings to clean the enlightened beings feet, we are really cleaning the "feet" of our own mind. With respect, devotion and confidence, we offer an ocean of this kind of water to all enlightened beings to purify all the temporary obscurations of ourselves and all sentient beings. Obscurations are called "temporary" because they can be purified. If they were permanent, we could not purify them even if we make an effort. So meditate on this when you make these offerings. All the different types of obscurations — gross, subtle, negative karma, afflictive emotions, and obscurations to enlightenment — all these different types of obscurations become fully purified.

### Offering Flowers-Generosity

Next is offering of a flower, the flower of the beauty of enlightenment. It signifies the practice of generosity and opens the heart. A flower is very beautiful; so you naturally want to keep it. But when you offer it to others, there is some special feeling in the mind. With that connection, make the offering and practice freedom from stinginess. Milarepa said there is no special practice of generosity if one is free from stinginess. Meditate on that by offering flowers, which signifies the practice of generosity.

May all sentient beings achieve the freedom and endowment of a precious human life.

Flowers are offered to the head of the enlightened beings, for them to wear on the crown of the head. Within the practice of generosity, we immediately think of giving wealth, giving fearlessness, giving wisdom — there are many different types of generosity. Usually when we say generosity, we immediately think of giving wealth, but it is not only that. For example, giving fearlessness means giving life. If someone is afraid for their life, like drowning in water, and if you give them safety from the water, this is called giving fearlessness, giving freedom from danger to life. Giving wisdom is very special generosity. When we give teaching to one who has no wisdom — does not know what samsara is, what enlightenment is, or what the cause of suffering is — that is such a great gift. To help them understand "Oh, that is samsara, that is enlightenment." Such a great gift! So, offering a flower symbolizes generosity.

## Offering Incense-Discipline, Moral Ethics

The fourth offering is incense, which symbolizes moral ethics or discipline. Moral discipline is one of the most important practices. In the West, maybe discipline and morality are a little bit different. What I mean here is that when we have good discipline, there is morality. Discipline is in the teaching of the Dharma. For instance, it says, "do this, this, this. Sit like this, meditate like this." It is taught like discipline. So when we do that, it is good moral ethics; when we cannot do these things that are taught to be done, then there is no morality, no ethics.

In Sanskrit, this is called "shila". Shila means coolness, freshness. When we have good discipline, it cools the mind free from suffering. When we stay in that position well, it relaxes the mind and frees it from agitation. All these disciplines are part of the process of progressing in our meditation practice. Unless these disciplines and moral ethics are there, it is not possible to achieve enlightenment. Therefore, Buddha gave these three teachings — moral ethics, samadhi and wisdom — called the Three Trainings. These Three Trainings are very important.

Wisdom or special insight comes from samadhi, the stability and strength of the mind. That kind of strength in the mind is based on discipline and morality. So they are all related to each other, are connected to each other and depend on each other. Therefore, moral ethics is a very important aspect of path.

Incense, which is the nature of morality, makes offerings to the nose of the enlightened beings. The enlightened beings are not attached to smell, but to our purity. All people respect those who have kept moral ethics well. It doesn't matter who they are, they get respect because they are trustworthy and dependable. That kind of person gives a good smell, good odour, and people are attracted to that. not only people, but the qualities of enlightened beings are also attracted by that morality. It is their foundation/basis, like the ground which grows all the "crops" of the enlightened qualities.

## Offering Light-Patience

Fifth is light or a lamp, which signifies the stability and clarity of patience, the beauty which dispels all ignorance. Light offering is made to the eyes of all the enlightened beings, who see clearly without mistake. Some people feel patience is showing weakness or pessimism. But, actually, patience shows the strength and clarity of mind, which are based on wisdom and compassion. Without proper wisdom and compassion, one cannot practice patience. So light shows that the strength of the mind, the clear, stable nature of the mind, achieved through the practice of patience. Because the mind is not disturbed by other forces, it has such great qualities: clarity knows what is to be done, which is necessary, which is not necessary. That dispels ignorance.

Patience can be practiced in all different forms, different ways, not just when people are faced with anger. For example, there is patience in Dharma practice and study. First, this is based on wisdom, so we should have such wisdom to really know how Dharma is, what quality it has, the depth and vastness of Dharma, and how we can achieve these qualities. Seeing those great qualities, then we need patience to study and practice. When we have that, there is a mind of clarity, of stableness.

On the other hand we should not be patient with our afflictive emotions. When we have anger, desire, jealousy, pride, don't practice patience with these! This is the wrong way to practice patience. Even if it is hard or painful, these are subjects to get rid of or purify; they don't do any good thing. Without sacrificing something, there is no chance that we will have peace and happiness. So no matter what kind of pain we face, what difficult circumstances we face, we have to go thru it. Even if we have to sacrifice this life, it is worthwhile to sacrifice. A lot of people commit suicide to get rid of all these afflictive emotions. They are overpowered by the afflictive emotions and they kill themselves. That is the wrong way to sacrifice this life. We have to sacrifice this life the other way around. Buddha said that if we have to lose our life to keep the moral discipline, it just finishes this life, but next lives will be higher and higher, better and better. But if we do it the other way around and sacrifice this life for the afflictive emotions, then we will go worse and worse.

In Shantideva's text it is said that we should not commit suicide or give this body without much purpose. Rather, we should cherish this precious human life. An explanation is given. When a medicinal tree is very small plant, it has to be protected in order to grow into a huge tree. If you pick it up when it is small, it will benefit only a few and then it is finished. But if you protect it well with many fences, it will grow into a huge tree that will bring fruits, flowers, roots, leaves, branches for the benefit of many, many sentient beings. Similarly we have a fragile mind at this time. We must protect this precious human life with all these antidotes, fences, and let it grow big. Then we can benefit many sentient beings. By the practice of patience, all the 112 major and minor marks of a Buddha will come. Of course, we should not expect it, but the result of patience is a healthy, good body, to which all people are attracted, which is respected and admired. All this comes from the practice of patience.

## OFFERING FRAGRANCE-PERSEVERANCE

Next is the offering of perfume or the fragrance from saffron or sandlewood. — all the different types of perfume. That signifies perseverance or joyous effort. Through that one quality, one develops all the qualities of enlightenment. Without perseverance, without joyous effort, nothing can be achieved. Even in samsara, we have to work so hard to achieve anything. A lot of people sacrifice a lot of things just for samsaric achievement. You sacrifice your life for your work; if you die, what will you do with your wealth? So now, see the other side — Dharma study and practice. When we could make such a great effort to study, practice Dharma, we have to sacrifice some little thing. It is said in Shantideva's text that studying Dharma is the cause to freedom from suffering. To achieve ultimate enlightenment, ultimate happiness, why can't we do that? Others in samsara, they even sacrifice their life for their achievements, but that becomes a cause only for suffering. So see that. As flowers were offered to the eyes of enlightenment, perfumes are offered to the Buddha's mind because perseverance is the heart of enlightenment. Perfect generosity, moral ethics, patience, samadhi, wisdom-these all depend on perseverance. Without joyous effort none of these can be accomplished, so it is the heart, the essence. Meditate that by this offering, may all sentient beings progress in their attainment of the qualities of enlightenment.

## Offering Delicious Food-Samadhi

Seventh is the offering of delicious food which has a lot of different tastes. The delicious, excellent quality of food signifies samadhi, which is a nectar or ambrosia to feed the mind. This is an offering to the tongue of the enlightened beings, the Buddhas and Bodhisattvas. Samadhi is also the source of all the siddhis like clairvoyance. There are two different types of clairvoyance — ordinary clairvoyance is usually from other lifetimes. The other type is special insight clairvoyance, which we achieve this lifetime through meditation practice. Flying in the sky, different types of miracle power, these can all be achieved through samadhi, the virtuous one-pointed mind.

The very stable mind, one-pointed, clear, calm, peaceful mind of samadhi becomes a basis to achieve all the enlightenment qualities. Food symbolizes samadhi because eating food maintains this body, and samadhi is a kind of food that maintains the mind as well as the physical body. When you achieve any kind of samadhi, it is the fruition of the effort you made before, and it can also become a path to get higher fruition. Generally, when we eat nutritious healthy food, it makes our health better. So if we have the nutritious food of samadhi, it keeps the health of the mind. It makes the mind healthy, clear, calm and peaceful. By making this offering of delicious food, may all sentient beings have the health which results from the samadhi food. May all sentient beings have the samadhi nature, quality.

## THE RITUAL

The Incense offering should be done in the morning on a clean and elevated outdoor site, free of insects., either on a hill or the top of a house and inhabited by many local gods and nagas.

If performed during a festival, all the inhabitants of a locality may assemble and, at the end of the offering, stand in a row and throw a handful of tsampa (roasted barley flour) in the air. As this is usually a happy occasion, a dance often follows. In the summer, incense offering is often associated with picnics on top of mountains. It is closely linked with the hanging of prayer flags from trees or tall poles, especially on the third day of the new year, but also on other auspicious days.

The incense should be burned in a large urn-shaped burner (sang-khun) and should not have been trampled by people or animals. Wood, not coal, should be used as fuel and the substance to be burned as incense should be fragrant, such as the leaves of fern or juniper, or the branches of coniferous tree, rhododendron, and red or white sandalwood. In addition, tsampa, butter, sugar, and medicinal plants, and other substances free from the taint of alcohol, onion or garlic are burned.

When offering incense, people should examine their motivation and reflect that by making this offering to lamas, meditational deities and religious protectors, they will accumulate merit, which they should dedicate to the benefit of all sentient beings. If they have any specific requests, such as prayers for longevity or the removal of obstacles to religious practice, they should be made at this point. Next the practitioners take refuge, meditate on the four immeasurable wishes, love, compassion, joy, equanimity, and visualize themselves as deities. The objects to be offered are then blessed, rid of their ordinary appearances and transformed by meditation, gestures, and mantras into an inexhaustible source of great bliss which will please those to whom they are offered.

The offering ends with the practitioners asking the deities to forgive them for any mistakes in the performance of the ritual, such as improperly or incompletely reciting the words of the text. the deities are then asked to return to their abodes and auspicious verses are recited.

## Talk by Khenpo Konchog Gyaltsen Rinpoche

The subject here today is an explanation of the significance of the eight offerings. We make these offerings to the enlightened beings in many practices-in the Vajrasattva practice, Guru Yoga, and a lot of other practices. We have been doing this for a long time, so I thought it would be useful if we studied a little about what that practice signifies.

The enlightened beings do not want or need these things. We make offerings for our own benefit, to accumulate great merit and wisdom. Enlightenment, Buddhahood, is achieved through the two great qualities-accumulation and purification. As you know, the Buddha has limitless qualities, which were gained through the great accumulations and purifications. Our offerings are a simple way to accumulate both merit and wisdom.

### OFFERING WATER TO CLEANSE THE MOUTH OR FACE-AUSPICIOUSNESS

First is the water offering to cleanse the mouth or face. It signifies auspiciousness or all the positive causes and conditions which bring positive effects. So, make an offering of water which is clean, fresh, cool, smooth, light, delicious, comfortable to the throat and stomach-these qualities are the qualities of auspiciousness. When you drink that kind of water, it is healthy; if you take a shower with it is healthy. While you make this kind of water offering to the enlightened beings, visualize an ocean of water. Then we dedicate this water to become a cause for all sentient beings to also collect positive causes and conditions. So this is the first water offering-to cleanse the mouth or face.

## HEALING : A TIBETAN BUDDHIST PERSPECTIVE

### What is Healing?

What do we mean by healing? Do we mean healing of the physical body, healing of the psyche/soul/mind, or both of these. What is the connection between body and mind? Many modern healing techniques regard successful healing as the cure of the presenting physical problem, whether this be symptoms of cancer, AIDS, chronic fatigue syndrome, or some other illness.

If the person does not recover from the presenting physical problem, or if that problem recurs or another develops at a later time, this may be regarded as failure. It is not uncommon in these situations for the therapist or organisation that has been helping the "sick" person to infer or state that the person must have done something wrong, that they haven't stuck strictly enough to the diet or meditated enough or done whatever else it was that they were supposed to do. In these situations the person can become very guilty, depressed or angry. In many cases, they just give up hope. To avoid these problems, it is necessary to consider a more comprehensive view of healing that incorporates not only physical healing but mental healing.

### Mind is the Creator

To understand healing from the Buddhist perspective, a useful starting point is to consider the Buddhist concept of mind. The mind is non-physical. It is formless, shapeless, colourless, genderless and has the ability to cognize or know. The basic nature of mind is pure, limitless and pervasive, like the sun shining unobstructedly in a clear sky. The problems or sickness we experience are like clouds in the sky obscuring the sun. Just as the clouds temporarily block the sun but are not of the same nature as the sun, our problems or sickness are temporary and the causes of them can be removed from the mind. From the Buddhist perspective, the mind is the creator of sickness and health. In fact, the mind is believed to be the creator of all of our problems. That is, the cause of disease is internal, not external.

## Unlimited Potential

You are probably familiar with the concept of karma, which literally means action. All of our actions lay down imprints on our mindstream which have the potential to ripen at some time in the future. These actions can be positive, negative or neutral. These karmic seeds are never lost. The negative ones can ripen at any time in the form of problems or sickness; the positive ones in the form of happiness, health or success. To heal present sickness, we have to engage in positive actions now. To prevent sickness occurring again in the future, we have to purify, or clear, the negative karmic imprints that remain on our mindstream. Karma is the creator of all happiness and suffering. If we don't have negative karma we will not get sick or receive harm from others. Buddhism asserts that everything that happens to us now is the result of our previous actions, not only in this lifetime but in other lifetimes. What we do now determines what will happen to us in the future.

In terms of present and future healing, the main objective is to guard our own actions, or karma. This requires constant mindfulness and awareness of all the actions of our body, speech and mind. We should avoid carrying out any actions that are harmful to ourselves and to others. Buddhism is therefore a philosophy of total personal responsibility. We have the ability to control our destiny, including the state of our body and mind. Each one of us has unlimited potential-what we have to do is develop that potential.

# HEALTHY MIND, HEALTHY BODY

Why do some people get ill while others remain in the best of health? Consider skin cancer. Of all the people who spend many hours out in the sun, some will develop skin cancer and others will not. The external situation is the same for all of them, but only some will be affected. The secondary cause of the skin cancer-the sun-is external, but the primary cause-the imprints laid down on the mindstream by previous actions-is internal.

Also, people with similar types of cancer will often respond quite differently to the same treatment, whether this be orthodox or alternative. Some will make a complete recovery. Some will recover temporarily and then develop a recurrence. Others will rapidly become worse and die. Logically one has to look to the mind for the cause of these differences.

Buddhism asserts that for lasting healing to occur, it is necessary to heal not only the current disease with medicines and other forms of treatment, but also the cause of the disease, which originates from the mind. If we do not heal or purify the mind, the sickness and problems will recur again and again.

This introduces the notion of "ultimate healing". By ridding the mind of all its accumulated "garbage", all of the previously committed negative actions and thoughts, and their imprints, we can be free of problems and sickness permanently. We can achieve ultimate healing-a state of permanent health and happiness. In order to heal the mind and hence the body, we have to eliminate negative thoughts and their imprints, and replace them with positive thoughts and imprints.

## The Inner Enemy

The basic root of our problems and sickness is selfishness, what we can call the inner enemy. Selfishness causes us to engage in negative actions, which place negative imprints on the mindstream. These negative actions can be of body, speech or mind, such as thoughts of jealousy, anger and greed. Selfish thoughts also increase pride, which results in feelings of jealousy towards those higher than us, superiority towards those lower than us and competitiveness towards equals. These feelings in turn result in an unhappy mind, a mind that is without peace. On the other hand, thoughts and actions directed to the well-being of others bring happiness and peace to the mind.

## Conscious Living, Conscious Dying

It is important to consider what happens to us when we die. The Buddhist view is that at the time of death the subtle consciousness, which carries with it all the karmic imprints from previous lives, separates from the body. After spending up to forty-nine days in an intermediate state between lives, the consciousness enters the fertilised egg of its future mother at or near the moment of conception. New life then begins. We bring into our new life a long history of previous actions with the potential to ripen at any time or in any of a myriad ways. The state of mind at the time of death is vitally important and can have a considerable effect on the situation into which we are reborn. Hence the need to prepare well for death and to be able to approach our death with a peaceful, calm and controlled mind. Death itself can be natural, due to exhaustion of the lifespan, or untimely, due to certain obstacles. These obstacles arise from the mind and can be counteracted in different ways. One method commonly employed in Tibetan Buddhism to remove life obstacles is to save the lives of animals that would otherwise have been killed. For example, animals can be rescued from being slaughtered or live bait can be purchased and released. For those with a life threatening illness, it is important to understand that being free of that illness doesn't mean that you will have a long life. There are many causes of death and death can happen to anybody at any time.

## Not just Pills and Potions

Tibetan medicine is popular and effective. It is mostly herbal medicine, but its uniqueness lies in the fact that in the course of its preparation it is blessed extensively with prayers and mantras, giving it more power. It is said that taking such medicine will either result in recovery, or, if the person is close to death, they will die quickly and painlessly. (Another theory, based on personal experience, is that it tastes so bad you want to recover quickly so that you can stop taking the medicine!)

Blessed pills and blessed water are also used extensively. The more spiritually developed the person carrying out the blessings or the healing practices, the more powerful is the healing result or potential. These pills often contain the relics of previous great meditators and saints, bestowing much power on the pills.

Many Tibetan lamas actually blow on the affected part of the body to effect healing or pain relief. I have seen a person with AIDS with intense leg pain have his pain disappear after a lama meditated intensely and blew on his leg for twenty minutes. Compassion is the power that heals.

Visualisation can also be very powerful healing. One method is to visualise a ball of white light above your head, with the light spreading in all directions. Imagine the light spreading through your body, completely dissolving away all sickness and problems. Concentrate on the image of your body as completely healed and in the nature of light.

This type of meditation is even more powerful when combined with visualising holy images and reciting mantras. I often tell my Christian patients to visualise the light as Jesus, with the light emanating from him.

In the Tibetan tradition, there are many Buddha figures (deities) which can be visualised while reciting their mantra. The Medicine Buddha; Chenrezig, or Avalokiteshvara (the Buddha of Compassion); or one of the long-life deities such as Amitabha are commonly used. Deities can be in peaceful or wrathful aspects. The wrathful ones are often used to cure heavy disease such as AIDS.

If you are not comfortable with these images, you can use other objects such as crystals, or simply visualise all the universal healing energy absorbing into you, transforming your body into light, and imagine yourself as totally healed.

Over the centuries many people have used these methods and have recovered from their illnesses, even from conditions such as leprosy, paralysis and cancer. The aim of these practises is to heal the mind as well as the body, so that the diseases or problems will not recur in the future. Also, many diseases are associated with spirit harm. Lamas and other practitioners will often recite certain prayers and mantras or engage in ceremonies to stop the spirit harm and allow the person to recover. A seven year old girl I knew had petit-mal epilepsy as the result of spirit harm; the epilepsy disappeared after various rituals and prayers had been performed. Whenever she had an epileptic attack, the girl would see a frightening apparition coming towards her. After the initial prayers had been performed, however, her attacks lessened and she would see a brick wall between her and the frightening figure. This wall was the colour of a monk's robes. Eventually the attacks and visions disappeared altogether.

In summary, we can say that the essential ingredients in the healing process, for both the person doing the healing and the person being healed, are compassion, faith, and pure morality.

## CHANGING OUR MINDS

Another powerful method of healing in Tibetan Buddhism is to meditate on the teachings known as thought transformation. These methods allow a person to see the problem or sickness as something positive rather than negative. A problem is only a problem if we label it a problem. If we look at a problem differently, we can see it as an opportunity to grow or to practice, and regard it as something positive. We can think that having this problem now ripens our previous karma, which does not then have to be experienced in the future.

If someone gets angry at us, we can choose to be angry in return or to be thankful to them for giving us the chance to practice patience and purify this particular karma. It takes a lot of practice to master these methods, but it can be done.

It is our concepts which often bring the greatest suffering and fear. For example, due to a set of signs and symptoms, the doctor gives the label 'AIDS' or 'cancer'. This can cause great distress in a person's mind, because they forget that it is only a label, that there is no truly existent, permanent AIDS or cancer. 'Death' is another label that can generate a lot of fear. But in reality 'death' is only a label for what happens when the consciousness separates from the body, and there is no real death from its own side. This also relates to our concept of 'I' and of all other phenomena. They are all just labels and have no true, independent existence.

Lama Zopa Rinpoche, a highly realised Tibetan Lama, says that the most powerful healing methods of all are those based on compassion, the wish to free other beings from their suffering. The compassionate mind-calm, peaceful, joyful and stress-free-is the ideal mental environment for healing. A mind of compassion stops our being totally wrapped up in our own suffering situations. By reaching out to others we become aware of not just my pain but the pain (that is, the pain of all beings).

Many people find the following technique powerful and effective: think "By me experiencing this disease or pain or problem, may all the other beings in the world be free of this disease, pain or problem" or "I am experiencing this pain/sickness/problem on behalf of all living beings."

One voluntarily takes on suffering in order for others to be free of it. This is similar to the Christian concept of regarding one's suffering as sharing the suffering of Jesus on the cross. Even death can be used in this way: "By me experiencing death, may all other beings be freed from the fears and difficulties of the death process." We have to ask ourselves "What is the purpose of my life? Why do I want to have good health and a long life?". The ultimate purpose of our life is to be of benefit to others. If we live longer and just create more negative karma, it is a waste of time.

Giving and taking is another powerful meditation. As you breathe in, visualise taking the suffering and the causes of suffering from all living beings, in the form of black smoke. When breathing in the black smoke, visualise smashing the black rock of selfishness at your heart, allowing compassion to manifest freely. As you breathe out, visualise breathing out white light that brings them happiness, enjoyment and wisdom.

Developing compassion is more important than having friends, wealth, education. Why? Because it is only compassion that guarantees a happy and peaceful mind, and it is the best thing to help us at the time of death

We can use our sickness and problems in a very powerful way for spiritual growth, resulting in the development of compassion and wisdom. The highest development of these qualities is the full realisation of our potential, the state of full enlightenment. Enlightenment brings great benefit to ourselves and allows us to work extensively for others. This is the state of ultimate healing.

I have outlined some of the concepts that are the basis of the Buddhist philosophy on healing. Many of these methods were taught by Lama Zopa Rinpoche at Tara Institute in Melbourne in August 1991 during the first course given by Lama Zopa specifically for people with life-threatening illnesses.

Some of these ideas may appear unusual at first, but please keep an open mind about them. If some of the ideas appear useful to you, please use them; if not, leave them aside.

## HYMN OF PRAISE

I hold aloft the scepter of compassion, the diamond thunderbolt of love. Its' five prongs showing the five wisdoms, conquering the five passions. I must be worthy to uphold it.

I hold aloft its' companion, the bell of wisdom, ringing freedom throughout the universes. I resolve never to separate from the perfect wisdom, to realize I cannot be separate. I will ring the bell throughout all worlds, throughout all lives.

I hold them together to show the non-duality of wisdom and compassion, with every fiber of my being, throughout all worlds.

I receive the bow and arrow, the bow of wisdom of selflessness, the arrow of communication, precise teaching, sending out the messages of wisdom to all beings. I shoot the arrow of freedom everywhere, in all directions, to slay the enemy of ignorance, and cynicism, and despair.

I receive the wheel of majesty and truth. I vow to turn the wheel, to liberate all beings, to preserve their freedoms.

I hold the gesture of sophisticated understanding, fine distinction between good and evil, beauty and ugliness.

I uphold the book, the teaching of the Buddha Yamantaka, conqueror of death. I accept responsibility for the teaching.

I remind all beings of the ground of freedom and the void.

I hold in reverence the ornaments of our teacher, His Holiness the Dalai Lama, always with us in our hearts.

The gesture of non-duality, the gesture of offering.

I receive the radiant wish-fulfilling jewel, to uphold the teachings of the jewel clan of the Buddhas.

I receive the vajra of the vajra clan.

My hands are dancing gods and goddesses of worship.

I receive the lotus of the lotus clan.

I touch the earth.

I uphold my vajra scepter and bell.

I uphold the sword of the sword clan, turning envy into all accomplishing wisdom and its' teachings.

## HEART SUTRA

Thus have I heard at one time.

The Lord was dwelling at Rajagriha, on Vulture-peak mountain, together with a great host of monks and a great host of Bodhisattvas.

At that time the Lord was composed in the concentration on the course of dharmas called 'Profound Illumination.'

At that time also the noble Lord Avalokita, the Bodhisattva and Mahasattva, in the practice of the profound Perfection of Wisdom, looked down; he beheld but five skandhas and that in their own-being they were empty.

Then, through the inspiration of the Buddha, the Venerable Sariputra said to the noble Lord Avalokita, the Bodhisattva and Mahasattva: "How should any child of good family train, who wishes to engage in the practice of the profound Perfection of Wisdom?" And the noble Lord Avalokita, the Bodhisattva and Mahasattva, spoke to the venerable Sariputra as follows.

"Sariputra, any son or daughter of good family who wishes to engage in the practice of the profound Perfection of Wisdom should look upon it thus: he or she beholds but five skandhas and that in their own-being they are empty.

Form is Emptiness, Emptiness is form.

Emptiness does not differ from form, and form does not differ from Emptiness.

Likewise feelings, recognitions, volitions and consciousnesses are empty.

So, Sariputra, all dharmas are Emptyness, without differentiating marks; they are not produced or stopped, not defiled and not immaculate, not deficient and not complete.

Therefore, Sariputra, in Emptyness there is no form, no feeling, no recognition, no volitions, no consciousness; no eye, no ear, no nose, no tongue, no body, no mind; no visible form, no sound, no smell, no taste, no tangible, no mental object; no eye-element, and so forth, up to no mind-element and no mental-consciousness-element; no ignorance and no extinction of ignorance, and so forth, up to no aging and death and no extinction of aging and death; likewise there is no Suffering, Origin, Cessation or Path, no wisdom-knowledge, no attainment and non-attainment.

Therefore Sariputra, because there is no attainment, Bodhisattvas abide relying on the Perfection of Wisdom, without obscurations of thought, and so are unafraid.

Transcending perverted views, they attain the end, Nirvana.

All Buddhas existing in the three times, relying on the Perfection of Wisdom, fully awaken to the highest, perfect Enlightenment.

Therefore one should know that the mantra of the Perfection of Wisdom is the mantra of great knowledge, the highest mantra, the unequalled mantra, the mantra that allays all suffering, the Truth, since it has nothing wrong.

The mantra of the Perfection of Wisdom is proclaimed:

Tad-yatha; Gate Gate Paragate Parasamgate Bodhi Svaha!

In this way, Sariputra, should a Bodhisattva and Mahasattva train in the profound Perfection of Wisdom."

Then the Lord rose from that concentration and commended the noble Lord Avalokita, the Bodhisattva and Mahasattva, saying: "Well said, well said, O son of good family!

So it is, O son of good family, so it is. Just as you have taught should the profound Perfection of Wisdom be practiced, and the Tathagatas will rejoice.

Thus spake the Lord. The Venerable Sariputra, the noble Lord Avalokita, the Bodhisattva and Mahasattva, and the whole world, that assembly with devas, human beings, asuras and gandharvas, were delighted and applauded the Lord's speech.

# 5

# Buddhist Temples in China

## TEMPLE OF BRIGHT FILIAL PIETY

The Temple of Bright Filial Piety on Guangxiao Road is one of the oldest Buddhist temples in Guangzhou and was the mansion of Prince Zhao Jiande of the Nanyue Kingdom during the Western Han Dynasty (206 B.C.-A.D.24).

The temple was initially built by an Indian monk during the Eastern Jin Dynasty (317-420) but the present temple, occupying an area of 31,000 square meters, dates from the Qing Dynasty (1644-1911). The temple has an important place in Buddhist history as Huineng of the Zen Buddhist sect was a novice monk here in the 7th century.

The Sixth Ancestor Hall in the temple was built in memory of Huineng, the sixth master of the Zen Sect of Buddhism, who is widely considered the most influential monk in the history of Chinese Buddhism. In the temple there is also a pagoda where Huineng's hair was buried. Other ancient structures in the temple include Sakyamuni Hall, Samgharama Hall, the King of Heaven Hall, and two iron towers.

## TEMPLE OF GREAT COMPASSION

The Temple of Great Compassion is a Buddhist temple in Hebei district, Tianjin, China. It was built during the Shunzhi period of the Qing Dynasty (1643-1661).

The temple was once famous for holding a skull relic of Xuanzang, however, the relic was presented to India in the 1950s and is now held in a Patna museum. Today the temple is a tourist attraction, with entry costing 4 Renminbi. It opens at 9 AM and is within walking distance of the main Tianjin train station.

## TEMPLE OF THE SIX BANYAN TREES

The Temple of the Six Banyan Trees is an ancient Buddhist temple built in 537 in the Liang Dynasty in Guangzhou, southern China. The temple's proximity to foreign consulates in Guangzou has made it a regular destination for families participating in the international adoption of children from China. Typically families receive blessings for their newly adopted children at this temple in front of the statue of Kuan Yin.

### History

The Temple of the Six Banyan Trees was originally called the Baozhuangyan Temple, but during the Northern Song Dynasty, a writer called Su Shi wrote the inscription *Liu Rong* (Six Banyan Trees) because of the six banyan trees he saw there and it has since been called the Temple of the Six Banyan Trees.

The temple was burned down and rebuilt in the Northern Song Dynasty. Flowery Pagoda, the main structure of the temple, was built in 1097, and was named for its colourful exterior.

## WANFU TEMPLE

Wanfu Temple is a temple on Mount Huangbo in Fujian province, China. It is famous as the original temple of Yinyuan Longqi, the temple's 33rd abbot and a Chan master. He later travelled to Japan with his disciple Muyan to found the Japanese Obaku school of Zen.

## WHITE HORSE TEMPLE

White Horse Temple was the first Buddhist temple in China, established under the patronage of Emperor Ming in the Eastern Han capital Luoyang in the year 68.

## Founding

One night, the emperor was said to have dreamed of a deity flying over his palace. The next day he told his ministers, and the minister Zhong Hu explained to him that he probably dreamed of Buddha in India.

The emperor then sent a delegation of 18 headed by Cai Yin, Qin Jing and Wang Zun to seek Buddhism. They returned from Afghanistan with an image of Gautama Buddha, the *Sutra of Forty-two Sections* and two eminent monks. The monks names have been variously romanized as Kasyapamatanga and Dharmavanya, Moton and Chufarlan.

The next year, the emperor ordered the construction of White Horse Temple three li west of the capital Luoyang, to remember the horse that carried back the sutras. It was China's first Buddhist temple.

## Naming

Notably, the emperor ordered the suffix (pinyin *si* to be used in the temple's name, as a display of respect. Previously, this character had been used to denote ministries of government. In later periods, all temples came to use this character in their name and it was dropped from the names of government ministries. As a result, the temple's name is sometimes translated as White Horse Ministry, a translation true to the time. However, White Horse Temple is the correct, literal reading to modern Chinese people.

## Significance

The first version of the Chinese *Sutra of Forty-two Sections* was produced within the temple. The temple then increased in importance as Buddhism grew within China, and spread to Korea, Japan and Vietnam. The introduction of Buddhism in China was also a significant influence on Chinese morals, thought and ethics.

## Location

The temple is located within Han and Wei Dynasty Luoyang,

which lies approximately 12km east of modern Luoyang, in Henan province.

## History

- 258 A royal Kuchean monk, Po-Yen, translated six Buddhist text in to Chinese at the temple, including the important *Infinite Life Sutra.*
- 1992 With the assistance of Thai and Chinese donors, the Hall of the Thai Buddha was constructed slightly west of the old temple.

## Description

The temple compound covers an area of 200 mu (13 hectares), and faces south. A stone paifang (archway) has been recently built 150 metres in front of the original gate. Between the archway and gate lies a pool with fountains, spanned by three stone bridges.

Entering the temple today, one sees the Hall of Heavenly Kings, Hall of the Great Buddha, Hall of Mahavira, Hall of Greeting, the Cool and Clear Terrace and the pavilion. On each side of the pavilion are the Sutra House and the Magic Weapon House.

## Visiting Today

The temple is open to the public, and can be reached by public bus number 56 from Luoyang Train Station. Standard tickets cost 35CQ and discounts are available to students at half price (17.5CQ).

# YONGHE TEMPLE

The Yonghe Temple, also known as the "Palace of Peace and Harmony Lama Temple", the "Yonghe Lamasery", or-popularly-the "Lama Temple" is a temple and monastery of the Geluk School of Tibetan Buddhism located in the northeastern part of Beijing, China. It is one of the largest and most important Tibetan Buddhist monasteries in the world. The building and the artworks of the temple combine Han Chinese and Tibetan styles.

## History

Building work on the Yonghegong Temple started in 1694 during the Qing Dynasty. It originally served as an official residence for court eunuchs. It was then converted into the court of the Prince Yong (Yin Zhen), a son of the Kangxi Emperor and himself the future Yongzheng Emperor. After Yongzheng's ascension to the throne in 1722, half of the building was converted into a lamasery, a monastery for monks of Tibetan Buddhism. The other half remained an imperial palace.

After Yongzheng's death in 1735, his coffin was placed in the temple. The Qianlong Emperor, Yongzheng's successor, gave the temple imperial status signified by having its turquoise tiles replaced with yellow tiles which were reserved for the emperor. Subsequently, the monastery became a residence for large numbers of Tibetan Buddhist monks from Mongolia and Tibet, and so the Yonghe Lamasery became the national centre of Lama administration. The temple is said to have survived the Cultural Revolution due to the intervention of Prime Minister Zhou Enlai. It was reopened to the public in 1981.

## Architecture and Artworks

The Yonghe Temple is arranged along a north-south central axis, which has a length of 480m. The main gate is at the southern end of this axis. Along the axis, there are five main halls which are separated by courtyards: the *Hall of the Heavenly Kings* (*Tian Wang Dian* or *Devaraja Hall*), the *Hall of Harmony and Peace* (*Yonghegong*), the *Hall of Everlasting Protection* (*Yongyoudian*), the *Hall of the Wheel of the Law* (*Falundian*), and the *Pavilion of Ten Thousand Happinesses* (*Wanfuge*).

The *Hall of the Heavenly Kings* is the southernmost of the main halls, it served originally as the main entrance to the monastery. In the Centre of the hall stands a statue of the Maitreya Buddha, along the walls statues of the four Heavenly Kings are arranged.

The *Hall of Harmony and Peace* is the main building of the temple. It houses three bronze statues of the Buddhas of the Three Ages, the statue of the Gautama Buddha (Buddha of the

Present) is in the Centre, it is flanked by the statue of Kasyapa Matanga (Buddha of the Past, right) and the Maitreya Buddha (Buddha of the Future, left). Along the sides of the hall, the statues of the 18 Arhats are placed. A mural in the hall shows the bodhisattva Avalokitesvara.

The *Hall of Everlasting Protection*was Emperor Yongzheng's living quarters as a prince and the place where his coffin was placed after his death. Today, a statue of the *Bhaisajya-guru* (healing Buddha) stands in this hall.

The *Hall of the Wheel of the Law* functions as a place for reading scriptures and conducting religious ceremonies. It contains a large statue of Je Tsongkhapa, founder of the Geluk School. The hall also contains the Five-Hundred-Arhat-Hill, a carving make of red sandalwood with statues of the arhats made from five different metals (gold, silver, copper, iron, and tin).

The *Pavilion of Ten Thousand Happinesses* contains an 18m tall statue of the Maitreya Buddha carved from a single piece of White Sandalwood. The statue is one of three artworks in the Temple which were included in the Guinness Book of Records in 1993.

## ZHANSHAN TEMPLE

Zhanshan Temple is a Buddhist temple in Qingdao, Shandong, China. It is located on the southern side of Zhanshan (literally 'clear' or 'deep mountain'), facing the sea.

It features a number of buildings, including a Buddhist scripture library and a large Yaoshi stupa.

In 2004 the temple underwent renovation.

As of April 2004, entry was priced at 5RMB, with discounts available for seniors and the disabled. During August 2004, the price was reported as 8RMB, which may be related to the renovations which were still underway.

## JING'AN TEMPLE

The Jing'an Temple is a Buddhist temple on West Nanjing Road, in Jing'an District, Shanghai, China.

## History

The first temple was built in 247 AD, at the time of the Kingdom of Wu, during the Three Kingdoms period. Originally located beside Suzhou Creek, it was relocated to its current site in 1216 during the Song Dynasty. The current temple was rebuilt in the Qing Dynasty.

During the Cultural Revolution, it was converted into a plastics factory. It was converted back to an active temple following reconstruction in 1983, and completely renovated in late 2003.

## Features Include

Three Southern-style main halls, each with its own courtyard, dating from the most recent reconstruction (1880):

- Hall of Heavenly Kings
- Hall of the Three Saints
- Hall of Virtuous Works
- The Precious Hall of the Great Hero, or main hall, currently under construction. When completed, it will be four to five stories tall
- To the east of the main hall is the Guanyin Hall. In the Centre of the hall is a statue of the goddess made out of camphor wood. Standing on a lotus-shaped base, it is 6.2 meters tall and weighs 5 tons
- Opposite to the hall is the Jade Buddha Hall, where a 3.8-meter jade Buddha sits in the Centre. It is the largest sitting jade Buddha statue in the country
- Abbot's Chambers
- Ming Dynasty copper bell (Hongwu Bell), weighing 3.5 tons
- Stone Buddhas from the Southern and Northern Dynasties period (420-589 AD).

## Transportation

The temple is served by the Jing'an Temple station of Shanghai Metro (Line 2).

## LINGYIN TEMPLE

Lingyin Temple is a Buddhist temple of the Chan sect located north-west of Hangzhou, Zhejiang province, China. The temple's name is commonly literally translated as Temple of the Soul's Retreat. It is one of the largest and wealthiest Buddhist temples in China. The monastery is the largest of several temples in the Wulin Mountains, which also features a large number of grottos and religious rock carvings, the most famous of which is the Feilai Feng.

### History

The monastery was originally founded in 328 AD during the Eastern Jin Dynasty by Indian monk Huili. From its inception, Lingyin was a famous monastery in the Jiangnan region. At its peak under the Kingdom of Wuyue (907-978), the temple boasted nine multi-storey buildings, 18 pavilions, 72 halls, more than 1300 dormitory rooms, inhabited by more than 3000 monks. Many of the rich Buddhist carvings in the Feilai Feng grottos and surrounding mountains also date from this era.

During the latter Southern Song Dynasty, the monastery was regarded as one of the ten most important temples of the Chan sect in the Jiangnan region. However, its prominence has not saved the temple from marauders. It has been rebuilt no less than sixteen times since then. The current buildings are modern restorations of late Qing buildings. During the Cultural Revolution, the temple and grounds suffered some damage at the hands of Red Guards during the Cultural Revolution. However, they escaped large scale destruction partly because of the protection of Premier Zhou Enlai.

Today the temple is thriving as a destination for both pilgrims and tourists. It is regarded as one of the wealthiest monasteries in China, and regular pilgrims have included former paramount leader Deng Xiaoping.

### Surrounds

The Wuling Mountains area is a major centre of Chan Buddhism in south-eastern China. A number of smaller temples are also located in the area. Today, Lingyin and the surrounding areas are marketed as the Lingyin-Feilai Feng Scenic Area, with ticketed admission. Visitors enter from a screen wall marked with a four character inscription "the Western Heaven is within reach". Proceeding down the road from the entrance, the visitor first sees Feilai Feng on the left, then Lingyin Hill on the right. The entire scenic area is dotted with historic buildings and artwork, including pagodas, pavilions, bridges, and statues. The largest stone pagoda is located near the entrance. Called Ligong Pagoda, it houses the ashes of Huili, the Indian monk who founded Lingyin. The area is thickly wooded, with some trees labelled as many centuries old.

## The Feilai Feng Grottos

Feilai Feng, or "the Peak that Flew Hither", also commonly translated as "Flying Peak", is located in front of the temple proper. The peak is so-named because it is made of limestone, giving it a craggy appearance very different to the surrounding mountains. Legend holds that the peak was originally from India (with some versions suggesting that it is Vulture Peak, but flew to Hangzhou overnight as a demonstration of the omnipotence of Buddhist law. A large number of carvings dot the surface of the peak. More are located in various caves and grottos throughout the peak. Within the main cave, dedicated to the bodhisattva Guanyin, there is a crack in the ceiling of the cave that stretches up to the surface, so that a person standing at a certain position can see a sliver of sunlight. This is known as the "one thread of heaven".

## Lingyin Temple

The main axis of Lingyin follows a traditional Song dynasty five-hall Chan sect structure. The main axis stretches up the Lingyin Hill. However, it should be noted that the five-hall axis is a recent recreation. Only the front three halls are a part of the Qing dynasty axis.

## Hall of the Heavenly Kings

The formal entrance of the temple is the Hall of the Heavenly

Kings. This hall is a double-eaved building. The front of the building carries a plaque, written by the Kangxi Emperor. The principal statue in this hall is that of the Maitreya Buddha in his manifestation as the clothes bag monk, or the Laughing Buddha. At the back, facing up the hill, is the Skanda Buddha, or Weituo as he is known in Chinese. This statue dates from the Southern Song Dynasty. Arranged along the left and right are the Four Heavenly Kings. The ceiling is ornately painted and decorated with phoenixes and dragons.

Visitors to the temple are often impressed by the size and majesty of the entrance hall and its statues of the heavenly kings. Indeed, the hall of the Heavenly Kings at the Lingyin Temple is as large or larger than the main hall at many temples, reflecting its status as the centre of Buddhism in south-eastern China.

## Grand Hall of the Great Sage

The second and principal hall is the Mahavira Hall, or the Grand Hall of the Great Sage. It is separated from the Hall of the Heavenly Kings by a large courtyard, featuring a raised lawn bordered with trees. To the left of the courtyard stands the Hall of the Five Hundred Arhats. The Grand Hall of the Great Sage is triple eaved and stands 33.6 metres tall. It houses, as is traditional, a statue of Shakyamuni, the historical Buddha. The present statue was carved in 1956 from camphor wood in Tang Dynasty style and coated with 60 taels of gold. It is the largest wooden Buddhist statue in China. At the back of the main statue is a statue of Guanyin, backed by a large screen that features the carved images of some 150 Buddhist personalities, including the pilgrims of the Journey to the West, Daoji, and arhats. Arranged along the sides of the hall are images of the 18 principal arhats, and other prominent Buddhists. The interior of the hall reaches about 30 metres, with a gold-painted ceiling featuring base relief images of traditional Buddhist symbols.

## Hall of the Medicine Buddha

Further uphill and behind the main hall is the Hall of the Medicine Buddha, housing a statue of the Bhaisajyaguru Buddha, commonly called the Medicine Buddha. The hall is currently undergoing exterior renovation and is not open to the public.

## Sutra Library

Uphill from the Hall of the Medicine Buddha is the Sutra Library. This, and the Huayan Hall behind it, were built from 2000 to 2002 to re-create the five-hall main axis. The Sutra Library does not house a major statue and is not open for worship.

## Huayan Hall

The fifth and last hall on the main axis is the Avatamsaka Hall, or Huayan Hall. Also built in 2002, this hall houses statues of the three sages of the Avatamsaka Sutra, known as the Huayan Sutra in Chinese-Shakyamuni, Manjusri, and Samantabhadra.

## Hall of the Five Hundred Arhats

The Hall of Five Hundred Arhats, also a modern addition, faces onto the western side of the court yard in front of the main hall. The building has a complex floor plan, shaped like a Buddhist swastika. Along the arms of the swastika are arranged the five hundred arhats as slightly larger-than-life bronze statues. Each statue is seated on a unique ornate seat. At the centre, where the arms of the swastika join, stands a bronze canopy housing statues of four bodhisattvas representing the four cardinal directions. This is currently the tallest solid bronze structure in the world.

## Famous people from Ling Yin Temple

- Daoji-A Buddhist monk revered as a Taoist god.

# NAN PUTUO SI TEMPLE

Nan Putuo Si Temple is a Buddhist temple founded in the Tang era in the Chinese city of Xiamen.

# NANHUA TEMPLE

Nanhua Temple is the Zen Buddhist monastery of the 6th

Patriarch of Zen Buddhism Hui Neng, located near the city of Shaoguan in China in the northern part of Guangdong Province.

## PUJI TEMPLE

Puji Temple is a Buddhist temple located on the island of Putuoshan in Zhejiang province, China.

The temple is now a tourist attraction as the island is significant in Chinese Buddhism. In January 2004, entry tickets to the temple cost 5CQ per person.

### History

Built in 916, at the time it was called (pinyin *bu ken qu guanyin yuan*).

Shen Zong donated lands to the temple, and a new monk was ordained every year. (After the temple was renamed, the old name for the temple was still used to refer to a nearby hill, (pinyin *zi zhu lin*), on which a 20 metre tall Guanyin now stands.) The monks studied Buddhism and the temple slowly prospered.

In 1214, still in the Song Dynasty, Emperor Ningzong of Song China donated tens of thousands of *min* (lines of cash) to the temple and presented them with a sign reading 'General Funds Hall'.

In 1298 by order of Emperor Chengzong of the Yuan Dynasty, Ngn, (*li ying*) repaired the temple, completing the work in 1301. The monks were given over 4000 mu (2.7 $km^2$) of land, and 20 *min* of government funds. In 1299, the abbot of the temple was appointed the director of Buddhist teaching for the region and was sent as an emissary to Japan by the emperor.

In the winter of 1313, the Emperor Renzong's mother sent an envoy to present the temple with 868 metal bars and three qing of land, and to make offerings.

In 1327, Emperor Taiding presented the temple with 1000 metal bars and 2 *qing* 26 *mu* of land.

In 1386, during the Ming Dynasty, Duke Tang was asked to come to the mainland to advise the Emperor. He brought with him 30,000 people from 46 islands, including the monks of

Putuoshan. At the same time, Duke Tang ordered the burning of 300 temples on Putuoshan. He also moved a large statue of Guanyin to a temple on the mainland. (The temple is now known as Qita Temple. It is located in Ningbo.)

In 1515, the Buddhist community began to recover through donations and alms.

In 1553, the Ming government under the Jiajing Emperor moved the monks and destroyed temples once more.

In 1572, a monk named Zhen Song came to Putuoshan to help rebuild it to its former glory.

In 1574, a monk named Zhen Biao wanted to ascend the mountain to locate the site of old Bao Guo Si, destroyed 200 years previously, but was not allowed. Despite this, he still ascended the mountain and located the old site of the temple, and managed to rebuild a small monastery, only to have it destroyed by a military commander named Xu Jing Xing. Afterwards, Zhou Liangbin, a Ningbo government official, had Zhen Biao and a group of nuns punished. Fours years later, Zhen Biao was made abbot. He had the Hall of Heavenly Kings and one other hall built.

## SHAOLIN

The Shaolin Monastery is a Buddhist temple, located in Henan province of the People's Republic of China, famous for its long association with Chan (Zen) Buddhism and martial arts, and is perhaps the Buddhist monastery best known in the Western world.

### History

Batuo an Indian dhyana master, was the founder and first patriarch of the Shaolin Monastery. Batuo went to China to preach Buddhism in AD 464. The Shaolin Temple was built thirty-one years later in AD 495, by the order of emperor Wei Xiao Wen (471–500). The temple originally consisted of a round dome used as a shrine and a platform where Indian and Chinese monks translated Indian Buddhist scriptures into native Chinese languages.

According to the *Continued Biographies of Eminent Monks* (AD 645) by Daoxuan, the Shaolin Monastery was built on the north side of Shaoshi, the western peak of Mount Song, one of the Sacred Mountains of China, by Emperor Xiaowen of the Northern Wei Dynasty for the monk Batuo. Yang Xuanzhi, in the *Record of the Buddhist Monasteries of Luoyang* (AD 547), and Li Xian, in the *Ming Yitongzhi* (1461 CE), concur with Daoxuan's location and attribution. The *Jiaqing Chongxiu Yitongzhi* (AD 1843) specifies that this monastery, located in the province of Henan, was built in the 20th year of the *Tàihe* era of the Northern Wei Dynasty, that is, the monastery was built in 497 CE.

Kangxi, the second Qing emperor, was a supporter of the Shaolin temple in Henan and he wrote the calligraphic inscription that, to this day, hangs over the main temple gate.

The monastery has been destroyed and rebuilt many times. Perhaps the most well-known story of the Temple's destruction is that it was destroyed in 1732 by the Qing government for supposed anti-Qing activities; this destruction is also supposed to have helped spread Shaolin martial arts through China by means of fugitive monks. This story commonly appears in martial arts history and in fiction.

However, accounts of the Qing Dynasty destroying the Shaolin temple may refer to a southern Shaolin temple, which Ju Ke, in the *Qing bai lei chao* (1917), located in Fujian Province. Additionally, some martial arts historians, such as Tang Hao and Stanley Henning, believe that the story is likely fictional, appearing only at the very end of the Qing period in novels and sensational literature.

In 1928, the warlord Shi Yousan set fire to the monastery, destroying many priceless manuscripts of the temple library, some of its halls, and damaging the aforementioned Stele.

The Cultural Revolution purged all monks and Buddhist materials from within its walls, leaving the temple barren for years. During most of the second half of the 20th century, the Chinese Communist Party (CCP) used Shao-lin for training bogus monks-actually Red Guard or Red Army soldiers/agents. The temple and grounds, including the cemetery of past priests known as Ta-lin (Big Forest) and the Pool of the Nine Dragons, was used as an artillery target by the CCP army for decades.

The target practice extended to Omei (Emei) Mountain Temple, a place that once housed the Shao-lin sister nuns. Shao-lin was subsequently rebuilt, repopulated and designated an official tourist site by the Chinese government after the overwhelming success of the Jet Li movie *Shaolin Temple* in 1982.

Martial arts groups from all over the world have made donations for the upkeep of the temple and grounds, and are subsequently honoured with carved stones near the entrance of the temple. In the past, many people have tried to capitalize on the Shaolin Monastery by building their own schools on Mount Song. However, the Chinese government eventually illegalized this, and so the schools all moved to the nearby towns. The CCP did not wish its monopoly on all things Shao-lin to be jeopardized, nor did it wish to lose the lucrative franchise of Shao-lin tourist trap souvenirs. A Dharma gathering was held between August 19 and 20, 1999, in the Shaolin Monastery, Songshan, China, for Buddhist Master Shi Yong Xin to take office as abbot. He is the thirteenth successor after Buddhist abbot Xue Ting Fu Yu. In March 2006 President Putin of Russia became the first foreign leader to visit the monastery.

## Martial Arts

The Shaolin monastery is the only temple in China that combines martial arts and Chan Buddhism. As such, monks at the monastery may be martial monks, scholarly or clerical monks, or both. However, even the martial monks also practice Chan Buddhism. It is said that Chan Buddhism allows you to store and build up qi, while martial arts is the act of releasing qi; therefore, the two complement and complete each other. Because of this dual focus, there are two abbots at the Shaolin Temple. The current martial abbot is Shi De Li, the thirty-first direct successor after Bodhidharma, or Da Mo. As martial abbot, the primary job is to train monks in shaolin wushu (shaolin kung fu). The monks have a very regimented schedule for training. For example, before even having breakfast, the trainees must wake up at 4 AM to run for an hour, to meditate for another hour, and train martial arts for a third hour. The monks do not get very much of a break; their only vacation is ten days near the Chinese New Year to see their parents. It must be noted, however, that this is reflective of the current schedule at Shaolin temple, and in no way reflects the historical focus or schedule of Shaolin prior to its most recent reconstruction. The current Shaolin temple is the subject of much controversy because it was reestablished by the Chinese government as a tourist attraction, rather than by the Shaolin order. Thus, many Chan Buddhist elements inherent in Shaolin training are no longer represented.

## STANDARD DESIGN FOR BUDDHIST TEMPLE CONSTRUCTION

*Standard Design for Buddhist Temple Construction* is a Chinese language text written by Dao Xuan in the early Tang Dynasty. It described a design for Buddhist temples influenced by mainstream Chinese architecture, and based upon a traditional layout composed of multiple, related courtyards. That tradition can be traced back to the Shang and Zhou Dynasties.

## TANZHE TEMPLE

The Tanzhe Temple is a Buddhist temple situated near China National Highway 108 in a mountainous area to the west of Beijing. It is relatively well-known in Beijing. At one time, it was one of the most important temples in the nation.

Built in the Jin Dynasty, it has an age of around 1,600 years. The area of the entire temple is 100 mu (6.8 hectares), and its arrangement of halls is akin to that found in the Ming and Qing dynasties.

The temple's central hall is its Mahavira Hall. 24 metres in length, 33 metres wide, and with a depth of 20 metres. Buddhist monks regularly perform chanting here, to the accompaniment of woodblocks, cup gongs, and bells.

Tanzhe Temple also has some other features. The bed of its former Dragon Pool, which has dried up sits on the hill at the back of the temple. The *zhè* trees (*Cudrania tricuspidata*), now few in number, are located in the temple as well. Their number has dwindled shockingly from the original thousand or so. There are also persimmon trees, as well as a stand of bamboo.

The township of Tanzhesi owes its origins to Tanzhe Temple. Recently, the tourist industry has expanded it.

## BADACHU

The Badachu, meaning Eight Great Sites, refers to the eight Buddhist temples and monasteries scattered across Cuiwei, Pingpo, and Lushi hills at the foot of Beijing's Western Hills Scenic Area. Located along the outskirts of Beijing, it was restored during the 1980's and has since become a famous tourist destination. There are a total of eight former Buddhist temples and monasteries in Badachu Park. These are the Temple of Eternal Peace (Chang'ansi), the Temple of Divine Light (Lingguangsi), Three-hill Nunnery (Sanshan'an), the Temple of Great Mercy (Dabeisi), the Temple of Dragon Spring Nunnery (Longquan'an), the Temple of Fragrant World (Xiangjiesi), The Cave of Precious Pearl (Baozhudong), and Zhengguo Temple.

Badachu Park is an attractive place to visit all year round. It has a pleasant temperate climate, remaining cool in summer and warm in winter. Visitors can stroll from one temple to another, enjoying the beautiful scenery and admiring the arbor and rare ancient trees. Some of these trees have been standing for over 6 centuries, but their roots and branches are still strong and in good shape. In September and October, when the leaves are turning red, crowds of tourists come to climb the mountains. You may also take a cable-car to the top of the hill and feast your eyes on the beautiful view from the mountain peak.

## BAOGUO TEMPLE

Baoguo Temple is a Mahayana Buddhist temple located in Jiangbei district, 15km north of Ningbo, in Zhejiang, China. It is famous as the oldest surviving wooden structure in southern China, as the main hall of the present temple dates back to 1013 in the Northern Song dynasty.

## History

The temple was originally named Lingshan Temple, but was later renamed to Baoguo Temple in 880, during the Tang. The main hall was rebuilt in 1013, during the Northern Song dynasty, and is one of the oldest and most well preserved wooden constructions in China. The temple also contains columns of the Tang dynasty, a hall dating from the Ming, and two halls and towers of the Qing.

Today the temple is a tourist attraction, and many of its rooms and halls are used to house various exhibitions, including:

- Guanyin statues
- Confucian bronzes
- Ningbo furniture
- Traditional Chinese wedding attire
- Carved stone screens
- Miscellaneous architectural pieces from the temple compound
- Famous places around China.

## Transport

The temple can be accessed by bus 232 from Ningbo city. The ride takes approximately 35 minutes.

## Entry

Standard tickets are 12 yuan per person. Guides are available for an additional fee.

# COLD MOUNTAIN TEMPLE

Coordinates: 31°182 44.673 N, 120°332 53.393 E Cold Mountain Temple or Hanshan Temple in Suzhou, China, has a history of 700 years. It is famous because of the poem "A Night Mooring by Maple Bridge" written by the famous Chinese poet, Zhang Ji.

## DAFO TEMPLE

The Dafo Temple is a famous Buddhist temple in Zhejiang and has a long history of more than 1000 years. This Temple is the symbol of the Xinchang prefecture and it attracts tens of thousands of visitors every year. Recently, the temple and its surroundings have often been used as a movie shooting area because of its exquisite natural beauty. During the Cultural Revolution, locals covered the giant Buddha statues in the temple with pictures of Mao Zedong to prevent the radical Red Guard from smashing the statues, which they were mandated to do so under the directive of "destroying all the old traditions".

## DONGLIN TEMPLE

Donglin Temple is a Buddhist monastery approximately 20km away from Jiujiang, Jiangxi, People's Republic of China. It was built in 386 at the foot of Lushan by Hui Yuan, founder of the Pure Land Sect of Buddhism.

The monastery reached its peak of influence during the Tang Dynasty, but was severely damaged during the Taiping Rebellion and all but destroyed during the Republican period. It currently houses a small community of monks supported by a small farming village in its immediate vicinity.

## GUANGHUA TEMPLE

Guanghua Temple is Buddhist, built in Northern Wei Dynasty as one of the eight temples around the Longmen Stone Cave, in the Fujian province of China. Guanghua is 500 metres south of the cave.

### History

In the period of Emperor Xuanzong of Tang, Indian monks came to the temple to discuss and lecture on Buddhism. After its decline in practical use, Emperor Xuanzong of Tang built a tower there.

Created in 558, the first master of the temple is Jinxian, hence called it was called the Jinxian Court. In 589, under Master

Shanwuwei, it was expanded in size and renamed Jinshan Monastery. Master Shanwuwei was one of the temple's founders who also visited Japan, so some Japanese Buddhists arrived here as well.

Major renovations took place in the Ming and Qing Dynasties.

As of 1949, there were 60 resident monks. In 1965, there were 57. During the Cultural Revolution, the temple is forcibly closed and turned into a factory, all statues of the deities were smashed, and all monks dispelled.

In February 1980, a provincial Putian County Guanghua Restoration Committee was created. Funded mostly by overseas Chinese, the reconstruction began four years later in December.

In 1983, the 36-year-old Master Yiran became the head monk of the temple. In 1990, the 24-year-old Master Xuecheng replaced him.

### Structure

- Gaoshan Gate (name literally means "Tall Mounatin"): two-story
- Tianwang Palace ("Heavenly King")
- Jialan Palace ("Monastery")
- Sanzang Palace ("Xuanzang")
- Dizang Palace ("Ksitigarbha").

There is a 10-metre stone staircase with 199 steps in front of the temple.

## HANGING TEMPLE

The Hanging Temple is a temple built into a cliff near Mount Heng in the province of Shanxi. The closest city is Datong, 65 kilometres to the northwest. Along with the Yungang Grottoes, the Hanging Temple is one of the main tourist attractions and historical sites in the Datong area. Built more than 1400 years ago, this temple is unique not only for its location on a sheer precipice but also because it includes Buddhist, Taoist, and Confucian elements.

# JADE BUDDHA TEMPLE

The Jade Buddha Temple is a Buddhist temple in Shanghai, China. As with most modern Chinese Buddhist temples, the current temple draws from both the Pure Land and Chan traditions of Mahayana Buddhism. It was founded in 1882 with two jade Buddha statues imported to Shanghai from Burma by sea. These were a sitting Buddha (1.95 metres tall, 3 tonnes), and a smaller reclining Buddha representing Buddha's death. The temple now also contains a much larger reclining Jade Buddha, donated from Singapore, and visitors may mistake this larger sculpture for the original, smaller piece.

## History

During the rule of emperor Guang Xu in the Qing Dynasty (1875-1908), Hui Gen, an abbot from Mount Putuo went on a pilgrimage to Tibet via the two famous Chinese mountains Mount Wutai and Mount Emei. After Tibet, he arrived in Burma. Whilst there, Mr. Chen Jun-Pu, an overseas Chinese resident in Burma, donated five Jade statues of Buddha to Hui Gen, who transported two of them back to Jiang-wan, Shanghai. Here Hui Gen had a temple built with donated funds, and died shortly thereafter. This temple was occupied during the 1911 uprising, and the statues were moved to Maigen Road.

An Abbot by the name of Ke Chen later had a new temple built on land donated by a Mr. Shen. The construction took ten years, and lasted from 1918-1928. Ke Chen also invited Reverend Di Xian from Tian Tai mountain to come and lecture on Buddhism in a magnificent ceremony.

In 1956, a ceremony was held at the temple by the Shanghai Buddhist Association to celebrate the 2500th anniversary of Gautama Buddha's enlightenment.

In 1966, during the cultural revolution, the monks made a living by selling handicrafts.

In 1983, Shanghai Institute of Buddhism was established at the temple under the Shanghai Buddhist Association.

In 1985, Monk Zhizhi Xuan and others made a trip to Dunhuang via Xinjiang. Shortly after their return regular scripture lectures, meditation and other features of temple life were resumed.

## Abbots

- ?-1942 Abbot Yuan Chen
- 1942-? Monk Zhen Hua (d. 1944, age 39).

## Modern Temple Layout

## Chamber of Four Heavenly Kings

The Chamber of Four Heavenly Kings contains the statues of Maitreya, Wei Tuo Bodhisattva and the Four Heavenly Kings, who represent favorable circumstance. The chamber is located on the southern-edge, or 'front' of the temple.

## Grand Hall

Also called the Great Hall, this hall contains many statues.

- Three Golden Buddhas. The central sculpture is of Gautama Buddha, the left Amitabha and the right Bhaisajyaguru.
- Gods of the Twenty Heavens. The Gods of the Twenty Heavens, covered in gold, line the eastern and western sides of the Grand Hall.
- 18 Arhats. 18 unique golden Arhats stand in two groups of nine.
- Guanyin, Shen Cai and his 53 teachers. A large golden statue of Guanyin stands on at northern entrance to the Great Hall, with Shen Cai at her side and sculptures representing the 53 teachers of his life above.

## Jade Buddha Chamber

The Jade Buddha Chamber is in the northern section of the temple, on the second floor. A fee of 10 yuan is charged to ascend to it. Some additional Buddhist sculptures are also viewable in the antechamber.

### Public Restaurant

The public restaurant is located on level two at the eastern edge of the temple and equipped with its own street entrance. Open daily, it serves a range of noodle dishes for five yuan per bowl, the most popular of which is 'double mushroom noodles'. Other dishes are served at moderate prices. Tickets are sold by colour and this ticket is turned in inside the main eating room and your soup is then delivered to your table which you might share with others. Upstairs is a much more upscale restaurant at much higher prices.

### Other

The temple also contains a private restaurant for the use of monks and temple volunteers, which is at the western edge of the temple complex. There is a visitor services office adjacent to the southern entrance, and a Buddhist library is also on the premises.

## JI LE TEMPLE

Ji Le Temple located at No.5, Dong-Dazhi Street, Nangang Dist, Harbin, is the biggest Buddhist building group in the Heilongjiang province,. It was constructed between 1921 and 1924. The grounds cover 27 570 square meters and the buildings 5 186 square meters.

# 6

# Buddhism in Europe

European contact with Buddhism first began after Alexander the Great's conquest of northwestern India in the 3rd century BC. Greek colonists in the region adopted Indian Buddhism and syncretized it with aspects of their own culture to make a sect called Greco-Buddhism which dominated the area of ancient India compromising modern day Pakistan and eastern Afghanistan for several centuries. Emperor Ashoka sent Buddhist missionaries to the Hellenistic world, where they established centers in places such as Alexandria, creating a noted presence in the region. Many prominent Hellenistic writers were well aware of Buddhist lore and tradition and wrote about it in detail. Some scholars believe that later Greek philosophers may have borrowed from the teachings of the Buddha and that Jesus Christ was influenced by certain principles. An interest in Buddhism had been circling among academic cicles in modern Europe since the 1870s, with philosophers like Arthur Schopenhauer and Friedrich Nietzsche and esoteric-minded scholars such as Helena Blavatsky.

Russia, and perhaps strangely, Austria are the only two European states today that recognize Buddhism as an "official", though not necessarily "state religion" in their respective countries. On top of that, Russia also recognizes it, along with Islam, Judaism, and of course Orthodox Christianity, as native to Russian soil in the 1993 Constitution of the Russian Federation – all other religious groups are unrecognized, and must officially register and be subject to rejection by the state. Apart from Siberian Buddhist nations, the Kalmyk people's 17th century migration into Europe has made them today's only traditionally Buddhist nation west of the Ural. They now live in the Republic of Kalmykia, a Russian Republic.

## BUDDHISM IN THE UNITED STATES

Buddhism is a religion with millions of followers in the United States, including traditionally Buddhist Asian Americans as well as non-Asians, many of whom are converts. The U.S. presents a strikingly new and different environment for Buddhists, leading to a unique history and a continuing process of development as Buddhism and America come to grips with each other.

### Early History

### Buddhism and the West

Occasional intersections between Western civilization and the Buddhist world have been occurring for thousands of years. Perhaps the most significant of these began in 334 BC, early in the history of Buddhism, when the Macedonian king Alexander the Great conquered most of Central Asia. The Seleucids and successive kingdoms established an important Hellenistic influence in the area, which interacted with the Buddhism that had been introduced from India to produce Greco-Buddhism. While this trend was very significant in the development of Mahayana Buddhism, it has yet to be established that it made a corresponding impact on Western thought.

In the Christian era, Buddhist ideas would periodically filter into Europe via the Middle East. A notable example is the story of Barlaam and Josaphat, folk heroes who were canonized by the Roman Catholic Church and whose story is believed to be an altered account of the life of Siddhartha Gautama, translated from Persian to Arabic to Greek. The first direct encounter between European Christians and Buddhists to be recorded was in 1253 when the king of France sent William of Rubruck as an ambassador to the court of the Mongol Empire. Later, in the 17th century, a group of Mongols practicing Tibetan Buddhism established Kalmykia, the only Buddhist nation in Europe, at the eastern edge of the continent.

## Buddhism in the New World

Because the above examples produced very little real religious interaction, the European settlers who would come to colonize the Americas had virtually no exposure to Buddhism. This almost complete isolation would last largely undisturbed until the 19th century, when significant numbers of immigrants from East Asia began to arrive in the New World. In the United States, the first immigrants from China entered around 1820, but they began to arrive in large numbers following the California Gold Rush of 1849. The first Buddhist temple in America was built in 1853 in San Francisco by the Sze Yap Company, a Chinese American fraternal society. Another society, the Ning Yeong Company, built a second in 1854; by 1875, there were eight such temples, and by 1900 there were approximately 400 Chinese temples on the west coast of the United States, most of them containing at least some Buddhist elements. These temples were often the subject of suspicion and ignorance by the rest of the population, and were dismissively referred to as *joss houses*.

The Chinese Exclusion Act of 1882 curtailed the growth of the Chinese American population, but large-scale immigration from Japan began in the late 1880s and from Korea around 1903. In both cases, immigration was at first limited primarily to Hawaii. Populations from other Asian Buddhist countries followed, and in each case, the new communities established Buddhist temples and organizations. For instance, the first Japanese temple in Hawaii was built in 1896 near Paauhau by the Honpa Hongwanji branch of Jodo Shinshu. In 1898, Japanese missionaries and immigrants established a Young Men's Buddhist Association, and the Rev. Soryu Kagahi was dispatched from Japan to be the first Buddhist missionary in Hawaii. The first Japanese Buddhist temple in the continental U.S. was built in San Francisco in 1899, and the first in Canada was built at the Ishikawa Hotel in Vancouver in 1905. The first Buddhist clergy to take up residence in the continental U.S. were Shuye Sonoda and Kakuryo Nishimjima, missionaries from Japan who arrived in 1899.

Henry David Thoreau, along with Ralph Waldo Emerson, edited *The Dial*, a magazine which published the first English translation of a portion of the Lotus Sutra into English from French.

At about the same time that Asian immigrants were first starting to arrive in America, some American intellectuals were beginning to come to terms with Buddhism, based primarily on information reaching them from British colonial possessions in India and East Asia. The Englishmen William Jones and Charles Wilkins had done pioneering work translating Sanskrit texts into English. The American Transcendentalists and associated persons, in particular Henry David Thoreau took an interest in Hindu and Buddhist philosophy. In 1844, *The Dial*, a small literary publication edited by Thoreau and Ralph Waldo Emerson, published the first English version of a portion of the Lotus Sutra; it had been translated by Elizabeth Palmer Peabody from a French version recently completed by Eugene Burnouf (this translation is often attributed to Thoreau himself, but this appears to be erroneous). His Indian readings may have influenced his later experiments in simple living: at one point in *Walden* he wrote: "I realized what the Orientals meant by contemplation and the forsaking of works." The poet Walt Whitman also admitted to an influence of Indian religion on his writings.

The first prominent American to publicly convert to Buddhism was Henry Steel Olcott. Olcott, a former U.S. army colonel during the Civil War, had grown increasingly interested in reports of supernatural phenomena that were popular in the late 19th century. In 1875, he, along with Helena Blavatsky and William Quan Judge founded the Theosophical Society, which was dedicated to the study of the occult and was partly influenced by Hindu and Buddhist scriptures. The group's leaders believed or claimed to believe that they were in contact, via visions and messages, with a secret order of adepts referred to as the "Himalayan Brotherhood" or "the Masters". In 1879, Olcott and Blavatsky travelled to India and then, in 1880, to Sri Lanka, where they were met enthusiastically by local Buddhists, who saw them as allies against an aggressive Christian missionary movement. On May 25 of that year, Olcott and Blavatsky took the pancasila vows of a lay Buddhist before a monk and a large crowd of onlookers. Although most of the Theosophists appear to have counted themselves as Buddhists, they held idiosyncratic beliefs that separated them from all known Buddhist traditions; only Olcott was enthusiastic about following mainstream Buddhism. He would return to Sri Lanka on two further occasions, where he worked to promote Buddhist education, and also visited Japan and Burma. Olcott authored a *Buddhist Catechism*, stating his view of the basic tenets of the religion.

A series of new publications greatly increased public knowledge of Buddhism in 19th century America. In 1879, Edwin Arnold, an English aristocrat, published *The Light of Asia*, an epic poem he had written about the life and teachings of the Buddha, expounded with much wealth of local colour and not a little felicity of versification. The book became immensely popular in the United States, going through eighty editions and selling more than 500,000 copies. Dr. Paul Carus, a German American philosopher and theologian, was at work on a more scholarly prose treatment of the same subject. Carus was the director of Open Court Publishing Company, an academic publishing house specializing in philosophy, science, and religion, and editor of *The Monist*, a journal with a similar focus, both based in La Salle, Illinois. In 1894, Carus published *The Gospel of the Buddha*, which was compiled from a variety of Asian texts and, true to its name, presented the Buddha's story in a form resembling the Christian Gospels.

Perhaps the most significant event in the 19th century history of Buddhism in America was the Parliament of the World's Religions, held in Chicago in 1893. Although most of the delegates to the Parliament were Christians of various denominations, the Buddhist nations of China, Japan, Thailand, and Sri Lanka sent representatives. Buddhist delegates included Soyen Shaku, a Japanese Zen abbott; Zenshiro Noguchi, a Japanese translator; Anagarika Dharmapala, a Sri Lankan associate of H. S. Olcott's; and Chandradat Chudhadharn, a brother of King Chulalongkorn of Thailand. Paul Carus also attended as an observer. The Parliament provided the first major public forum from which Buddhists could address themselves directly to the

Western public; Dharmapala was particularly effective in this role because he spoke fluent English.

A few days after the end of the Parliament, in a brief ceremony conducted by Anagarika Dharmapala, Charles T. Strauss, a New York businessman of Jewish descent, became, it is believed, the first person to formally convert to Buddhism on American soil. A few fledgling attempts at establishing a Buddhism for Americans followed. One of the most interesting, in fact, had initially appeared prior to the Parliament, met with little fanfare, in 1887: *The Buddhist Ray*, a Santa Cruz, California-based magazine published and edited by Phillangi Dasa, born Herman Carl (or Carl Herman) Veetering (or Vettering), a recluse about whom little is known. The *Ray*'s tone was, in the words of Rick Fields, "ironic, light, saucy, self-assured... one-hundred-percent American Buddhist" (Fields, 1981), which was by all means a novel development in that time and place. It ceased publication in 1894. Elsewhere, six white San Franciscans, working with Japanese Jodo Shinshu missionaries, established the Dharma Sangha of Buddha in 1900 and began publishing a bimonthly magazine, *The Light of Dharma*. In Illinois, Paul Carus wrote further books about Buddhism and attempted setting portions of Buddhist scripture to Western classical music.

## The Early 20th Century

In the first half of the 20th century, it would prove to be Buddhist teachers from Japan who played the most active role in disseminating Buddhism to the American public, perhaps because Japan was the most developed and self-confident Buddhist country at the time. In 1905, Soyen Shaku was invited to stay in the United States by a Mr. and Mrs. Russell, a wealthy American couple. He lived for nine months in their home near San Francisco, where he established a small zendo in their home and gave regular zazen lessons, making him the first Zen Buddhist priest to teach in North America. This short sojourn eventually produced an effect on American Buddhism that continues to the present. Shortly after Shaku settled in to his erstwhile home, he was followed by Nyogen Senzaki, a young monk from Shaku's home temple in Japan. Senzaki briefly worked for the Russell family and then, expressing his desire to stay in America, he was reportedly advised by Shaku to spend seventeen years as an ordinary worker before teaching Buddhism. Thus, it was in 1922 that Senzaki first rented a hall and gave an English talk on a paper by Soyen Shaku; his periodic talks at different locations became known as the "floating zendo". In 1931, he established a permanent sitting hall in Los Angeles, where he would teach until his death in 1958.

Another Zen teacher, Sokatsu Shaku, one of Soyen Shaku's senior students, arrived in late 1906. Although he stayed only a few years and had limited contact with the English-speaking public, one of his disciples, Shigetsu Sasaki, made a permanent home. Sasaki, better known under his monastic name, Sokei-an, spent a few years wandering the west coast of the United States, at one point living among American Indians near Seattle, and reached New York City in 1916. After completing his training and being ordained in 1928, he returned to New York to teach. In 1931, his small group incorporated as the Buddhist Society of America, later renamed the First Zen Institute of America. By the late 1930s, one of his most active supporters was Ruth Fuller Everett, a British socialite and the mother-in-law of Alan Watts. Shortly before Sokei-an's death in 1945, he and Everett would wed, at which point she took the name Ruth Fuller Sasaki.

In 1914, under the leadership of Koyu Uchida, who succeeded Shuye Sonoda as the head of Jodo Shinshu missionary effort in North America, several Japanese Buddhist congregations formed the Buddhist Mission of North America (BMNA). This organization would later form the basis of the Buddhist Churches of America, currently the largest and most influential ethnic-based Buddhist organization in the U.S. The BMNA focused primarily on social and cultural activities for and ministering to Japanese American communities. In the late 1920s, it first began to develop programs to train English-speaking priests, for the benefit of the growing number of American-born parishoners. Also, in 1927, the Soto sect of Japanese Zen opened its own mission with Zenshuji temple in Los Angeles, although it did not make attempts at the time to attract non-Japanese members. One American who made his own attempt to establish an American Buddhist movement was Dwight Goddard (1861 – 1939). Goddard had been a Christian missionary to China, when he first came in contact with Buddhism. In 1928, he spent a year living at a Zen monastery in Japan. In 1934, he founded "The Followers of Buddha, an American Brotherhood", with the goal of applying the traditional monastic structure of Buddhism more strictly than Senzaki and Sokei-an. The group was largely unsuccessful: no Americans were recruited to join as monks and attempts failed to attract a Chinese Chan (Zen) master to come to the United States. However, Goddard's efforts as an author and publisher bore considerable fruit. In 1930, he began publishing *ZEN: A Buddhist Magazine*. In 1932, he collaborated with D. T. Suzuki, on a translation of the Lankavatara Sutra. That same year, he published the first edition of *A Buddhist Bible*, an anthology of Buddhist scriptures focusing on those used in Chinese and Japanese Zen, which was enormously influential.

However, another Japanese person, also an associate of Soyen Shaku's, had an even greater literary impact. This was D. T. Suzuki. At the World Parliament of Religions in 1893, Paul Carus befriended Soyen Shaku and requested his help in translating and preparing Oriental spiritual literature for publication in the West. Shaku instead recommended Suzuki, then a young scholar and former disciple of his. Starting in 1897, Suzuki worked from Dr. Carus's home in Illinois; his first projects were translations of the *Tao Te Ching* and Asvaghosa's *Awakening of Faith in the Mahayana*. At the same time, Suzuki began writing his first major book, *Outlines of Mahayana Buddhism*, which was published in 1907. Suzuki returned to Japan in 1909 and married an American Theosophist and Radcliffe graduate in 1911. Through English language essays and books, such as *Essays in Zen Buddhism* (1927), he established himself as the most visible literary expositor of Zen Buddhism, its unofficial goodwill ambassador to Western readers, until his death in 1966. His 1949 book, *An Introduction to Zen Buddhism*, featured a 30-page introduction by Carl Jung, an emblem of the deepening relationship between Buddhism and major Western thinkers.

## Modern American Buddhism

Some scholars, such as Charles Prebish, have suggested that the social phenomenon of Buddhism in America can be seen to be comprised of three broad types. The oldest and largest of these is "immigrant" or "ethnic Buddhism", those Buddhist traditions that arrived in America along with immigrants who were already believers and that largely remained with those immigrants and their descendants. The next oldest and arguably the most visible and best-heralded type is referred to as "import Buddhism", because it came to America largely in response to the demand of interested American converts who sought it out, either by going abroad or by supporting foreign teachers; this is sometimes also called "elite Buddhism" because its practitioners, especially early in the process, tended to come from social elites. The newest trend in Buddhism is "export" or "evangelical Buddhism", groups which are based in another country and who are actively recruiting members in America from various backgrounds; by far the most successful of these has been Soka Gakkai, which will be discussed below.

## Immigrant Buddhists

Immigrant Buddhist congregations in North America come in an extremely wide variety, exactly as wide a variety as exists in the different peoples of Asian Buddhist extraction who have settled there. The New World is home to Chinese Buddhists, Japanese Buddhists, Korean Buddhists, Sri Lankan Buddhists, Vietnamese Buddhists, Thai Buddhists, and Buddhists with family backgrounds in nearly every Buddhist country and region in the world. The passage of the 1965 Immigration Act in the United States greatly increased the number of immigrants arriving from China, Vietnam, and the Theravada-practicing countries of southeast Asia.

It is common for Buddhist temples and societies to serve as foci for the social life of an immigrant community, helping to maintain a connection to Old World traditions in a foreign environment. However, as the passing of time produces congregations increasingly dominated by persons born in America, which is especially common among Japanese Buddhists, questions arise about how their religious customs should adapt.

The largest and most influential national immigrant Buddhist organization in the United States is the Buddhist Churches of America and the Honpa Hongwanji Mission of Hawaii. The BCA is an affiliate of Japan's Nishi Hongwanji, a sect of Jodo Shinshû, which is in turn a form of Pure Land Buddhism. Tracing its roots to the Young Men's Buddhist Association founded in San Francisco at the end of the 19th century and the Buddhist Mission of North America founded in 1914, it took its current form in 1944. All of the Buddhist Mission's leadership, along with almost the entire Japanese American population, had been interned during World War II. The name Buddhist Churches of America was adopted at Topaz Relocation Centre in Utah; the use of the word "church", which normally implies a Christian house of worship, was significant. After internment ended, some members returned to the West Coast and revitalized churches there, while a number of others moved to the Midwest and built new churches. During the 1960s and 1970s, the BCA was in a growth phase and was very successful at fund-raising. It also began to publish two periodicals, one in Japanese and one in English. However, since 1980, BCA membership has declined markedly. The Honpa Hongwanji Mission of Hawaii has 36 temples throughout the state of Hawaii. The history and organization of the Mission is quite similar to the BCA.

It is interesting to note that, while a very large majority of the Buddhist Churches of America's membership are ethnically Japanese, it does have some members from non-Asian backgrounds. Thus, it can be seen as having some, currently very limited, aspects of an export Buddhist institution. As declining involvement by its ethnic community creates questions about its future, there has been internal discussion as to whether it should devote more attention to attracting the broader public.

Another institution with some appeal both to a specific ethnic group as well as to Americans generally is Hsi Lai Temple in Hacienda Heights, California. Hsi Lai is the American headquarters of Fo Guang Shan, an enormously successful modern

Buddhist group in Taiwan. Hsi Lai was built in 1988 at a cost of $10 million and is often described as the largest Buddhist temple in the Western hemisphere. Although it continues to cater primarily to Chinese Americans, it also has regular services and outreach programs in English. Hsi Lai was at the centre of a bizarre incident in the history of American Buddhism when a 1996 fund-raising event by Vice President Al Gore provoked a controversy; at the time Hsi Lai was often referred to in the media as simply "the Buddhist temple".

## Import Buddhists

Since Henry Steele Olcott travelled to Sri Lanka in 1880, interested Americans have sought out Buddhist teachers from a variety of countries in Asia, many of which have now established their teachings in America. The three most notable trends of this type are Zen, Tibetan Buddhism, and Vipassana, which is an outgrowth of Theravada Buddhism. Because its membership tends strongly to be among educated, white, native English speakers, import Buddhism has come to enjoy a higher level of prominence and prestige than other types of Buddhism in America.

## Zen

Beginning with Soyen Shaku's invitation to San Francisco and then the ministries of Nyogen Senzaki and Sokei-an, Zen Buddhism was the first import Buddhist trend to put down roots in North America. In the late 1940s and 1950s, writers associated with the Beat Movement, including Gary Snyder, Jack Kerouac, Allen Ginsberg, and Kenneth Rexroth, took a serious interest in Zen, which helped increase its visibility. In 1951, an octagenarian Daisetz Teitaro Suzuki returned to the United States to take a visiting proffessorship at Columbia University, where he began a long series of public lectures on Zen; Kerouac and Ginsberg were among the attendees. In 1956, the Zen Studies Society was formed to support his work. After moving to Cambridge, Massachusetts in 1957, Suzuki was also involved in founding the Cambridge Buddhist Association, which was likely the first Buddhist group in America which was dedicated primarily to practicing zazen meditation. The Zen Studies Society, which had become completely dormant when Daisetz Teitaro Suzuki left Columbia, would be revived in 1965 by Eido Tai Shimano, a New York–based Rinzai Zen teacher.

One of the most influential figures in 20th century American Zen was Shunryu Suzuki. After serving as a temple priest in Japan, Suzuki requested to be sent to America, and, in 1959, at the age of 54, he travelled to San Francisco to manage Sokoji, the city's Soto sect mission. When he arrived, his congregation consisted almost exclusively of older Japanese people, although his predecessors had begun to make some efforts at a broader outreach. Suzuki himself proved to be more comfortable teaching Americans than Japanese. He quickly attracted a group which met for regular zazen sittings and lectures in English. The group incorporated as the San Francisco Zen Centre and, in 1966, purchased a tract of land near Los Padres National Forest to began building Tassajara Zen Mountain Centre, described as the first Buddhist training monastery located outside of Asia. In 1969, Suzuki left Sokoji when the Zen Centre started its own new temple in San Francisco, operating largely independently of the Soto Sect in Japan. In 1970, *Zen Mind, Beginner's Mind*, an edited collection of talks given by Suzuki, was published and became one of the most popular brief introductions to Zen practice. The San Francisco Zen Centre remains one of America's largest and most influential Buddhist groups and is now part of a network of related centers.

Sanbo Kyodan Zen is a contemporary Japanese Zen lineage which had an impact in the West disproportionate to its size Japan. It is rooted in the reformist teachings of Harada Daiun (1871-1961) and his disciple Yasutani Hakuun (1885-1971), who argued that the existing Zen institutions of Japan, the Soto and Rinzai sects, had become complacent and, with few exceptions, were unable to teach real Dharma. Harada had studied with both Soto and Rinzai teachers and Yasutani founded Sanbo Kyodan in 1954 to preserve what he saw as the vital core of teachings from both schools. Sanbo Kyodan's first American member was Philip Kapleau, who first travelled to Japan in 1945 as a court reporter for the war crimes trials. In 1947, Kapleau visited D.

T. Suzuki at Engaku-ji in Japan and in the early 1950s, he was a frequent attendee of Suzuki's Columbia lectures. In 1953, he returned to Japan, where he met with Nakagawa Soen, a protege of Nyogen Senzaki. At Nakagawa's recommendation, he began to study with Harada and later with Yasutani, whose disciple he became. In 1965, he published a book, *The Three Pillars of Zen*, which recorded a set of talks by Yasutani outlining his approach to practice, along with transcripts of dokusan interviews and some additional texts. The book quickly became popular in America and Europe, contributing to the prominence of the Sanbo Kyodan approach to Zen. Later in 1965, Kapleau returned to America and, in 1966, established the Rochester Zen Centre in Rochester, New York, making him the first American-born Zen priest to found a training temple. In 1967, Kapleau had a falling out with Yasutani over some of Kapleau's moves to Americanize the style of his temple, after which it became independent of Sanbo Kyodan. The Rochester Zen Centre is now part of a network of related centers in the United States, Canada, Europe, Mexico, and New Zealand, referred to collectively as the Cloud Water Sangha. One of Kapleau's most notable early disciples was Toni Packer, who herself left Rochester in 1981 to found a nonsectarian meditation centre, not specifically Buddhist or Zen.

Robert Aitken is another important American member of Sanbo Kyodan. He was first introduced to Zen as a prisoner in Japan during the Second World War. After returning to the United States, he began studying with Nyogen Senzaki in Los Angeles in the early 1950s. In 1959, while still a Zen student himself, he founded the Diamond Sangha, a zendo in Honolulu, Hawaii. Three years later, the Diamond Sangha hosted the first U.S. visit by Yasutani Hakuun, who would visit various locations in the U.S. six more times before 1969. Aitken travelled frequently to Japan and became a disciple of Yamada Koun, Yasutani's successor as head of the Sanbo Kyodan. Aitken became a dharma heir of Yamada's, authored more than ten books, and developed the Diamond Sangha into an international network with temples in the United States, Argentina, Germany, and Australia. In 1995, he and his organization split with Sanbo Kyodan in response to reorganization of the latter following Yamada's death. The Pacific Zen Institute led by John Tarrant, Aitken's first Dharma successor continues as an independent Zen line.

Another influential Japanese Zen teacher was Taizan Maezumi, who arrived as a young priest to serve at Zenshuji, the North American Soto sect headquarters in Los Angeles, in 1956. Like Shunryu Suzuki, he showed considerable interest in teaching Zen to Americans of various backgrounds and, by the mid-1960s, had formed a regular zazen group.

In 1967, he and his supporters founded the Zen Centre of Los Angeles. He was later instrumental in establishing the Kuroda Institute and the Soto Zen Buddhist Association, the latter an organization of American teachers with ties to the Soto tradition. In addition to his membership in Soto, Maezumi was also recognized as an heir by a Rinzai teacher and by Yasutani Hakuun of the Sanbo Kyodan. Maezumi, in turn, had several American dharma heirs who have become prominent, such as Bernie Glassman, John Daido Loori, Charlotte Joko Beck, and Dennis Genpo Merzel. His successors and their network of centers have organized as the White Plum Asanga.

Not all the successful Zen teachers in the United States have been from Japanese traditions. There have also been teachers of Chinese Zen (also known as Chan), Korean Zen (or Seon), and Vietnamese Zen (or Thien).

The first Chinese Buddhist priest to teach Westerners in America was Hsuan Hua, a disciple of the preeminent 20th century Chan master, Hsu Yun. In 1962, Hsuan Hua moved to San Francisco's Chinatown, where, in addition to Zen, he taught Chinese Pure Land, Tiantai, Vinaya, and Vajrayana Buddhism. Initially, his students were mostly ethnic Chinese, but he eventually attracted a range of followers. In 1970, Hsuan Hua founded Gold Mountain Monastery in San Francisco and in 1976 he established a retreat centre, the City Of Ten Thousand Buddhas, on a 237 acre (959,000 $m^2$) property near Ukiah, California. These monasteries are noted for their close adherence to the vinaya, the austere traditional Buddhist monastic code. Hsuan Hua also founded the Buddhist Text Translation Society, which works on the translation of scriptures into English.

Another Chinese Zen teacher with a Western following is Sheng-yen, a master trained in both the Caodong and Linji schools (equivalent to the Japanese Soto and Rinzai, respectively). He first visited the United States in 1978 under the sponsorship of the Buddhist Association of the United States, an organization of Chinese American Buddhists. In 1980, he founded the Ch'an Mediation Society in Queens, New York. In 1985, he founded the Chung-hwa Institute of Buddhist Studies in Taiwan, which now sponsors a variety of Chinese Zen activities in the United States.

The most prominent Korean Zen teacher in America was Seung Sahn. Seung Sahn had been the abbot of a temple in Seoul and had also lived in Hong Kong and Japan when, in 1972, not speaking any English, he decided to move to America. On the flight to Los Angeles, a Korean American passenger offered him a job at a laundry in Providence, Rhode Island, the city which was to become the headquarters of Seung Sahn's Kwan Um School of Zen. Shortly after arriving in Providence, he attracted a group of America students and founded the Providence Zen Centre. The affiliated Kwan Um School now has more than 100 Zen centers on six continents. Another notable Korean Zen teacher in America is Samu Sunim, who moved to America in 1968 and founded Toronto's Zen Buddhist Temple in 1971. He is now the head of the Buddhist Society for Compassionate Wisdom, which has temples in Ann Arbor, Chicago, and Mexico City.

Two notable Vietnamese Zen teachers have been influential in America: Thich Thien-An and Thich Nhat Hanh. Thich Thien-An came to America in 1966 as a visiting professor at UCLA and taught traditional Thien meditation. Thich Nhat Hanh was a monk in Vietnam during the Vietnam War, during which he was a peace activist.

In response to these activities, he was nominated for the Nobel Peace Prize in 1967 by Martin Luther King, Jr. In 1966, he left Vietnam in exile and now resides at Plum Village, a monastery in France. He has written more than one hundred books about Buddhism, which have made him one of the very few most prominent Buddhist authors among the general readership in the West. In his books and talks, Thich Nhat Hanh emphasizes mindfulness (*sati*) as the most important practice in daily life.

## Tibetan Buddhism

Perhaps the most widely visible Buddhist teacher in the world is Tenzin Gyatso, the current Dalai Lama, who first visited the United States in 1979. As the exiled political leader of Tibet, he has become a popular cause celèbre. His early life was depicted in glowing terms in Hollywood films such as *Kundun* and *Seven Years in Tibet.* He has attracted celebrity religious followers such as Richard Gere and Adam Yauch. The first Western-born Tibetan Buddhist monk was Robert A. F. Thurman, now a noted academic supporter of the Dalai Lama. The Dalai Lama maintains a North American headquarters at Namgyal Monastery in Ithaca, New York.

The best-known Tibetan Buddhist lama to live in the United States was Chogyam Trungpa. Trungpa, part of the Kagyu school of Tibetan Buddhism, moved to England in 1963, founded a temple in Scotland, and then relocated to Barnet, Vermont, and Boulder, Colorado in 1970.

He established a series of what he named Dharmadhatu meditation centers, which were eventually organized under a national umbrella group called Vajradhatu (later to become Shambhala International). The methods and techniques he developed for teaching Westerners he termed Shambhala Training. Following Trungpa's death, his followers built the Great Stupa of Dharmakaya, a traditional reliquary monument, near Red Feather Lakes, Colorado. Consecrated in 2001, it is the largest stupa in the United States.

The first Tibetan Buddhist lama to come to the United States was Geshe Ngawang Wangyal, a Kalmyk-Mongolian of the Gelug lineage, who came to the United States in 1955 and founded the "Lamaist Buddhist Monastery of America" in New Jersey in 1958. Among his students were the future western scholars Robert Thurman, Jeffrey Hopkins and Alexander Berzin. Other early arrivals included Deshung Rinpoche, a Sakya lama who settled in Seattle, WA, in 1960, and Tarthang Tulku Rinpoche, the first Nyingma teacher in America, who arrived in the U.S. in 1968 and established the "Tibetan Nyingma Meditation Centre" in Berkeley, California in 1969.

There are four major schools of Tibetan Buddhism: the Gelug, the Kagyu, the Nyingma, and the Sakya. Of these, the greatest impact in the West was made by the Gelug, which is led by the Dalai Lama, and the Kagyu, specifically its Karma Kagyu branch, which is led by the Karmapa. As of the early 1990s, there were four significant strands of Kagyu practice in the United States: Chogyam Trungpa's Shambhala movement; the Karma Triyana Choling, a network of centers affiliated directly with the Karmapa's North American seat in Woodstock, New York; a network of centers founded by Kalu Rinpoche; and an organization established by Ole Nydahl, a Danish-born lama with many supporters in Europe. (Lehnert, 1997)

In the 21st century, the Nyingma lineage is increasingly represented in the West, by both Western and Tibetan teachers. Lama Surya Das is a Western-born teacher carrying on the great rime, or non-sectarian, branch of Tibetan Buddhism. H.E. Chagdud Tulku Rinpoche, before his death in 2002, founded centers in Seattle and Brazil. Khandro Rinpoche is a modern female Tibetan teacher who has a strong presence in America. Jetsunma Ahkon Lhamo, the first Western woman to be recognized and enthroned as a Tulku, has also established Nyingma centers in Sedona, AZ and Poolesville, MD.

The Gelug tradition is most strongly represented in America by the Foundation for the Preservation of the Mahayana Tradition (FPMT), founded by Lama Thubten Yeshe and Lama Zopa. Another prominent Gelugpa teacher is Geshe Michael Roach, the first American to be awarded a Geshe degree, who has established centers in New York, NY, and at Diamond Mountain University in Arizona.

Also quite active in the United States is the self-described New Kadampa Tradition (NKT) established by Geshe Kelsang Gyatso. A schismatic offshoot of the Gelug school founded in the

1990s in the UK, the NKT has over 50 Kadampa (NKT) Buddhist Centers and branches in the United States. Geshe Kelsang Gyatso is the only Tibetan associated with the movement—most of its followers are Westerners or in the far east, principally in Hong Kong and Singapore.

## Vipassana

Vipassana, also referred to by the rough translation "insight meditation" is an ancient meditative practice described in the Pali Canon of the Theravada school of Buddhism, and in similar scriptures of other schools. Vipassana also refers to a distinct movement which was begun in the 20th century by reformers such as Mahasi Sayadaw, a Burmese monk. Mahasi Sayadaw was a Theravada bhikkhu and Vipassana is rooted in the Theravada teachings, but its goal is to simplify ritual and other peripheral activities in order to make meditative practice more effective and available both to monks and to laypeople. This openness to lay involvement is an important development in Theravada, which has sometimes appeared to focus exclusively on monasticism.

In 1965, monks from Sri Lanka established the Washington Buddhist Vihara in Washington, D.C., the first Theravada monastic community in the United States. The Vihara was fairly accessible to English-speakers, and naturally vipassana meditation was part of it activities. However, the direct influence of the Vipassana movement would not reach the U.S. until a group of Americans returned there in the early 1970s after studying with Vipassana master in Asia. Joseph Goldstein, after journeying to Southeast Asia with the Peace Corps, had lived in Bodhgaya, where he was a student of Anagarika Munindra, the head monk of Mahabodhi Temple and himself a student of Mahasai Sayadaw's. Jack Kornfield had also been in the Peace Corps in Southeast Asia, after which he studied with Ajahn Chah, perhaps the most influential figure in 20th century Thai Buddhism. Sharon Salzberg went to India in 1971 as a spiritual seeker and studied with Dipa Ma, a former Calcutta housewife trained in vipassana by Mahasai Sayadaw.

Goldstein and Kornfield met in 1974 while teaching at the Naropa Institute in Colorado. The next year, Goldstein, Kornfield, and Salzberg, who had very recently returned from Calcutta, along with Jacqueline Schwarz, founded the Insight Meditation Society on an 80 acre (324,000 $m^2$) property near Barre, Massachusetts. IMS became the central Vipassana instituation in America, hosting visits by Mahasi Sayadaw, Munindra, Ajahn Chah, and Dipa Ma. In 1981, Kornfield moved to California, where he founded another Vipassana centre, Spirit Rock Meditation Centre, in Marin County. In 1985, Larry Rosenberg founded the Cambridge Insight Meditation Centre in Cambridge, Massachusetts. Another important Vipassana centre is the Vipassana Metta Foundation, located on Maui.

In 1989, the Insight Meditation Centre established the Barre Centre for Buddhist Studies near the IMS headquarters, with the goal of promoting scholarly investigation of Buddhism from various perspectives. It director is Mu Seong, a former Korean Zen monk.

S. N. Goenka is a Burmese-born meditation teacher who can also be considered part of the Vipassana movement. His teacher, Sayagyi U Ba Khin of Burma, was a contemporary of Mahasi Sayadaw's, and taught a style of Buddhism with similar emphases on simplicity and accessibility to laypeople. Goenka has established a method of instruction which has proven very popular in Asia and throughout the world. In 1981, he established the Vipassana Research Institute based in Igatpuri, India. He and his students have built several active centers in North America.

## Export Buddhists

Although ethnic-based institutions, such as Hsi Lai Temple and the Buddhist Churches of America, show some evangelical tendencies, there is only one Buddhist group in North America which has focused on recruiting converts from among the general public and been successful: Soka Gakkai, a Japan-based society which promotes Nichiren Buddhism. Soka Gakkai, which literally means "Establishing Value Education Society", was founded in Japan in 1930 as a fraternal auxiliary to Nichiren Shoshu, the largest sect of Nichiren Buddhism. It was perhaps the most successful of Japan's new religious movements, which enjoyed tremendous growth after the end of the Second World War. During the occupation of Japan, some American soldiers became aware of it, and it was the Japanese wives of veterans who became the first active Soka Gakkai members in the West. A U.S. branch was formally organized on October 13, 1960. Its Korean-Japanese leader took the name George M. Williams to emphasize his commitment to reaching the English-speaking public. Soka Gakkai expanded rapidly in the U.S. through an aggressive recruitment technique called shakubuku. One of the results of this outreach is that Soka Gakkai has been much more effective than any other group at attracting non-Asian minority converts, chiefly African American and Latino, to Buddhism. It has also been successful in attracting the support of celebrities, such as Tina Turner, Herbie Hancock, and Orlando Bloom.

Soka Gakkai has no priests of its own and was originally part of Nichiren Shoshu, a formal religious sect in Japan. In fact, its United States branch was originally named Nichiren Shoshu America (NSA). However, in 1991 Soka Gakkai split from Nichiren Shoshu and became a separate organization; at that time, the U.S. branch changed its name to Soka Gakkai International-United States of America (SGI-USA). Nichiren Shoshu proper maintains six temples of its own in the U.S. and another Nichiren group exists which is primarily the domain of ethnic Japanese.

The main religious practice of Soka Gakkai members, like other Nichiren Buddhists, is chanting the mantra *Nam Myoho Renge Kyo* and sections of the Lotus Sutra. Unlike import Buddhist trends such as Zen, Vipassana, and Tibetan Buddhism, Soka Gakkai does not teach meditative techniques other than chanting.

## Demographics of Buddhism in the United States

For various reasons, it is not easy to arrive at an accurate idea of the number of Buddhists in the United States. The simplest reason is that it is not at all clear how to define who is and who is not a Buddhist. The easiest and most intuitive definition is one based on self-description, but this has its pitfalls.

Because Buddhism exists as a cultural concept in American society, there may be individuals who self-describe as Buddhists but have essentially no knowledge of or commitment to Buddhism as a religion or practice; on the other hand, others may be deeply involved in meditation and committed to the Buddhadharma, but may refuse the label "Buddhist". Despite these difficulties, several scholars have investigated this question. Most studies have indicated a Buddhist population in the United States of between 1 and 4 million. The U.S. State Department's International Religious Freedom Report for 2004 indicates that 1.0% of the U.S. population is Buddhist, which would mean a total of 3,000,000 Buddhists (give or take about 100,000). Other estimates, perhaps relying on a greater degree of intuition, are larger: in the 1990s, Robert A. F. Thurman stated his opinion that there were 5 to 6 million Buddhists in America, and others might speculate there are more. Whatever the total number, it appears that roughly 75 to 80 percent of Buddhists in the U.S. are of Asian descent and inherited Buddhism as a family tradition; the remaining 20 to 25 percent are non-Asians.

## Ethnic Divide

Discussion about Buddhism in America has sometimes focused on the issue of the visible ethnic divide separating ethnic Buddhist congregations from import Buddhist groups. Although many Zen and Tibetan Buddhist temples were founded by Asians, they now tend to attract very few Asian-American members. With the important exception of Soka Gakkai, almost all active Buddhist groups in America can be readily classed as either ethnic or import Buddhism based on the demographics of their membership. There is often very limited contact between these Buddhists of different ethnic groups. This divide can be disturbing in view of the historical necessity of relying on Asian peoples to transmit Buddhism, and in light of ongoing and complex tensions surrounding ethnicity and immigration in America. Some Asian-American Buddhists feel that their non-Asian counterparts ignore the many contributions of their ethnic communities toward the development of American Buddhism.

However, the cultural divide should not necessarily be seen as pernicious. It is often argued that the differences between Buddhist groups arise benignly from the differing needs and interests of those involved. Convert Buddhists tend to be interested in meditation and philosophy, in some cases eschewing the trappings of religiosity altogether. On the other hand, for immigrants and their descendants, preserving tradition and maintaining a social framework assume a much greater relative importance, making their approach to religion naturally more conservative. Further, Kenneth K. Tanaka suggests, based on a survey of Asian-American Buddhists in San Francisco, that "many Asian-American Buddhists view non-Asian Buddhism as still in a formative, experimental stage" and yet they believe that it "could eventually mature into a religious expression of exceptional quality".

Additional questions come from the demographics within import Buddhism. Researchers and casual observers alike report that the vast majority of American converts practicing at Buddhist centers are white people with Christian or Jewish backgrounds. Only Soka Gakkai has attracted significant numbers of black or Latino members. A variety of ideas have been broached regarding the nature, causes, and significance of this racial uniformity. A key question is the degree of importance ascribed to discrimination, which is suggested to be mostly unconscious, on the part of white converts toward potential minority converts. To some extent, the racial divide is indicative of a class divide, because convert Buddhists tend strongly to be drawn from the more educated segments of society. Among the African American Buddhists who have commented on the dynamics of the racial divide in convert Buddhism are Jan Willis and Charles R. Johnson.

## TRENDS IN AMERICAN BUDDHISM

### Engaged Buddhism

An important trend that has developed in Buddhism in the West is socially engaged Buddhism. While some critics have asserted that the term is redundant, as it is mistaken to believe that Buddhism in the past has not affected and been affected by the surrounding society, others have suggested that Buddhism is sometimes seen as too quietistic and passive toward public life. This is particularly true in the West, where almost all converts to Buddhism come to it outside of an existing family or community tradition. Engaged Buddhism is an attempt to apply Buddhist values to larger social problems, including war and environmental concerns. The term *engaged Buddhism* was coined by Thich Nhat Hanh, who developed the idea during his years as a peace activist in Vietnam. The most notable engaged Buddhist organization is the Buddhist Peace Fellowship, which was founded in 1978 by Robert Aitken, Anne Aitken, Nelson Foster, and others and received early assistance from Gary Snyder, Jack Kornfield, and Joanna Macy. Another engaged Buddhist group is the Zen Peacemaker Order, which was founded in 1996 by Bernie Glassman and Sandra Jishu Holmes.

## Buddhist Education in the United States

A variety of Buddhist groups have established institutions of higher learning in America. The first four-year Buddhist college in the U.S. was the Naropa Institute (now Naropa University), which was founded in 1974 by Chogyam Trungpa. It has enjoyed consistent involvement both from convert Buddhists and counterculture personalities, such as Allen Ginsberg, who christened the Institute's poetry department the "Jack Kerouac School of Disembodied Poetics". Naropa is currently fully accredited and offers degrees in some subjects not directly related to Buddhism. Another Buddhist university is the University of the West, which is affiliated with Hsi Lai Temple and was, until recently called Hsi Lai University. Soka Gakkai also sponsors two branches of Soka University, which is based in Japan. The City of Ten Thousand Buddhas is the site of Dharma Realm Buddhist University, a four-year college teaching courses primarily related to Buddhism but including some general-interest subjects. The Buddhist Churches of America runs its Institute of Buddhist Studies in Berkeley, California, which offers a master's degree in Buddhist Studies but is primarily a seminary affiliated with the Graduate Theological Union. It recently opened a Jodo Shinshu Centre also in Berkeley. The first Buddhist high school in the United States, Developing Virtue Secondary School, was founded in 1981 by the Dharma Realm Buddhist Association at their branch monastery in the City of Ten Thousand Buddhas in Ukiah, California. Another Buddhist high school, the Pacific Buddhist Academy, opened in Honolulu in 2003. It is affiliated with the Hompa Hongwanji Jodo Shinshu mission, which had already run an elementary and middle school.

## BUDDHISM IN BRAZIL

Buddhism in Brazil has practitioners of various Buddhist schools, as well as a fair number of somewhat Buddhist-inspired cults and "New Age" movements. Many Japanese schools have a strong presence mainly as a result of World War II, which encouraged emigration of Japanese people. A considerable number of those chose to settle in Brazil, including teachers of schools such as Soto Zen, Honmon Butsuryu Shu (a Nichiren Buddhism school), Jodo Shinshu (also known as True Pure Land Buddhism) and the controversial Soka Gakkai movement. Buddhist schools of Japanese descent are the most expressive in Brazil, although they face a number of challenges that make their influence somewhat smaller than one would expect. One of those challenges is the mismatch of goals and expectations between the more traditional, Japanese-born people and the native Brazilians (many of them of Japanese descent).

Adherence to Buddhism is not particularly widespread among descendants of Japanese immigrants, who are largely Roman Catholic. The descendants that do follow Buddhism tend to display a wide variety of stances regarding their relationships to the ethinicity and the religious tradition. To various degrees most of them attempt to simmultaneously meld with local Brazilian culture according to their personal preferences. As of 2005 most such schools are attempting to become receptive to Brazilians not of Japanese descent, often facing considerable internal resistance in the process. Shingon, Tendai and Nichiren Shu and Nichiren Shoshu schools are also present in Brazil, albeit in somewhat modest numbers. Recent years saw a growth of interest in the practice Zen variants from Korea and Vietnam in Brazil. Theravada school also has Brazilian presence. There are active groups in Belo Horizonte and Sao Paulo, as well as a Theravada temple in Rio de Janeiro.

All four major Vajrayana schools from Tibet have some centers in Brazil-Nyingma, Gelug, Sakya and Kagyu. Particularly, Chagdud Tulku Rinpoche relocated the headquarters of his international organization to Tres Coroas, Rio Grande do Sul, Brazil, where he spent the last few years of his life. The Chinese Chan school (which gave birth to Zen) gained a major presence in Brazil with the inauguration of the Zu Lai Temple and its companion Buddhist University in 2003. There is considerable Internet activity among Brazilian Buddhists, with a number of websites and mailing lists, as well as Orkut Communities dedicated to clarifying doubts about the Dharma and its practice. Many of those lists and communities are in practice open to various schools and lineages. A few schools and movements are more isolated and do not emphasize dialog with other schools.

## BUDDHISM IN CANADA

There is a small, growing Buddhist community in Canada. As of the 2001 census, roughly 300,000 Canadians identified their religion as Buddhist. Buddhism arrived in Canada with the arrival of Chinese laborers in the territories during the 19th century. The first Japanese Buddhist temple in Canada was built at the Ishikawa Hotel in Vancouver in 1905. A substantial expansion of Buddhism in Canada began in the last half of the 20th century. Changes in Canadian immigration pattern saw a massive influx of immigrants from China, India, Sri Lanka, Japan, and Southeast Asia, countries with strong Buddhist histories and demographics. In addition, the immense popularity and goodwill ushered in by Tibet's Dalai Lama (who has been made honorary Canadian citizen) put Buddhism in the forefront of Canadian spirituality. Many non-Asian Canadians embraced Buddhism (in various traditions) and have become leaders in their respective sanghas in their own right.

Buddhism in the United States had a strong influence on the development of Western Buddhism in Canada, and continues to today. Canadian Buddhism is dominated primarily by the Tibetan, Zen, and Theravada schools.

## BUDDHISM IN AUSTRIA

Buddhism is a legally recognized religion in Austria and it is followed by more than 10,000 Austrians. Although still small in absolute numbers (10,402 at the 2001 census), Buddhism in Austria enjoys widespread acceptance if not popularity. A majority of Buddhists in the country are Austrian nationals (some of them naturalized after immigration from Asia, predominantly from the People's Republic of China and Vietnam), while a considerable number of them are foreign nationals.

As in most European countries, different branches and schools of Buddhism are represented by groups of varying sizes. Vienna not only has the largest number of foreign residents, but is also the place with the longest tradition of Buddhism in the country. Most of Austria's Buddhist temples and centres of practice can be found there; some with a specific Chinese, Vietnamese, Tibetan or Japanese appearance. The latest development has been the establishment of a "Buddhist Cemetery" around a stupa-like building for funeral ceremonies at the Vienna Central Cemetery.

Buddhism was officially recognized under Austrian law in 1983. Russia is the only other "European" country to forwardly recognize Buddhism as "native" to its own soil, giving it official status, along with Orthodox Christianity, Islam, and Judaism.

### History

### Early Years

By the late 19th century, due to the influence of Arthur Schopenhauer and Richard Wagner, artists and intellectuals in the capital city of the Austro-Hungarian Empire started to take interest in Buddhism. Karl Eugen Neumann (1865-1915), who had met the composer Wagner in his father's house. took great interest in what he had heard about Buddhism. In 1884 he decided to become a Buddhist and study the original languages to be able 'to see for himself'. He managed to translate large parts of the Pali Canon into German before dying in Vienna at the age of fifty.

In 1913 in Java, a man from Graz became the first recorded Austrian to be ordained as Buddhist monk, taking the name Bhikkhu Sono.

1923 saw the foundation of a "Buddhist Society" in Vienna and Austrians were among the participants at the 2nd International Buddhist Congress in Paris in 1937. The political situation — an alliance between the Fascist regime and the Catholic Church from 1933 to 1938 followed by Hitler's conquest of Austria and the Second World War — was highly unfavourable to the development of Austrian Buddhism.

## After World War II

In 1949 the "Buddhist Society of Vienna" was founded and interest for Buddhism started to flourish again. Due to personalities like Fritz Hungerleider, who had returned from exile in the People's Republic of China in 1955 to become the society's president, and Dr. Walter Karwath, who had spent years in Asia practicing medicine, Buddhism took a step out of literary and intellectual circles toward the world of daily life.

The late 1970s saw the establishment of Dannebergplatz, the first Buddhist Centre in Vienna; the purchase of a rural property intended to become a retreat centre (Buddhist Centre Scheibbs); and the establishment of the first Buddhist Association outside Vienna (the Salzburg Buddhist Association). The latter was founded by Friedrich Fenzl, who had been a student at the Ryukoku University in Kyoto and who invited Kosho Otani, the Patriarch of the Nishi-Honganji branch of Jodo Shinshu to visit Austria. Hemaloka Thero, Geshe Rabten, the 16th Karmapa, the 14th Dalai Lama, and other eminent representatives from different Buddhist traditions visited the country, gave talks, and attracted dharma students.

In 1979, Genro Koudela, who was ordained as a Zen priest in California by Joshu Sasaki, returned to Vienna, his city of origin, and established the "Bodhidharma Zendo" there. The new Buddhist Centre at Fleischmarkt, in the very centre of Vienna, became the home for Zen, Kagyu and Theravada groups.

## Buddhism recognized

When official recognition was granted by the government in early 1983 a new era of Austrian Buddhism was ushered in. A widely visible 'Peace Stupa' was opened at the banks of the river Danube and a retreat and study centre, Letzehof, affiliated with the Geluk school of Tibetan Buddhism was opened in the western province of Vorarlberg. Vanja Palmers, a Zen monk of the Japanese Soto school, and Brother David Steindl-Rast, an Austrian-American Bendedictine monk, founded a retreat centre high up in the Salzburg alpine region. The first centre in the south of the country, a retreat centre in the Burmese Theravada tradition was established in the early 1990s. In 1993, Austria hosted an annual general meeting of the European Buddhist Union, which drew participants from a dozen European countries. A series of visits to the city of Graz by the Dalai Lama in 1995, 1998 (for the consecration of a large stupa), and in 2002 (to speak on "Kalachakra for World Peace") became a strong encouragement for Buddhists in Austria.

## Buddhist Religious Instruction at Austrian Schools

Official recognition also opened the doors for Buddhist religious education at schools. In 1993, the first few groups of Buddhist children were given the chance to hear about the Buddhadharma on a regular basis as part of their syllabus. Twelve years after the project was started in the cities of Vienna, Graz and Salzburg, Buddhist religious education is being made available to school children of all age groups (6 to 19) at different types of schools in all of nine federal provinces of the Republic. A Teachers' Training Academy was founded in 2001 to offer in-service teacher training for the teachers concerned.

## BUDDHISM IN FRANCE

France has over two hundred Buddhist meditation centers.

It mainly consists of Chinese and Vietnamese immigrants, but has also managed to attract a large number of converts.

### History

Alexandra David-Neel was an important early French Buddhist. She is most known for her visit to the forbidden (to foreigners) city of Lhasa, capital of Tibet (1924) and wrote more than 30 books, about Buddhism, philosophy, and her travels. In 1911 Alexandra travelled for the second time to India, to further her study of Buddhism.

She was invited to the royal monastery of Sikkim, where she met Maharaj Kumar (crown prince) Sidkeon Tulku. She became Sidkeong's "confidante and spiritual sister" (according to Ruth Middleton), perhaps his lover (Foster & Foster). She also met the thirteenth Dalai Lama twice in 1912, and had the opportunity to ask him many questions about Buddhism—a feat unprecedented for a European woman at that time.

Taisen Deshimaru was a Japanese Zen Buddhist who founded some dojos in France. Thich Nhat Hanh, a Nobel Peace Prize-nominated, Vietnamese-born Zen Buddhist is influential in the Engaged Buddhism movement in France and around the world.

## BUDDHISM IN SWITZERLAND

According to the 2000 census of Switzerland, 21,305 Swiss residents (0.29% of the total population) self-identified as Buddhists. About a third of them was born in Thailand.

### History

In 1978 the Swiss Buddhist Union *(Schweizerische Buddhistische Union/Union Suisse des Bouddhistes/Unione Buddhista Svizzera)* was founded by the Czech Buddhist *Mirko Fryba (Bhikku Kusalananda)*.

The German Buddhist Nyanatiloka was an important early Buddhist in Switzerland, who planned to found a Buddhist monastery in Switzerland. The writings of Swiss psychologist Carl Gustav Jung have many allusions to Buddhism. Max Ladner founded a Buddhist group in Zurich in 1942. In 1948, Ladner published the Buddhist journal "Die Einsicht". Geshe Rabten Rinpoche founded in 1977 in Mont-Pèlerin a Buddhist monastery and study centre for European monks. There are also Tibetan-Buddhist and Zen monasteries in Switzerland.

In earlier censuses, Buddhism figured together with other non-Abrahamic traditions (mainly Hinduism) as "other churches and communities". These accounted for 0.12% in 1970, 0.19% in 1980, 0.42% in 1990 and 0.78% in 2000 (0.38% Hinduism, 0.29% Buddhism, 0.11% other).

## BUDDHISM IN ITALY

Buddhism was first known in Italy at the start of the past century under the auspices of notable scholars like Giuseppe Tucci. Presently not all centres and schools in Italy are collected under UBI (Unione Buddhista Italiana).

### Religion in Italy

Italy is an overwhelmingly Catholic country (Catholics make up for the 87.8% of the populations, with 36.8% considering themselves practicing Catholics and 30.8% attending Church every Sunday).

There are also some important religious minorities:

- Other Christians: 1,800,000 (3.1%)
  - o Protestants: 1,100,000 (1.9%)
    - * Jehovah's Witnesses: 500,000 (0.85%)
    - * Evangelicals and Pentecostalists: 450,000 (0.76%)
    - * Assemblies of God: 300,000 (0.5%)
    - * Waldensians and Methodists: 35,000 (0.06%)
    - * Waldensians: 30,000 (0.05%)
    - * Methodists: 5,000 (0.01%)
    - * Seventh-day Adventists: 25,000 (0.04%)
    - * Latter-day Saints: 22,000 (0.04%)
    - * Others: 60,000 (0.1%)
    - * Baptists: 20,000 (0.03%)
    - * Lutherans: 7,000 (0.01%)

    * Others (Reformed Christians, Anglicans, Mennonites, Brethren, etc.): 30,000 (0.05%)
  - o Eastern Orthodoxes: 700,000 (1.2%)
- Muslims: 850,000 (1.4%)
- Buddhists: 110,000 (0.2%)
- Sikhs: 70,000 (0.1%)
- Hindus: 70,000 (0.1%)
- Jews: 45,000 (0.1%).

## BUDDHISM IN KALMYKIA

The Kalmyks are the only inhabitants of Europe of Mongolian origin, and the only ones whose national religion is Buddhism. They live in the Republic of Kalmykia, a federal subject of the Russian Federation. It has borders with the Republic of Dagestan in the south; the Stavropol Krai in the southwest; the Rostov Oblast and the Volgograd Oblast in the west and the northwest, respectively. Its eastern border is the Astrakhan Oblast.

The Kalmyks are the descendants of several Oirat tribes that migrated to Europe during the early part of the 17th century. As Tibetan Buddhists, the Kalmyks regard His Holiness the Dalai Lama as their spiritual leader.

The Sajin Lama (Supreme Lama) of the Kalmyks is Erdne Ombadykow, a Philadelphia-born man of Kalmukian origins who was brought up as a Buddhist monk in a Tibetan monastery in India from the age of seven and who was recognized by the Dalai Lama as the reincarnation of the Buddhist saint Telo Rinpoche. Ombdaykow divides his time between living in Colorado and living in Kalmykia.

Kalmyk political refugees opened the first Buddhist temple in Central Europe, located in Belgrade, Serbia. Their offspring relocated to the United States in late 1951 and early 1952, where they established several Kalmyk Buddhist temples in Monmouth County, New Jersey. Geshe Wangyal, a Kalmyk Buddhist monk, established the Tibetan Buddhist Learning Centre and monastery in Washington County, NJ.

## BUDDHISM IN RUSSIA

Historically, Buddhism was incorporated into Russian lands as early as the late 15th century, when Russian explorers travelled to and settled in Siberia and what is now the Russian Far East. It is also believed that Indian King Ashoka had sent monks to spread Buddhism all over the world including Siberia. Mongolian and Tibetan lamas first appeared on the eastern shores of Lake Baikal in the middle of the 17th century and quickly spread Buddhism in the area. Later in that century Buddhism emerged as the dominant religion in Tuva. The Kalmyks who migrated from China to the lower reaches of the Volga River in the later half of the 17th century also professed Buddhism. Tzarist authorities were fairly tolerant with respect to Buddhists.

Later, religious centers-Buddhist monasteries, or datsans-appeared in other areas of Buryatiya, too. Within a short time most of the Buryats living east of Lake Baikal were converted to Buddhism. In 1764, Damba Dorzhi Zayayev, the high priest of the Tasongolski datsan-the oldest in the Baikal region-became head of the entire Buddhist clergy with the title Bandido Khambo Lama.

In the late sixteenth century the Kalmyks were converted to Buddhism by Mongolian lamas in Dzungaria (China). In the seventeenth century, they moved to the lower reaches of the Volga River, retaining their religion. At that time the Kalmyks gained access to the first works of Buddhist literature translated from the Tibetan language.

The main form of Buddhism in Russia is the Gelukpa school of Tibetan Buddhism. Although Tibetan Buddhism is most often associated with the peoples of Tibet, in the north the school spread into southwestern and northern China, Mongolia, and finally Russia. In the south, it took hold in Bhutan and parts of northern India and Nepal.

Afterwards, it began to spread into the geographically and culturally adjacent Russian constituent regions known today as: Amur Oblast, Buryatia, Chita Oblast, Tuva Republic, and Khabarovsk Krai. There is also Kalmykia, another constituent republic of Russia that is in fact the only Buddhist region in Europe, perhaps paradoxically located to the north of the Caucasus. Buddhism has been in Russia for four centuries.

In the second half of the XVIIth century Buryats were incorporated into Russia. Beginning from 1727 when the treaty determining the borders between Russia and Manchu-Chinese empires was signed the Buryats started the official development within the Russian state. In Czarist Russia, where Orthodoxy was the predominant state religion, Buddhists were subjected to certain restrictions. Buddhist monks (lamas) were made dependent on the local police and were subordinated to the chief provincial board. The regulations for the lamaist clergy, introduced in 1853, established the almost despotic reign of officials under the czar. The latter made the most important assignments concerning even the clerical posts; in official documents the Buddhists were called "the followers of the alien belief" (*inovertsi*) and the religious problems of the Buddhist were the concern of a special department for foreign religions. Nevertheless, Buddhism began spreading among the Buryats in the 17th century and became an essential and significant element of social, spiritual and material life of most Buryat ethnic groups, and has played a great role in their political and spiritual consolidation. This process of consolidation was stimulated by the formation of a centralized system of the Buryat Buddhist religious administrative structure.

The spread of the Shambhala myth and the Kalachakra Tantra in the West has a history of its own. It does definitely not first begin with the expulsion of the lamas from Tibet (in 1959) and their diaspora across the whole world, but rather commences at the beginning of the twentieth century in Russia with the religious political activity of an ethnic Buryat by the name of Agvan Dorjiev. He was convinced that the union of Tibet with Russia would provide the Highlands with an extremely favorable future, and was likewise able to convince the hierarch upon the Lion Throne of the merits of his political vision for a number of years. He thus advanced to the post of Tibetan envoy in St. Petersburg and at the Russian court. His work in the capital was extremely active and varied. Since the end of the 19th century Buddhism had become fashionable among the Russian high society.

Tibetan medical doctor Badmajev was head of the most famous private hospital in St. Petersburg. There the cabinet lists for the respective members of government were put together under his direction. R. Fulop-Miller has vividly described the doctor's power-political activities: "In the course of time medicine and politics, ministerial appointments and 'lotus essences' became more and more mingled, and a fantastic political magic character arose, which emanated from Badmajev's sanatorium and determined the fate of all Russia. The miracle-working doctor owed this influence especially to his successful medical-political treatment of the Tsar. Badmajev's mixtures, potions, and powders brewed from mysterious herbs from the steppes served not just to remedy patient's metabolic disturbances; anyone who took these medicaments ensured himself an important office in the state at the same time" (Fulop-Miller, 1927,).

For this "wise and crafty Asian" too, the guiding idea was the establishment of an Asian empire with the "White Tsar" at its helm. Buryats had received initiations into the Time Tantra from the Ninth Panchen Lama which were supposed to have been of central significance for Russias future vision. At the centre of Agvan Dorjiev's activities in Russia stood the construction of the Buddhist temple in St. Petersburg. The shrine was dedicated to the Kalachakra deity. A painter by the name of Nicholas Roerich, who later became a fanatic propagandist for Kalachakra doctrine, produced the designs for the stained-glass windows. Work commenced in 1909. In the central hall various main gods from the Tibetan pantheon were represented with statues and pictures, including among others Dorjiev's wrathful initiation deity, Vajrabhairava. Regarding the decor, it is perhaps also of interest that there was a swastika motif which the Bolsheviks knocked out during the Second World War.

Stalinist secret police agents tried to oppress all religious groups, leading to a decline in Buddhism.

Tibetan Buddhism is primarily practiced by the indigenous peoples in various regions of central and eastern Russia, except for a few Russian converts based mainly in the larger cities such as St. Petersburg or Moscow, where there is greater access to urban Buddhist centers or similar facilities.

The other major form of Buddhism found in Russia is the more commonly known Mahayana Buddhism, primarily practiced by the Vietnamese or Chinese immigrant communities based mainly in the large cities.

The Russian Federation and Austria are the only two European states today that recognize Buddhism as an "official", though not necessarily "state religion" in their respective countries. On top of that, Russia also recognizes it, along with Islam, Judaism, and of course Orthodox Christianity, as native to Russian soil in the 1993 Constitution of the Russian Federation. All other religious groups are unrecognized, and must officially register and be subject to rejection by the state.

There are a few dozen Buddhist university-monasteries throughout Russia, but concentrated in the Russian Far East and Siberia, known in Russian as Datsans. Adherents to Buddhism account for approximately 700,000 in the Russian Federation, about 0.5% of the total population.

Organizations: The highest authority for Russian Buddhists is the Central Buddhist Board based in the Ivolginski Datsan in the Buryat. (A permanent office in Moscow is concerned with external relations). The congress of clergy and laity convenes once in four years and elects the members of the Board. Head of the Central Buddhist Board is Bandido Khambo-Lama.

Russian Buddhism is representative of the Gelugpa school ("the School of Virtue"), which is a branch of Tibetan Buddhism in the Mahayana tradition, that is, "the broad path" of salvation from endless rebirth in the world of suffering. Russian Buddhism has a number of specific ritual peculiarities that have taken shape over the course of history. Historically it has been marked by the prevalence of rural lamas living outside datsans because of the nomadic way of life. To some extent, this tradition has survived to this day. In keeping with tradition, six major holidays, khurals, are celebrated annually and are attended by a large number of people who bring various gifts to datsans as well as money and food for lamas. Tsagaalgan is a holiday celebrated on the eve of the lunar new year, which usually falls in February. This khural is devoted to the twelve miracles of Buddha during his dispute with six preachers of heresy. Services and a series of religious rites are conducted to mar the occasion. Buddhists, dressed in their best clothes, come to pray together for well-being and more happiness. On the eve of the new year, a solemn evening ritual is performed during which food is served to the doksheetsi, the protectors of the faith. This involves the ritual burning of Dugzhub, a magic pyramid of paper and wood; according to a Buddhist belief, a ritual fire consumes all evil thoughts.

A long note from a big white conch proclaims the first day of the lunar new year. A traditional service is held to celebrate the Sagaan Sar ("white month") holiday.

In the main temple lamas, replacing one another, pray for fifteen days for peace and goodness.

The khural Duyn-khor, a second major holiday, lasts three days in April. It is dedicated to the preaching of the sacred teaching of Kalachakra.

The third major holiday is Gandun-Shunserme, devoted to the birth and enlightenment of Buddha and his attainment of nirvana. It is celebrated in early summer.

The fourth holiday Maidari is dedicated to Maidari, the Buddha of the future (Maitreia). It is always celebrated for two days in midsummer. People spend the first day in many hours of devout prayer. On the second day the gilded statue of Maidari is solemnly carried out of the temple and placed on a chariot twined with silk ribbons. It is surrounded by lamas in ceremonial dress. A green horse of plaster is harnessed to the chariot, and the procession sets off around the datsan. This ceremony symbolizes Maidari's tour of the universe and the spread of his grace throughout it. Several thousand people gather in the datsan for the procession. A kharang, a big copper shield, is struck with a mallet, and its sounds can be heard far away. There is a fanfare, the drums roll, and conchs are blown. The procession stops at every turn of the monastery walls for a reading of scared

Scriptures. Many Buddhists attending the procession try to approach the chariot, to hold onto its beam and harness, and to throw money at the feet of the statute of Maidari.

The last two khurals are celebrated with less splendour, but they also attract large crowd of believers. Lkhabab Duysen, marked in autumn, is devoted to the Buddha's return from the thirty-third heaven. The holiday Zula is dedicated to the passing away of the father of lamaism, Bogdo Tsongkhapa. A thousand candles are lit during the service.

During the khurals prayers are said in honour of the protectors of the faith and for well-being and peace on earth.

Lamas who live in monasteries observe the Dulva, a traditional moral and ethical code. Depending on the level of ordination, they participate in services and philosophical discussions and perform special religious rites at the people's request.

Recently, in addition to Buryats, Kalmyks, and Tuvinians, more and more Russians, Ukrainians, and people from the Baltic republics have been attending Buddhist services. Previously, they all went to pray at the Ivolginsk datsan, but today, with the 1991 reopening of the temple in Leningrad, followers of Buddhism from the European part of the country will travel there, too.

## Buddhism in Science

In Russia academic Buddhist studies began from the middle of the XIXth century. Already by the end of the century the Russian buddhological school had won international prestige. With the discovery of the Buddhist manuscripts in Central Asia in the beginning of the XXth century a newstage in the study of Buddhism began.

The Central Asian, Sak and Uigur Buddhist texts with their Chinese and Tibetan translations have been published. The international series "Bibliotheca Buddhica" founded in Russia by S.F. Oldendurg and F.I. Tsherbatsky became the centre of Buddhist studies which attracted the greatest scholars of the world L. de La Vallee Poussen, Max Walleser, Sylvan Levi and others.

Beginning with 1897 and up to 1937 the most important Buddhist texts in Sanskrit, Tibetan and Uigur on Buddhist philosophy, logic, etc. were printed in 30 volumes within this series. In 1960 V.N. Toporov published the translation of "Dhammapada", which became the 31st volume, and A.I. Vostrikov's book "The Tibetan historical literature"-the 32nd.

Many of the works published, particularly on Buddhist logic, have been regarded unsurpassed. In the enormous volume of buddhological works the quantitative contribution of the Russian scientists is rather modest, but their qualificative aspect is of high value. In 1985 with the publication of the "Monuments of the Indian texts from Central Asia" by G.M.Bongard-Levin and M.I. Vorobyova-Desyatovskaya the edition of this series was continued. Later on a few other publications appeared. Among them one can mention the study and the translation from Sanskrit of the 1st part of the "Abhidharmakosa" done by V.I.Rudoi, the translation from the Pali of the "Thequestions of Milinda" (Milindapanhi) carried out by A.V. Paribok and also the publication of the work by the Chinese author Huei Tsyao "Biographies of the distinguished monks" (Gao sen chuan) carried out by M.E. Ermakov. At present Buddhism is studied at the research centers in Moscow, St.-Petersburg, aswell as in Ulan-Ude, Elista and Kyzyl.

The buddhologists in Moscow concentrate their efforts on therole of the Buddhist cult as well as the place and role of Buddhism in social and political life of Asian countries, and its influence on the culture and traditions of oriental peoples. In St.-Petersburg scholars are mainly engaged in deciphering ancient Indian inscriptions and textological researches in the field of Buddhist art and old Uyghur, Tibetan, Mongolian and Chinese texts and treatises. In the buddhological studies which were pursued mainly in the field of sinology and indology notable achievements have been made, whereas in the field of Tibetan and Mongolian studies the scope of research has not been so wide.

Nevertheless all the buddhological studies are closely interrelated. A great many texts in the Tibetan language translated from Sanskrit are accessible now though their original texts in

Sanskrit have been lost. Therefore the value of the Tibetan texts becomes all the more significant. The fact that in Russia there is the living tradition of the Tibetan Buddhism, spread among Buryats, Kalmycks and Tyvanians, greatly contributed to the development of Tibetan and Mongolian studies and within their frame to the buddhological studies.

Buddhism in Buryatia is one of the Buddhist regions of Central Asia and South Siberia, which was the extreme point of the spread of Buddhism northwards. The Buryats were and still are the largest Buddhist population in Russia. The Buryats, Kalmycks and the Tyvanians are the three Buddhist nationalities in Russia historically belonging to the common Mongolian spiritual realm and to the Tibetan and Mongolian cultural and religious tradition of the great Central Asian civilization. Tibetan religious and cultural influence has been playing up to now an important role in the culture and history of these peoples.

At the beginning Buddhist monasteries were the centers not only of culture and learning, but in fact they became moral and ethical regulators of everyday life of Buryat families. Buddhism stimulated the formation of the nation's intellectual potential. There appeared different monastic educational faculties with many learned monks and scholars. Among them we can mention Agvan Dorjiev (1857-1930), one of the tutors of the 13th Dalai Lama, who was his representative at the Russian court and played a great role in the international political life, establishing various relations between Tibet and Russia. By the beginning of the century Buddhism has become quite strong and this caused the anxiety on the part of the Christian church. In order to adapt the Buddhist teaching and church to the rapidly developing and changing world Agvan Dorjiev and some prominent Buryat scholars initiated a modernization movement among Buddhist clergy and intellectuals, proclaiming the necessity of combining the Buddhist philosophy with the best achievements of Western culture and civilization. The movement has gained a wide scope in Buryatia. It was due to the fact of mutual interest of both: the Buddhist clergy wanted to preserve somehow the church by means of modification, whereas local intelligentsia regarded

Buddhist ideas as a cultural and social basis for the further national development after being freed from pagan elements. Though "modernists" played an important role in national liberation movement of Buryats and promoted national and cultural Autonomy of Buryats within the Russian Federation and establishing of the Buryat-Mongolian Autonomous Republic after the revolution, still the movement was doomed to failure because it was unrealistic to expect gaining self-administration for Buryat people by means of religious reforms and revival of national culture neither before the revolution nor after it.

The attempt of "modernists" to emphasize similarity of ideas in Marxism and early Buddhism also failed. This movement is all the more noteworthy because no comparable developments took place in Tibetan Buddhism until after the confrontation with Chinese communism in 1949. By 1935 in Buryatia there were about 45 or 46 Buddhist temples and monasteries.

## BUDDHISM IN GERMANY

Buddhism in Germany looks back to a history of over 150 years. Arthur Schopenhauer was one of the earliest Germans who were influenced by Buddhism. Schopenhauer got his knowledge of Buddhism from authors like Isaac Jacob Schmidt (1779-1847). German Buddhists or Orientalists like Karl Eugen Neumann, Paul Dahlke, Georg Grimm, Friedrich Zimmermann (Subhadra Bhikschu) and the first German Buddhist monk Nyanatiloka were also influenced by Schopenhauer and his understanding of Buddhism. But also German Indologists like Hermann Oldenberg and his work "Buddha, sein Leben, seine Lehre, seine Gemeinde" had an important influence on German Buddhism.

In 1888 Subhadra Bickshu (Friedrich Zimmermann) published the first edition of the "Buddhistischen Katechismus", a work based on the "Buddhist Catechism" of Henry Steel Olcott.

In 1903 the first German Buddhist organisation was founded by the Indologist Karl Seidenstucker in Leipzig. In 1904 Florus Anton Gueth became the Theravada monk Nyanatiloka. Some important Pali texts were translated into German in the early part of the 20th century by scholars like Karl Eugen Neumann (1865-1915), Nyantiloka and others.

In 1922 Hermann Hesse published his famous work "Siddhartha", which has been translated into many languages.

In 1924 Dr. Paul Dahlke established the first German Buddhist monastery, the "Buddhistische Haus" in Berlin.

The German Dharmaduta Society, initially known as the Lanka Dhammaduta Society and dedicated to spreading the message of the Buddha in Germany and other Western countries, was founded in 1952.

In 1957 The German Dharmaduta Society purchased the premises of "Das Buddhistische Haus" from the heirs of Dr. Dahlke. It is now a Centre for the spread of Theravada Buddhism in Europe. The German authorities have designated it, as the oldest Buddhist institution in Europe), a National Heritage site.

# 7

# Millennial Buddhism

The Notion of Buddhist Economics may seem a contradiction in terms. The Buddhist doctrine of non-self would appear to discourage both production and accumulation, and, moreover, to undermine concern for the economic welfare of others. Its doctrine of nibbana (nirvana) appears both to deny the importance of economic activity and to encourage withdrawal from this world.

Its doctrine of kamma (karma) appears to erode any critical analysis of the existing economic order. From such considerations respected authorities on religion, such as Max Weber [1958], argue Buddhism takes an "asocial course" so that there is no "nexus" between the Buddhist ideology and the social order which includes the economy.

Nevertheless, governments, in the Asian nations where Buddhism is a living force, are faced with problems in making or implementing economic policy, creating economic institutions, and raising the level of economic development. In this context Buddhist intellectuals have been re-examining their religion to obtain theological perspectives on suchpolicy problems. Further, in the West, scholars of Buddhism are turning, from their focus on Buddhist salvation and contemplation, toward an examination of individual and social ethics of Buddhism (e.g., Sizemore and Swearer [1988]) Finally, certain Western intellectuals are also using Buddhist ideas to describe their view of desirable economic policy. The topic of Buddhist economics, therefore, seems deserving of consideration.

The purpose is to determine whether the most important parts of the Buddhist canon contain a set of doctrines which allow us to gain some coherent ideas about how a modern economic system based upon it should function. Certainly, one finds no systematic exposition about economics in these scriptural sources (or, for that matter, in more modem commentaries; however, despite their discursiveness and vagueness, enough is available to see a coherent framework. Such an attempt, involves a certain subjectivity, especially since I view these matters through the lenses of a Western trained economist and can only take into account readily available (and translated) primary and secondary source materials, which represent only a fraction of the canon.

This discussion of ideas in the formal Buddhist canonical sources does not tell us anything very specific about how Buddhism is actually practiced today, i.e., we cannot easily infer from doctrine to behaviour, especially without specification of the social matrix and those particular aspects which a particular group has chosen to adopt or to ignore. To draw a parallel with Christianity, at face value, there is little in the formal doctrines of Calvinism or, for that matter, of the Old Believers of the Russian Orthodox Church which would directly lead someone to suspect that the groups practicing these religions were extremely active in the rise in capitalism that occurred in Western Europe or Russia in the 17th through 19th centuries.

To limit further the scope of discussion, I focus primary attention on Theravada rather than Mahayana Buddhism. The former is found in Burma, Cambodia, Laos, Sri Lanka, and Thailand; the latter, in China, India, Japan, Korea, and Vietnam. I also deal only with the formal sources, rather than the legends and myths; the latter may have more direct influence, however, on the actual behaviour of practicing Buddhists.

## TEACHINGS ON PROPERTY, WEALTH, AND INCOME

A well known buddhist analysis of the origins of private property is contained in the "Aganna Sutta" [Suttanta No. 27 in

Digha Nikaya] sometimes called the "Buddhist Book of Genesis." According to this text, in the beginning there was general prosperity and property in common. Rice was so abundant that when gathered in the evening for supper, a new crop was ready to be gathered for breakfast in the morning. However, certain inequalities—based on physical characteristics—arose and such differentiation led to transgressions from the path of the dhamma, as the more handsome people scorned those with less fortunate endowments. Somewhat later, further transgressions occurred as people maximized utility by collecting and storing rice for several meals, thereby saving some work for themselves and acting in a self-interested manner. A consequence of this latter transgression was a decline in the fecundity of rice, which seems to indicate diminishing returns to the land. Following these events, the Sutta says that the fields were divided and assigned to specific individuals as private property, which in turn gave rise to the stealing of land, lying and other undesirable activities.

Three aspects of this story of differentiation leading to "attachment" appear particularly important for our purposes. First, private property in land arose as a pragmatic response to human frailities and economic scarcities which were induced by transgressions from the moral law. Second, private property is by no means a perfect institution and it can give rise to undesirable activities. Nevertheless, I have been unable to find any suggestion in the canon that alternative property arrangements, e.g, a system of community or public ownership, would be better, given the condition of human kind which we find on earth. Third, a later part of the story derives the origins of the caste system from such events.

From this story of the origins of property, it should come as no surprise that Buddhist teachings on the nature of wealth reveal some fundamental ambivalences. Fortunately, a recent scholarly conference on this topic has provided a useful exegesis of these doctrines.

Property per se for the layman is not despised. For instance, in the Anguttara-Nikaya, IV, vii, 61) we read of the Fourfold Deserved Bliss of a Layman: the bliss of ownership, the bliss of enjoyment, the bliss of debtlessness, and the bliss of blamelessness. Later in the same source we learn of the five reasons why a person should desire to be rich (by riches obtained by moral means). By his diligence he could make himself happy as well as his family and work people; he could also make happy his friends and companions; he would be able to keep his property from the depredations of weather, robbers, and enemies; he could make suitable offerings to kin, guests, the deceased, and kings; and finally he could offer to recluses and monks.

Further, practical advice is given so that one's property is maintained. For instance, in the "Sigalovada Suttanta" (op. cit.), the Buddha cites six ways condicive to loss of property and wealth which should be avoided, of which one is idleness. The property owner is also advised to divide his wealth into four parts one part for living and doing one's duties for others; one part for times of need; and two parts to business (presumably buying intermediate products). If these four parts are of equal size and if the passage refers to the division of income (this is ambiguous), it implies a high amount of savings.

Despite these positive views toward wealth, two basic moral ideas must be stressed. First, the owner of such wealth should not be unduly attached to it, nor must he accumulate it by immoral means. To cultivate this non-attachment, a person must be generous and give large parts of it away, specially to the monks. Moreover, the more that is accumulated and then given away, the more a person can cultivate non-attachment (a matter discussed by Kemper, 1988; Reynolds, 1988; and others in Sizemore and Swearer, 1988). Thus wealth is a means for gaining merit. Second, such generosity leads to the accumulation of merit which, in turn, means that a person is reborn to a higher position of wealth and social status; thus inherited wealth is a sign of virtue in a previous life, i.e. accumulated merit. However, such amassing of wealth can also lead to rebirth in a lower social and economic status—even perhaps in hell—if it is carried out by improper means or unskillful mental habits if it is not generously shared; or if it gives rise to pride or greed or other types of improper behaviour.

In sum, there is a high risk but also a high spiritual and economic return in amassing wealth. The optimal path for accumulating and then giving away wealth does not seem to be specified in the canon; clearly, however, a person's discount rate for wealth in future rebirths cannot be an important factor in arriving at a solution, for a person approaching the problem in this manner would reveal too much attachment to wealth. In possessing wealth, one must not be possessed by wealth.

To complete this discussion it should be emphasized that the Buddha saw no virtue in poverty; indeed, that poverty can be an impediment to virtue. In an oft-cited passage from the Dhammapada Commentary [1969], Book 15, Story 5) the Buddha notes that if he is preaching the dhamma while a nearby poor man is suffering from pangs of hunger, he will not be able to be comprehended. However, as soon as the poor man's physical suffering becomes relieved, his mind becomes tranquil and he is open to reason. The same source notes that the ideal city, as described by Buddha, is one where prosperity reigns. Further, poverty raises improper desires—greed and craving—and does not permit a person to be generous. Indeed, in one dialogue, "Cakkavatti-Sihanada Suttanta," the Buddha notes that poverty leads to stealing, violence, and murder which is hardly conducive to the conditions leading to the spiritual enrichment of the society or the individual ording to Swearer and Sizemore (1988), "[f]or the individual, following the d/gamma is not only morally the best and religiously the highest life; it is prudentially the wisest, and ultimately the most profitable. And yet, non-attachment is still the dominant motif: if self-serving greed becomes the motive for such a life, the virtue of even the best action will be lost. Craving destroys the merit of any action and so conformity to the dhammic code for the sake of gain is self-defeating." It should be added that the spiritually most developed look upon all worldly success, even in a future world, as a snare and delusion; and they attempt to transcend this cycle of rebirths by achieving nibbana; but such spiritual virtuosity is only for a self-elected few who, moreover, are capable (in terms of accumulated merit) of carrying out such a task.

## IMMIGRATION IN BHUTAN

Since the twentieth century, Bhutanese immigration and citizenship laws have been promulgated as acts of the royal government, often by decree of the *Druk Gyalpo* on advice of the rest of government. Immigration policy and procedure are implemented by the Lhengye Zhungtshog (Council of Ministers) Ministry of Home and Cultural Affairs, Department of Immigration. Bhutan's first modern laws regarding immigration and citizenship were the Bhutanese Citizenship Act 1958 and subsequent amendments in 1977. The 1958 Act was superseded by the Bhutanese Citizenship Act 1985. The Constitution of 2008 included some changes in Bhutan's immigration laws, policy, and procedure, however prior law not inconsistent with the 2008 Constitution remained intact. Bhutan's modern citizenship laws and policies reinforce the institution of the Bhutanese monarchy, require familiarity and adherence to Ngalop social norms, and reflect the social impact of the most recent immigrant groups.

Historically, there have been at least five distinct waves of human migration into Bhutan. The first record of human movement into Bhutan is the settlement of the region by Tibetan Buddhists, thoroughly established by AD 600. Before Tibetans settled Bhutan, the area was populated by the aboriginal Monpa, who practiced the shamanistic Bon religion. The second wave is represented by Bhutan's Sharchop population, who arrived from Burma or Assam sometime in the first millennium. The third wave of human migration was that of Nepalis in the late nineteenth and early twentieth centuries. A fourth, much smaller wave of Tibetans came to Bhutan beginning in 1959, followed fifth by a wave of Indians and Nepalese during Bhutan's development projects in the 1960s.

Bhutan's first modern laws regarding immigration and citizenship were the Bhutanese Citizenship Act 1958 and subsequent amendments in 1977. The Act was pronounced by the Druk Gyalpo King Jigme Dorji Wangchuck among a series of legal and social reforms in 1958 designed to begin modernizing Bhutan, including the abolition of slavery. The 1958 Act defined Bhutanese citizenship in patrilineal terms, and provided a basic framework for the process of naturalization in Bhutan. Initially, applicants other than wives of Bhutanese citizens were required to show a ten year residency, five years of service to the government, and ownership of agricultural land. The 1958 Act originally defined no procedural framework for immigration. It also allowed the King to make *ad hoc* changes to the law, and left decisions largely to the discretion of the King and government officials.

In 1977, an amendment lengthened the residency requirement for naturalization to 20 years (15 years if in service to Bhutan), and the requirement of owning agricultural land was eschewed. Deprivation of citizenship as a punishment for sedition was expanded to associates and family relatives of seditious citizens. The amendment introduced other requirements, such as knowledge of Dzongkha and adherence to Ngalop customs. The amendment also introduced a procedural framework for citizenship and naturalization; namely it codified procedural requirements for census registration and births abroad and designated the Ministry of Home Affairs as the government agency to oversee immigration matters. The 1958 Act and 1977 amendments were superseded by the Bhutanese Citizenship Act 1985, though much of the procedural framework established in 1977 remains *de jure* in effect because it was not overridden.

Since the Bhutanese Citizenship Act 1985, immigration policy and procedure have been implemented by the Lhengye Zhungtshog (Council of Ministers) Ministry of Home and Cultural Affairs, Department of Immigration. Procedural safeguards for both naturalization and bona fide citizenship remained largely absent: applicants could be rejected for no reason at all, such decisions were final and binding, and even bona fide Bhutanese citizens faced deprivation of citizenship for sedition. Placement and maintaining one's placement in the national census registry is of central importance to legitimizing and proving one's citizenship. Placement by government workers into census registry categories, which ranged from "Genuine Bhutanese" to "Non-nationals: Migrants and Illegal Settlers," has been arbitrary, and could be arbitrarily changed. In some cases members of the same family have been, and still are, placed in different categories.

Furthermore, only the entries recorded at the*Dzongkhag* (second highest) level are deemed valid; official local *Dungkhag*, *Gewog*, *Chewog* or other civil records are disregarded.

Bhutanese immigration policy, as reflected in its citizenship laws, can be described as highly assimilatory, requiring familiarity with the dominant Ngalop culture and allegiance to the Ngalop King of Bhutan. Its broader citizenship policy toward both immigrants and citizens alike can also be described as assimilatory, and on its face, a tool against dissent.

### History

Historically, there have been at least five distinct waves of human migration into Bhutan: two ancient and three since the 19th century. These migrant groups have, to varying degrees, shaped Bhutanese society, culture, and politics. They have also assimilated into the dominant Tibetan-Ngalop culture to varying degrees, one of the foremost concerns of modern Bhutanese immigration policy.

## SOCIAL CUSTOMS AND TRADITIONS IN BHUTAN

Men and women in Bhutan customarily wear traditional clothing. Clothing for men consists of a gho, which is a garment that wraps around the body like a coat that reaches the knee and is worn with a belt.

The kira is what women wear as a custom. Kira is a garment that is made from a piece of cloth (in the shape of a rectangle) that reaches the ankles. Kira is secured at the shoulders with a clip, while a woven belt holds the garment closed and in place.

It is custom for both sexes to use scarves or shawls and on occasion, men will wear earrings as well. The majority, roughly 75 percent, of Bhutan's population practices Mahayana Buddhism which is similar to Tibetan/Lamaist Buddhism.

After Buddhism, Hinduism is the next most popular religion.

There is a broad range of Hinduism that is practiced ranging from traditional Hinduism to a combination of Buddhism/

Hinduism where gods in both religions are worshipped. Monasteries and convents are common throughout Bhutan. Monks and nuns kept their heads shaved and wore distinguishing maroon robes. Days are spent in study and meditation but also in the performance of rituals honouring various bodhisattvas, praying for the dead, and seeking divine intercession on behalf of the ill. Some of their prayers involved chants and singing accompanied by conch shell trumpets, thighbone trumpets (made from human thighbones), metal horns up to three meters long, large standing drums and cymbals, hand bells, temple bells, gongs, and wooden sticks. Such monastic music and singing, not normally heard by the general public, has been reported to have "great virility" and to be more melodious than its Tibetan monotone counterparts.

Bhutanese have unique lifestyle, manners and customs that are still intact after thousands of years because of its continued policy of keeping itself isolated from the rest of the world. Religion has a big role in the life of the people of Bhutan. Social conventions of Bhutan are very much influenced by the country's state religion. Buddhism and Bonism, the original religion of Tibet have become so integrated with Bhutanese culture that they have become almost inseparable. Most of the Bhutanese people lead an agrarian lifestyle. Men and women share equal rights and there are no rigid clan systems in the nation. You will see all Bhutanese citizens wear national dresses in public, which is made compulsory by law since 1990. Men wear robes called gho while women wear kira in bright colors with ornate brooches and a wraparound skirt.

It is illegal in Bhutan to sell or buy tobacco products and smoking in public places is banned too. The religious leaders of the country have always had much of their say in the political affairs of Bhutan and have been political leaders in the past too. So, the lifestyle conforms to the religious beliefs mostly. The country had isolated itself for years to preserve its uniqueness of culture and to keep its traditions alive but has only recently opening up to the outside world. Bhutanese government however controls the foreign influence with a keen eye and is trying hard to keep it under control. This is the reason the old-world feel in

Bhutan is still intact. Bhutanese inherit strange and peculiar customs that have their origin in the country's history and mythological legends and folk tales of the country.

Giant phalluses painted outside the homes of otherwise conservative and reserved Bhutanese represent the Divine Madman, who is believed to ward off evil spirits. Tipping is not very common in Bhutan and old people relish doma (betel nut) very much. Dogs are treated with reverence in Bhutan as they are considered to be the highest animal life form, with the best chance of being reborn as humans. Thus, you can see dogs run freely and noisily through Bhutanese villages. Keep in mind that the King and royal family is respected very much throughout Bhutan and you should avoid any criticisms or negative comments on them while conversing with the local people. Always pass sacred sites and objects such as mani stones, stupa and other religious objects with your right side nearest to the object. Prayer wheels should only be turned in a clockwise direction.

The Bhutanese people can perceive turning them in the wrong direction as a sign of disrespect. It is considered derogatory and disrespectful to sit on mani stones or stupa, so never do that. Before visiting any sacred site and temples, remember to remove your shoes and hats and wear respectful clothing. Though, it is not compulsory but it is customary to offer a small donation to the monks and Buddhist statues and idols at the monasteries as a sign of respect and is considered as a means of developing a generous and spacious mind. It is not only disrespectful but also illegal to smoke at monasteries and other public places.

## TRADITIONAL BUILDING MATERIALS

Local construction materials and building materials used traditionally in Bhutan to build bridges, chortens, dzongs, houses, palaces, temples, monasteries and even utilitarian items mostly consisted of stone, rammed earth, local timber or wood and bamboo. The construction of the outer walls of palaces, temples, monasteries, stupas and large fortresses along with other buildings used masonry and stone arts. Wood and timber is easily available in Bhutan and is used extravagantly for structural elements including windows, doors, stairs, balconies, columns, beams and ornate decorative cornices to be placed around the upper edges of the structure, just below the roof and above doors and windows. On the lower floors, you will often find very narrow timber windows while larger three-lobed windows can be found at the top floor.

Bhutanese often paint windows and doors profusely in bright colors giving a colourful and festive appearance to their houses and buildings. Colourful paintings using floral, animal and religious motifs are quite common. Wooden flooring and ceilings are quite popular in Bhutan. The 'flying roof' is unique to Bhutanese houses. This type of rood is high and made of wooden shingles kept in place with small stones, thus, leaving a large, open and breezy space just under the roof. Staircase often consists of a single log of wood with ledges cut on one side. Murals and carvings on Lord Buddha and other deities can be seen on walls and altars of religious places in Bhutan and almost every house in the country has a wooden altar with statues of the Buddha and the great gurus.

## BHUTAN PALACES

Palaces were constructed much recently in Bhutan, only after Wangchuck dynasty came to power. Jigme Namgyal, the father of the first king, built some of the first Bhutanese palaces. Most of the palaces were built between 1870 to 1940. During this time, Bhutan had a relatively peaceful and stable period. With the diminishing use of dzongs or fortresses, palaces were built in the Bumthang and Trongsa regions. Similar to a dzong in terms of architecture, the main architectural elements of a Bhutanese palace is the central building that usually had the residence of the master and a private chapel on the upper floor.

A courtyard surrounded this building while the kitchen and the servants' quarters were situated in an outer structure. Elaborate and ornate, places usually had rich and intricate wood work and the windows in the outer building were painted profusely. The most notable palaces in Bhutan are the palaces of Lamey Goemba, Wangdue Choeling and Ugyen Choeling in Bumthang;

Kuenga Rabten and Samdrup Choeling situated south of Trongsa Dzong and the mansions of Gangtey in Paro. Ugyen Pelri Palace built around 1930 in Paro is unique in terms of palatial architecture of Bhutan as it as built on the model of the Zangdopelri (the celestial abode of Guru Rinpoche). Paro Poenlop Tshering Penjor built it.

## TRADITIONAL BHUTANESE HOUSES

Traditional Bhutanese houses serve as a home or residential dwelling for the family, a shelter for domestic livestock, a place for weaving and other household activities and also a religious space. The architecture of vernacular houses in Bhutan has an open or semi-covered courtyard in front of the building, which is used to grow vegetables and other agricultural produce, drying things, as a shelter for the animals and other functions that are performed in the open. Most of the indigenous rural houses are two or three stories high and each level has a unique function. The ground floor is simply a space to keep animals, the living quarters, the family room, the kitchen and the store find their place on the first floor while the religious rituals are performed in the upper storey, which is considered sacred.

Architectural elements and construction materials may vary a bit according to environment and climatic conditions of a place. In most houses in southern Bhutan, spaces are laid out in straight lines in rectangular shapes and walls are either masonry or made up of thick-rammed mud finished with plaster. They have ridged roof and inner walls are made of closely woven bamboo matting. Traditional homes, in the Bumthang area in central Bhutan, are made of stone and sparsely decorated. You can see houses made of bamboo matting and built on stilts in eastern Bhutan. Lungshi, Laya, Lunana yak herders and semi nomadic people of northern Bhutan live in dry stone walled houses. Bhutanese villages are often close hamlets of 5 to 15 houses, as a mutual protection against the wind and cold. Trees are sometimes planted around the village to act as windbreaks.

Typical Bhutanese houses found at altitudes of 1000 to 3000 meters have timber frame structures assembled with a system of pegs. Glass panes are rare in rural Bhutan and sliding wooden shutters are used instead to close the window. The trefoil arches are striking and outer walls are often painted black or brown with motifs such as clouds, lotus flowers or other auspicious signs. Phallic images on the exteriors of Bhutanese homes look startling against conservative Bhutanese background that are painted or carved to chase away demons and bring fertility and prosperity to the household. Elaborate cornices and wide overhanging eaves adorn larger houses. Traditionally, the kitchens had no chimney and smoke escaped through the windows, leaving a thick layer of soot over everything. This protected the wood from insects.

## TEMPLES AND MONASTERIES

Temples in Bhutan are known as Lhakhangs while monasteries are known as Gompas or Goenpas. They are found everywhere in the country, from every valley to every village to almost every mountain.

They serve as the religious centres, as the venue for social and cultural functions and events and as a place for employment for laymen who work as help, artisans and agricultural labourers. Lhakhangs or temples in Bhutan can be a part of a dzong or a monastery as the main and central building or can be a separate building by itself. Some of the most sacred Bhutanese temples are situated outside the boundaries of dzongs and monasteries.

The temples are often surrounded by a courtyard lined with rows of prayer wheels on all four sides and pilgrims revolve them while circumambulating the temple. The courtyard forms the entrance of the temple and you have to cross it to reach the main shrine or the assembly room and the sanctum of the temple. The courtyard is used for communal gatherings, festivals and dance performances. Every temple as 'gonkhangs' or 'chamber of horrors', the secret chamber for Mahakala Vajra Bhairav, the chief protective deity of the Gelukpas. Here, the masks, weapons and skulls used in rituals, are kept. The origin of the gonkhang lies in the mixing of Mahayana tantric Buddhism and older beliefs.

'Dukhangs' in monasteries are large rooms devoted to communal ceremonies and shared meals. Roof of the temple has bell-shaped domes. The number of the domes depends upon the number of shrines attached to the temple. Templesand monasteries have an important place in Bhutanese history and saints and lamas often supervised their construction. Temples were considered to be the home of Gods and monasteries were solitary places where monks used to live and receive spiritual training. Boththe places were used for prayer and meditation.

Temple used to house only a few monks that were responsible for its maintenance and upkeep while monasteries often accommodated large community of over 100 monks who used to study and get trained there. Mani walls, chortens and prayer flags are often found around any religious building in Bhutan and are some of the major architectural elements of temples and monasteries of Bhutan. Like most of the buildings, Bhutan's temple and monastery too are made up of stone or rammed mud. Timber is used in their construction and they have shingle roofs. However, the interiors of these lhakhangs and gompas are quite different from vernacular houses. Walls painted in bright colors with symbols, designs and images of Buddhist deities, lamas and saints make these religious buildings unique. Monasteries may have chapels or lhakhands portraying protective spirits in most fearsome and angry forms that comes as a surprise to most visitors. They represent defenders of religion who can destroy any enemies around us.

The cockerel, snake and pig at the centre of the Wheel of Life symbolize desire, anger and ignorance in our hearts. Some Bhutanese temples are built in unusual shapes though. The Dungtse Lhakhang in the Paro valley, built in 1433, looks like a chorten. Thangtong Gyelpo, the famous chain-bridge builder, built it around a central axis and in the spirit of the mandala. The buildings of temples and monasteries are examples of exquisite architectural skills and fine craftsmanship. Though, the names of most of the founders of dzongs and monasteries are known, records related to the architects, workmen and artists who helped to build them, have not been maintained as the artistic creations in Bhutan are not considered a form of personal expression but the reflection of a shared state of mind.

## CHORTENS ARCHITECTURE IN BHUTAN

Chortens, known as 'stupas' in India, are quite common in the countryside of Bhutan. Thousands of chortens can be found all over the country, at crossroads, near a dzong or a monastery and even on high mountain passes. They range from being very small and just two meters in height to being huge and over ten meters in height. Serene and peaceful, chortens are religious monuments that are built in a precise way and are a receptacle for worship or offering. Chortens were originally built to keep the relics of the Buddha and other Buddhist saints but with time, building a stupa is considered a pious thing to do and the builders and those who pay to make a chorten are believed to earn merit for it. Chorten or a stupa is considered to support faith and represent Buddha's Body.

Chortens or stupas also symbolize the five elements of the Universe. Its square base represents earth, the dome represents water, the shaft represents fire, the crescent represents air and the circle represents ether. One of the five 'Jina' (also known as Dhyani Buddhas or primordial Buddhas) corresponds to each of these elements. For religious and didactic reasons, the chorten has always been an object of faith and devotion for the entire Buddhist world. All the major gompas or monasteries have their own chortens, preserving the remains of the Head or Senior Lama. The walls of the chorten are painted from inside with murals, each telling a different story. Sometimes thick prayer walls called 'mani' connect chortens. Chortens may be built in various ways. The most common one in Bhutan is called 'Khangtseg, that' or house chorten, which is simply a building with a square base, enclosed on all four sides sealing sacred objects and relics inside it and perhaps an ornamental roof.

There is a wooden square known as 'sokshing' that acts as the central post of the chorten, around which it is built. It is adorned and has inscriptions of sacred text representing the vital principle and 'life spirit' of the chorten. While building a chorten, there are special rituals and ceremonies for each stage of work as it commemorates the death (Parinirvana) of the Buddha Sakyamuni and his spiritual progress towards enlightenment.

The other types of chortens are Chendebji or Chorten Kora that follow the model of Bodnath in Nepal, made up of lime washed stone and are huge; smaller Tibetan style chortens; and pure Bhutanese square chortens or stupas with four-sided roofs. The red stripe below the roof called 'khemar' mark the religious nature of chortens, just like dzongs.

## FOLK HERITAGE MUSEUM

Inaugurated by Her Majesty, the Queen Ashi Dorji Wangchuck on 28th July 2001, Phelchey Toenkhyim or the Folk Heritage Museum at Thimphu provides you a glimpse of lifestyle, items and artifacts of Bhutanese villages and rural households. Besides the display, the museum also organizes demonstrations of rural traditions, skills, habits and customs, educational programs for children and research and documentation on rural life of Bhutan. The museum building itself is one of the star exhibits of the library. It is a restored three-storey traditional rammed mud and timber house that resembles the average rural household in the Wang area during the mid-19th century, complete with typical household objects, domestic tools and equipments that were used by rural families of that period.

The age of the building proves how durable and long lasting, the building materials used in those times, were. The activities of the museum follow a seasonal rhythm, just like the activities of a true rural household, offering you something new to see, every time you visit Phelchey Toenkhyim. The rural setting and flavor has been well-preserved and you can see paddy, wheat and millet fields here, a traditional water-mill with mill stones more than 150 years old, traditional style kitchen gardens with vegetables that were grown over the past 100 years and the famous traditional hot stone bath. Native trees and plants that had domestic uses in Bhutanese rural household are being grown here in an effort to keep indigenous knowledge about the use of natural resources alive and have a patch of greenery, right in the heart of the capital city of Thimphu.

Tourists may also avail the special offers of the museum at a nominal fee and advance booking of at least one week. They include demonstrations of the traditional way of extracting oil or Markhu Tsene, brewing ara or Ara Kayne, roasting rice or Zaw Ngowni and pounding rice or Thom Dhungni within the museum premises and organizing an open air buffet lunch and dinner offering a taste of the traditional cuisine at the museum. The menu for such arrangements is available at the Museum and consists of a variety of traditional food items from all parts and regions of the Kingdom of Bhutan. However, lunch and dinner arrangements are only arranged for groups with five or more than five members at a time. Phelchey Toenkhyim or the Folk Heritage Museum at Thimphu closes only on government holidays. The museum remains open from 10:00 am to 4:30 pm from Monday to Friday, from 10:30 am to 1:00 pm on Saturdays and 11:30 am to 3:30 pm on Sundays.

## BHUTANESE CUISINE

Bhutanese cuisine is as varied and splendid as its landscapes and scenic beauty. Cooking methods are given immense importance in Bhutan and every region has its own specialty. Rice is the staple meal with vegetable or meat dishes cooked with chili and cheese often accompanies the meal as a side dish.

Chili dominates all Bhutanese food and if you do not like spicy-hot flavor, be sure to point that out very clearly before you order a meal in Bhutan. The famous traditional vegetarian dishes in Bhutan are 'Ema-Datsi' (literally meaning 'chili and cheese' and the hottest of all the dishes), 'Kewa-Datsi' (comprising of potato, cheese and chili) and 'Shamu-Datsi' (made up of mushrooms, cheese and chili).

'Matar-Paneer' is a North-Indian dish readily available here for vegetarians. You may also like to taste 'Cheese Momos', small steamed buns with cheese, potato and onion and buckwheat cakes that are considered a specialty of the Bumthang area. People of Bhutan also relish Yak meat along with pork, beef, fish, poultry, goat and corn dishes. Daily food of upland people often consists of corn or rice, yak cheese, meat soups and spiced chilies. Tea is quite a popular beverage in Bhutan, though people often prefer butter tea or 'suja' to sweet milk tea. Local beer made from cereal grains, such as rice or corn, is called 'ara' and is very popular among village folk.

Attention to detail and using just the right amount of spices is considered important in Bhutani cuisine. In rural areas, people often use red rice variety as opposed to white rice variety popular in urban areas. Visual attractiveness of the dish is considered important and balance between colors and proportions are paid attention to. Cured and smoked hams are often parts of delicious dishes. Wheat noodles of the east and dried and coarsely ground corn kernels known as 'Kharang' from the south are some of the traditional Bhutanese dishes. People also eat 'Thukpa' or porridge and in traditional feasts, hot eggs and butter are served and 'Ara' is poured over them. In the Kheng region, people eat raw meat people with special drinks. During weddings or traditional Bhutanese gatherings, local cuisine is preferred.

## INDIGENOUS PEOPLES AND ANCIENT MIGRATIONS

### Monpa

The Monpa are a major people of Arunachal Pradesh in northeastern India. Currently they are also one of the 56 officially recognized ethnic groups in China. Most Monpas live in the Indian state of Arunachal Pradesh, with a population of 50,000, centred in the districts of Tawang and West Kameng. Around 25,000 Monpas can be found in the district of Cuona in the Tibet Autonomous Region, where they are known as Menba. Of the 45,000 Monpas who live in Arunachal Pradesh, about 20,000 of them live in Tawang district, where they constitute about 97% of the district's population, and almost all of the remainder can be found in the West Kameng district, where they form about 77% of the district's population. A small number of them may be found in bordering areas of East Kameng and Bhutan (2,500). They also share very close affinity with the Sharchops of Bhutan. Their language belongs to the Tibeto-Burman family, but it is significantly different from the Eastern Tibetan dialect. It is written with the Tibetan script.

The Monpa are sub-divided into six sub-groups because of their variations in their language. They are namely:

- Tawang Monpa
- Dirang Monpa
- Lish Monpa
- Bhut Monpa
- Kalaktang Monpa
- Panchen Monpa.

## Religion

The Monpa are generally adherents of the Gelugpa sect of Tibetan Buddhism, which they adopted in the 17th century as a result of the evangelical influence of the Bhutanese-educated Mera Lama. The testimony to this impact was the central role of the Tawang monastery–which aligns with the Gelugpa tradition–in the daily lives of the Monpa folk. Nevertheless, some elements of the pre-Buddhist Bon faith remained strong among the Monpas, particularly in regions nearer to the Assamese plains. In every household, small Buddhist altars placed with statues of Buddha are given water offerings in little cups and burning butter lamps.

The belief in transmigration of the soul and reincarnation is widespread, as their life is largely centred on the Tawang monastery in Tawang district, where many of the young Monpa boys would join the monastery and grow up as Buddhist Lamas.

The Bhut Monpa led a hunter-gather lifestyle and believed that the main totem and clan idol is the spirit of the tiger, who will torment any initiate while he sleeps. It is also believed that the spirit of the tiger is the manifestation of the ancestral forest spirit, who took a young shaman into the jungle to be initiated.

## Culture

The Monpa are known for wood carving, Thangka painting, carpet making and weaving. They manufactured paper from the pulp of the local sukso tree. A printing press can be found in the Tawang monastery, where many religious books are printed on local paper and wooden blocks, usually meant for literate Monpa

Lamas, who use it for their personal correspondence and conducting religious rituals.

Principal Monpa festivals include Choskar harvest, Losar, Ajilamu and Torgya. During Losar, people would generally pray pilgrimage at the Tawang monastery to pray for the coming of the Tibetan New Year. The Pantomime dances are the principle feature of Ajilamu.

The Buddhist Lamas would read religious scriptures in the Gompas for a few days during Choskar. There after, the villagers will walk around the cultivated fields with the sutras on their back. The significance of this festival is to pray for better cultivation and protect the grains from insects and wild animals. The prosperity of the villagers is not excluded as well.

It is a rule that all animals except men and tigers are allowed to be hunted. According to tradition, only one individual is allowed to hunt the tiger on an auspicious day, upon the initiation period of the shamans, which can be likened a trial of passage. Upon hunting the tiger, the jawbone, along with all its teeth, is used as a magic weapon. This is believed that its power will enable the tigers to evoke the power of his guiding spirit of the ancestral tiger, who will accompany and protect the boy along his way.

## Society

The traditional society of the Monpa was administered by a council which consists of six ministers locally known as *Trukdri*. The members of this council were known as the *Kenpo*, literally the Abbot of Tawang. The Lamas also hold a respectable position, which consists of two monks known as *Nyetsangs*, and two other *Dzongpon*.

The man is the head of the family and he is the one who takes all decisions. In his absence, his wife takes over all responsibilities. When a child is born, they have no strict preference for a boy or a girl. Some, however, prefer a daughter for she stays in the house of her parents once she is married. Her husband is the one who moves to the house of his parents-in-law. The same type of tradition is found among the Khasi tribe of Meghalaya, India.....

## Lifestyle and Dress

The traditional dress of the Monpa is based on the Tibetan Chugba, although woolen coats and trousers may be worn as well. The men wear a skull cap of felt with fringes or tassels. The women tend to wear a warm jacket and a sleeveless chemise that reaches down to the calves, tying the chemise round the waist with a long and narrow piece of cloth. Ornaments include silver rings, earrings made of flat pieces of bamboo with red beads or turquoises are worn as well. One can see a person wearing a cap with a single peacock feather round their felt hats.

Due to the cold climate of the Himalayas, the Monpa, like most of the other Buddhist tribes, construct their house of stone and wood with plank floors, often accompanied with beautifully carved doors and window frames. The roof is made with bamboo matting, keeping their house warm during the winter season. Sitting platforms and hearths in the living rooms are also found in their houses.

## Economy

The Monpa practice shifting and permanent types of cultivation. Cattle, yaks, cows, pigs, sheep and fowl are kept as domestic animals, and meat is hunted using primitive methods.

To prevent soil erosion by planting crops on hilly slopes, the Monpa have terraced many slopes. Cash crops such as rice, maize, wheat, barley, chili pepper, pumpkin, beans, tobacco, indigo and cotton are planted.

## History

Earliest records to the area which the Monpas inhabited today indicated the existence of a kingdom known as Lhomon or Monyul which existed from 500 B.C to 600 A.D. Subsequent years saw Monyul coming under increasing Tibetan political and cultural influence, which was apparent during the years when Tsangyang Gyatso, an ethnic Monpa, became the Dalai Lama. At that time, Monyul was divided into thirty two districts, all of which spanned the areas of Eastern Bhutan, Tawang, Kameng and Southern Tibet. However, Monyul, also known as Tawang Tract remained thinly populated throughout its history. In the 11th century, the Northern Monpas in Tawang came under the influence of Tibetan Buddhism of the Nyingma and Kagyu denominations. It was at this time when the Monpas adopted the Tibetan script for their language. Drukpa missionaries made the presence felt in the 13th century and the Gelugpa, in the 17th century, which most Monpas belong to today.

Monyul remained an autonomous entity, of which local monks based in Tawang held great political power within the community, and direct rule over the area from Lhasa was established only in the 17th century. From this time until the early 20th century, Monyul was ruled by the authorities in Lhasa, and, through them, by the Qing Emperor of China. However, in the 19th century, the area began to interest British India. One of the first British-Indian travellers into Monyul, Nain Singh, who visited the area from 1875-6 noted that the Monpas were a conservative people who shunned off contact with the outside world and were making efforts to monopolise trade with Tibet. Owing to its strategic position, subsequently the British sought to make their political influence felt.

In 1914, Britain and its colonial authorities in India drew the McMahon Line, which they claimed to be the border between Chinese Tibet and British India. The line divided the land in which the Monpas inhabited, and became a source of contention in the subsequent years to come owing to ambiguities to the specific location of the McMahon Line.

In subsequent years, China continued to claim the pre-McMahon border as the border between Tibet and India, while British India gradually established effective control over Monyul south of the McMahon line. Following the independence of India and a change of government in China, the dispute became a major issues in the relations between the People's Republic of China and the Republic of India. The McMahon Line was the effective line of control in this period, though the border was somewhat porous. In 1962, a Chinese military patrol which ventured *south* of the McMahon Line drew a military response from India, which resulted in the Sino-Indian War. During the war, China took effective control of the entire Monyul area south of the McMahon Line as well as some other surrounding areas. However, the war ended with China's voluntary withdrawal north of the McMahon Line. Negotiations on the dispute remain active.

## Notable Monpas

- Tsangyang Gyatso, 6th Dalai Lama
- Geshe Ngawang Tashi Bapu, popularly known as Lama Tashi, Grammy Awards Nominee of the Traditional World Music category in 2006.
- Dorjee Khandu, Chief Minister of Arunachal Pradesh.

Before Tibetans settled Bhutan, much of the region was populated by the aboriginal Monpa who practiced the shamanistic Bon religion. Earliest records to the area which the Monpas inhabited today indicated the existence of a kingdom known as Monyul or Lhomon from 500 BC to 600 AD. Monyul spanned the areas of Eastern Bhutan, Tawang, Kameng and Southern Tibet. However, it remained thinly populated throughout its history. By the 7th century, Monyul had come under increasing Tibetan political and cultural influence. King Songtsen Gampo, who ruled Tibet from AD 627–649, was responsible for the construction of Bhutan's oldest surviving Buddhist temples, the Kyichu Lhakhang in Paro and the Jambay Lhakhang in Bumthang.

The Sharchop (meaning "easterner"), are thought to have migrated next from Assam or Burma during the past millennium. Sharchop is a collective term for the populations of mixed Southeast Asian and South Asian descent found in the eastern districts of Bhutan.

A few other indigenous groups, however, remained largely beyond the pale of Tibetan settlement and cultural influence. Among these are the Tibetan Buddhist Lhop and Hindu Toto peoples in the southwest.

In the seventeenth century, a Tibetan expatriate Drukpa monk, Ngawang Namgyal established a theocratic government independent of political influence from Tibet proper, and premodern Bhutan emerged. Ngawang Namgyal arrived in Bhutan in 1616 seeking refuge from the domination of the Gelugpa sect led by the Dalai Lama in Lhasa. He established a new base in western Bhutan, founding Cheri Monastery at the head of Thimphu valley. In 1627 he built Simtokha Dzong at the entrance to Thimphu valley.

From this dzong he exerted control over traffic between the powerful Paro valley to the west and Trongsa valley to the east. In the 1634 Battle of Five Lamas, Ngawang Namgyal prevailed over the Tibetan and Bhutanese forces allied against him and was the first to unite Bhutan into a single country. He took the title shabdrung, becoming the temporal and spiritual leader of Bhutan. He promulgated a code of law and built a network of impregnable dzongs, a system that helped bring local lords under centralized control and strengthened the country against Tibetan invasions. Thus, more than 1,000 years of Tibetan influence and migration into the region brought about the formation of Bhutan.

Today, the term Ngalop refers to those Bhutanese of ancient Tibetan descent who came to dominate Bhutan culturally and politically. The Ngalop are concentrated in the western and central valleys of Bhutan. They practice mostly Tibetan Buddhism and speak Dzongkha. The Sharchop comprise most of the population of eastern Bhutan. Although long the biggest ethnic group in Bhutan, the Sharchop have largely assimilated into the Tibetan-Ngalop culture.

## SHARCHOP

Sharchop is a collective term for the populations of mixed Southeast Asian and South Asian descent that live in the eastern districts of Bhutan and constitute around 45 percent of the Bhutanese population. They have largely adopted the cultural practices of the Tibet-derived culture of central and western Bhutan. They speak Tshangla, also known as Sharchopkh, a Tibeto-Burman language. Tshangla is also spoken by the Monpa (Menba) national minority across the border in China, where it is classified as a branch of Monpa, distributed in Mêdog, Nyingchi and Dirang. Tshangla is similar to the language of the Kalaktang Monpa.

Most Sharchops follow Tibetan Buddhism with some elements of Bon, although those who live in the Duars follow Animism.

## Immigration from Nepal and India (1600–1958)

Since Bhutan emerged as an independent state, the most significant immigrant groups have been from Nepal and India. These people are collectively called *Lhotshampa* (meaning "southerner"), though a collective name may present an oversimplification because of the diversity within the group. The first reports of people of Nepalese origin in Bhutan was around 1620, when Shabdrung Ngawang Namgyal commissioned Newar craftsmen from the Kathmandu valley in Nepal to make a silver stupa to contain the ashes of his father Tempa Nima.

The next small groups of Nepalese emigrated primarily from eastern Nepal under British Indian auspices in the late nineteenth and early twentieth centuries. The beginning of Nepalese immigration largely coincided with Bhutan's political development: in 1885, Shabdrung Ugyen Wangchuck consolidated power after a period of civil unrest and cultivated closer ties with the British in India. In 1910, the government of Bhutan signed a treaty with the British in India, granting them control over Bhutan's foreign relations.

## Tibetan Refugees in Bhutan (1959)

In 1959, Bhutan granted asylum to several thousand refugees after the Chinese took control of Tibet. The Tibetan refugees were fleeing famine, uprising, suppression, and persecution during Chinese Chairman Mao Zedong's Great Leap Forward. Chinese demographers have estimated that 90,000 Tibetans became refugees. The people of Bhutan deeply sympathized with the refugees and extended assistance as much as possible within their capacity. Those Tibetan refugees renounced the right to return to Tibet were granted Bhutanese citizenship, however the majority told Bhutanese authorities they would like to return to Tibet one day. As a result, they remained refugees.

In 1981, many Tibetan refugees in Bhutan chose to permanently resettle in India and they were allowed to do so.

About half of the initial Tibetan refugees chose to remain in Bhutan and continued to live in these in seven settlements located across Bhutan. The seven Tibetan settlements in Bhutan are: Khunpheling (village of Karche), Namling (village of Badgarnang), Yidmonling (village of Lhongtso), Raptenling, Kunga Rabtenling, Kelsangling, and Kungaling. Most of settlements have a small monastery, a primary school, and a small heath clinic.

In 1998, there were about 1,500 Tibetans living in Bhutan, and in 2007 there were about 1,883.

Life remains relatively difficult for Tibetan refugees in Bhutan. Without a security clearance — something they claim is virtually impossible to obtain — Tibetans cannot get government jobs, enrol their children in higher education or obtain licenses to run private business. Many get around that rule by renting shop licenses off native Bhutanese, but it leaves them in an uncomfortable limbo.

## Immigration from Nepal and India (1959–present)

Immigrants from Nepal and India continued to enter Bhutan with a spurt from the 1960s when Bhutan's first modern 5-year plan began, many arriving as construction workers. Like the prior Nepalese immigrants, they came to be called Lhotshampa, blurring the line between citizens, legal residents, and persons illegally present. From 1961 onward, with Indian support, the government began planned developmental activities consisting of significant infrastructure projects. Uncomfortable with India's desire to bring in large numbers of workers from India, the government initially tried to prove its own capacity by insisting that the planned Thimphu-Phuntsholing highway be done with its own workforce. However, the import of workers from India was inevitable; most Bhutanese worked as farmers and were unwilling to take up the major infrastructure projects. Thus, many skilled and unskilled construction workers from India came to Bhutan, and most were of Nepali origin.

The government traditionally attempted to limit immigration and restrict residence and employment of Nepalese to the southern region. Liberalization measures in the 1970s and 1980s encouraged intermarriage and provided increasing opportunities for public service. The government allowed more internal migration by Nepalese seeking better education and business opportunities. Large-scale assimilation into Tibetan-Ngalop culture, however, has not occurred among the Nepalese as it did among other groups.

By the late 1980s, the Bhutanese government estimated 28 percent of the Bhutanese population were of Nepalese origin, though without distinguishing between earlier and later immigrants. Unofficial estimates of the ethnic Nepalese population ran as high as 30 to 40 percent, constituting a majority in the south. The number of legal permanent Nepalese residents in the late 1980s may have been as few as 15 percent of the total Nepalese population, however.

## BHUTANESE REFUGEES

The Bhutanese refugees are Lhotshampas, a group of people of Nepalese origin, including some Kirat, Tamang, and Gurung peoples. These refugees registered in refugee camps in eastern Nepal during the 1990s claiming to be Bhutanese citizens forcibly expelled from Bhutan.

### Historical Background

The earliest surviving records of Bhutan's history show that Tibetan influence already existed from the 6th century. King Songtsen Gampo, who ruled Tibet from 627 to 649 AD, was responsible for the construction of Bhutan's oldest surviving Buddhist temples, the Kyichu Lhakhang in Paro and the Jambay Lhakhang in Bumthang. Settlement in Bhutan by people of Tibetan origin happened by this time.

The first reports of people of Nepalese origin in Bhutan was around 1620, when Shabdrung Ngawang Namgyal commissioned a few Newar craftsmen from the Kathmandu valley in Nepal to make a silver stupa to contain the ashes of his father Tempa Nima.

During the late 19th Century, contractors working for the Bhutanese government began to organise the settlement of Nepali-speaking people in uninhabited areas of southern Bhutan in order to open those areas up for cultivation. The south soon became the country's main supplier of food. By 1930, according to British colonial officials, much of the south was under cultivation by a population of Nepali origin that amounted to some 60,000 people.

Settlement in Bhutan of large numbers of people from Nepal happened for the first time in the early 20th century. This settlement was encouraged by the Bhutan House in Kalimpong for the purpose of collecting taxes for the government. In the 1930s, the Bhutan House settled 5,000 families of Nepali workers in Tsirang alone. In the 1940s, the British Political Officer Sir Basil Gould was quoted as saying that when he warned Sir Raja Sonam Tobgye Dorji of Bhutan House of the potential danger of allowing so many ethnic Nepalese to settle in southern Bhutan, he replied that "since they were not registered subjects they could be evicted whenever the need arose"

## Bhutan's Citizenship Act of 1958

Toward the end of the reign of the second King Jigme Wangchuck in the 1950s, the numbers of new immigrants had swelled causing tension between the King and the Dorji family in the Bhutan House. Amnesty was given through the Citizenship Act of 1958 for all those who could prove their presence in Bhutan for at least 10 years prior to 1958.

From 1961 onward however, with Indian support, the government began planned developmental activities consisting of significant infrastructure development works. Uncomfortable with India's desire to bring in workers in large numbers from India, the government initially tried to prove its own capacity by insisting that the planned Thimphu-Phuntsholing highway be done with its own workforce.

While the project was a success, completing the 182-kilometer highway in just two years, the import of workers from India was inevitable. With most Bhutanese self-employed as farmers, Bhutan lacked a ready supply of workers willing to take up the major infrastructure projects. This led eventually to the large-scale import of skilled and unskilled construction workers from India. These people were most of Nepali origin who were able to slowly settle down under the guise of the naturalized immigrants. With the pressures of the developmental activities, this trend remained unchecked or inadequately checked for many years. Immigration check posts and immigration offices were in fact established for the first time only after 1990.

## Bhutan's Citizenship Act of 1985

By the 1980s, the government had become acutely conscious not just of widespread illegal immigration of people of Nepali origin into Bhutan, but also of the total lack of integration even of long-term immigrants into the political and cultural mainstream of the country. Most of the immigrants knew very little of the culture of Bhutan and most could not understand any of the local languages including Dzongkha. In the rural areas they remained so "Nepalese" in their culture they were indistinguishable from the Nepalese in Nepal itself. For its part, government officials had long ignored the situation and assumed that most of these people who were most often observed in non-Bhutanese clothes were in fact non-Bhutanese visitors or foreign residents. There was also a perception of a Greater Nepal movement emerging from the Nepali-dominated areas in Nepal, Darjeeling, Kalimpong and West Bengal which the Bhutanese feared as Nepali chauvinism.

Perceiving this growing dichotomy as a threat to national unity, the government promulgated directives in the 1980s that sought to preserve Bhutan's cultural identity as well as to formally embrace the citizens of other ethnic groups in a "One Nation One People" policy. The government implied that the "culture" to be preserved would be that of the various northern Bhutanese groups. To reinforce this movement, the government forced the use of the *Driglam Namzha*, the Bhutanese national dress and etiquette code. This policy required citizens to wear the attire of the northern Bhutanese in public places and reinforced the status of Dzongkha as the national language. Nepali was discontinued as a subject in the schools, thus bringing it at par with the status of the other languages of Bhutan, none of which are taught. Such policies were criticized at first by human rights groups as well as Bhutan's Nepalese economic migrant community, who perceived the policy to be directed against them.

The Citizenship Act of 1985 clarified and attempted to enforce the Citizenship Act of 1958 in order to control the flood of illegal immigration. In 1988, the government conducted its first real census exercise. The basis for census citizenship classifications was the 1958 "cut off" year, the year that the Nepali population had first received Bhutanese citizenship. Those individuals who could not provide proof of residency prior to 1958 were adjudged to be illegal immigrants.

## Bhutan's First Census (1988)

The issue was brought to the fore when the government of Bhutan discovered in its first census the magnitude of the Lhotsampa population.

Lhotsampa of Nepali descent who had been living in southern Bhutan since the late nineteenth and early twentieth centuries were induced to leave Bhutan after the country carried out its first census in 1988.

The government however failed to properly train the census officials and this led to some tension among the public. Placement in the census categories which ranged from "Genuine Bhutanese" to "Non-nationals: Migrants and Illegal Settlers" was often arbitrary, and could be arbitrarily changed. In some cases members of the same family have been, and still are, placed in different categories. The government also attempted to enforce the Bhutanese driglam namzha dress and language code at the same time. These measures combined to alienate even bona fide citizens of Nepali descent. As the census exercise came to an end, the southern border of Bhutan became a hotbed of militancy for several years.

## Interethnic Conflict

Matters reached a climax in September 1990 after organized groups of 10,000 or more ethnic Nepalis from the Indian side of the border organized protest marches in different districts, burned down schools, stripped local government officials of their national attire which they burned publicly, and carried out kidnappings and murders of other ethnic Nepalis who did not join their protests. Some of the organizers of the marches were arrested and detained. They were led by the Bhutan Peoples' Party, a political party and militant group that was subsequently banned by the government. However the Bhutanese government later released most of these detainees. Those with ties to the groups responsible for murders and kidnappings were forced to leave Bhutan, but many other innocent ethnic Nepali citizens were coerced to leave by the angry ethnic Nepali dissidents. The Kyodo News Agency reported the "massacre" of the demonstrators at the hands of the Bhutanese army. This report was reportedly submitted by a Nepali reporter based in Siliguri. The Kyodo News Agency reportedly apologized to the government of Bhutan for the incorrect report even though the government of Bhutan did not demand the apology in writing, not wanting to even acknowledge the claim. In 1989, Tek Nath Rizal, a Lhotshampa and trusted official of the Royal Advisory Council who acted as a chief liaison between the government and the Nepalese population in the south, was also accused of instigating the racial riots in Southern Bhutan and was arrested; he was sentenced to life imprisonment in 1993. In 1998 after being granted a royal pardon, he left for Nepal to form the "People's Forum for Human Rights."

## Refugees Outside Bhutan

A group of several thousand left and settled in refugee camps set up by UNHCR. The UNHCR began to distribute aid to the refugees, it recognized most of the refugees from Bhutan who arrived in Nepal between 1990 and 1993 on a *prima facie* basis Many poor, border-dwelling Nepalese claimed to be refugees as well to receive aid, and within a year the camps population exploded from around 5,000 to 100,000. The Bhutanese refugee issue remains unresolved.

Most of the refugees were received by camps in Nepal which currently have about 103,000 Bhutanese refugees according to UNHCR.

## Resettlement Efforts

The U.S. has offered to resettle 60,000 of the 107,000 Bhutanese refugees of Nepalese origin now living in seven U.N. refugee camps in southeastern Nepal, and began receiving this group in 2008. Five other nations — Australia, Canada, Norway, Netherlands and Denmark — have offered to resettle 10,000 each. New Zealand has offered to settle 600 refugees over a period of five years starting in 2008. As of January, 2009, more than 8,000 Bhutanese refugees were resettled in various countries. Other countries also operate resettlement programs in the camps. Norway has already settled 200 Bhutanese refugees, and Canada has agreed to accept up to 5000 through to 2012.

## TRADITIONAL BUDDHIST ECONOMIC BELIEFS AS REFLECTED IN THE CANON

Buddhism stems from the teachings of Siddhartha Gautama (ca. 566-ca. 483 B.C.E.) sometimes called Gautama Buddha or the Buddha Sakyamuni (the Enlightened sage of the Sakya clan, to which he belonged). Born in what is now southern Nepal, his teachings—called dhamma (a word also meaning truth, law, norm)-focused on penetrating the obvious, visible aspects of life to determine their essential and true aspects. The ultimate aim of the teachings of the Buddha is the attainment of nibbana (understanding of this reality; dispassion; bliss), transcending the rounds of existence or the cycle of rebirth, and leading a life based on such understanding. A noble but less lofty aim is expressed in the doctrine of kamma (moral justice): to live a life such that sufficient merit has been accumulated to be reborn in a better situation to attain nibbana in a later life.

The ethical teachings of the Buddha can only be understood in the light of some of his views about the nature of the world, of which three are of particular relevance for this discussion:

First, all mental and physical phenomena are impermanent and life is a process subject to constant change. Thus, our state of material wealth may not last and we must not develop undue attachment to our possessions.

Second, the nature of causation regulating the movement of this flux is very broad Our actions and attitudes today, as well as our treatment of nature, have a variety of future consequences not only in this life but our succeeding lives as well (this is part of the doctrine of rebirth). Such an approach provides the basis for a "deep ecology." It also means that moral action (which includes both activity and thoughts) on the part of a group can influence the happiness and prosperity of both the group members and the members of the larger community, both in the near and the far future.

Third, in its most essential sense, the self does not exist; and that which we call "self" is the result of a misunderstanding about our separation from nature. Thus self-centred ambition is at best only temporarily satisfying; and we must learn to transcend such base passions as selfishness and greed.

Personal ethics are an important part of the Buddhist doctrine. In his first sermon, the Buddha pronounced the Four Noble Truths dealing primarily with the nature of suffering on this earth and its transcendence.

The fourth truth is that cessation of such suffering requires a person to follow the Noble Eightfold Path, which consists of a set of prescriptions for attitudes and behaviour (discussed below) in our world. Theory and practice (i.e., behaviour in this world) are interrelated; suffering is rooted in sensory craving and attachment; and that attachment is fundamentally a state of bondage to the wheel of rebirth operating according to the inevitable law of cause and effect which bring about a moral justice (kamma). That is, suffering is conditioned by both the mind and behaviour and through right understanding and activity, a new relationship to the world can be fashioned both now and in our future lives.

# Bibliography

Arthur F.: *Buddhism in Chinese History,* Stanford University Press, Stanford, 1959.

Banerji, Aparna: *Traces of Buddhism in South India,* Scientific Book Agency, Calcutta, 1970.

Barua, Dipak Kumar: *Viharas in Ancient India: A Survey of Buddhist Monasteries,* Indian Publications, Calcutta, 1969.

Buddhadasa, Bhikkhu: *Teaching Dhamma by Pictures,* Social Science Association Press of Thailand, Bangkok, 1968.

Chakravarti, Balaram : *A Cultural History of Bhutan,* Chittaranjan, West Bengal, India: Hilltop, 1979.

Clifford, Terry : *Tibetan Buddhist Medicine and Psychiatry: The Diamond Healing,* York Beach, ME: 1984.

Cook, Elizabeth: *Holy Places of the Buddha,* Dharma Publishing, Berkeley, 1994.

Coomaraswamy, Ananda K.: *Elements of Buddhist Iconography,* Harvard University Press, Cambridge, 1935.

Cummings, Mary: *The Lives of the Buddha in the Art and Literature of Asia,* University of Michigan, Ann Arbor, 1982.

Dagyab, Loden Sherap: *Tibetan Religious Art,* Otto Harrassowitz, Wiesbaden, 1977.

Dallapiccola, Anna: *The Stupa: Its Religious, Historical, and Architectural Significance,* Franz Steiner Verlag, Wiesbaden, 1980.

Daniel L. : *Folk Buddhist Religion: Dissenting Sects in Late Traditional China,* Cambridge, MA: Harvard University Press, 1976.

Das, Nirmala : *The Dragon Country: The General History of Bhutan,* Bombay: Orient Longman, 1974.

David P. : *Tibetan Thangka Painting: Methods and Materials,* London: Serindia Publ., 1984.

Davidson, J. Leroy: *The Lotus Sutra in Chinese Art,* Yale University Press, New Haven, 1954.

Dehejia, Vidya: *Discourse in Early Buddhist Art: Visual Narratives of India,* Munshiram Manoharlal, Delhi, 1997.

Della Santina, Peter : *Madhyamaka Schools in India,* Delhi: Motilal Banarsidass, 1995.

Dowman, Keith : *Masters of Mahamudra: Songs and Histories of the Eighty-Four Buddhist Siddhas,* Albany, NY: State University of New York Press, 1985.

Dumoulin, Heinrich: *Zen Buddhism: A History,* MacMillan, New York, 1988.

Dunnell, Ruth W.: *The Great State of White and High: Buddhism and State Formation in Eleventh-Century Xia,* University of Hawai'i Press, Honolulu, 1996.

Gehlek, Rinpoche Nawang : *Good Life, Good Death: Tibetan Wisdom on Reincarnation,* New York: Riverhead Books, 2001.

Goldstein, Melvyn C. : *The Snow Lion and the Dragon: China, Tibet and the Dalai Lama,* Berkeley, CA: University of California Press, 1997.

Grant, Beata : *Mount Lu Revisited: Buddhism in the Life and Writings of Su Shih,* Honolulu, HI: University of Hawaii Press, 1994.

Gregory Schopen : *Essays on Buddhism and Chinese Religion,* Oakville, Ontario: Mosaic Press, 1992.

Hayashi, Yukio : *Practical Buddhism among the Thai-Lao: Religion in the Making of a Region,* Melbourne: Trans Pacific Press, 2004.

Hopkins, Jeffrey : *Reflections on Reality: The Three Natures and Non-Natures in the Mind-Only School,* Berkeley, CA: University of California Press, 2002.

James P.: *Karma and Rebirth in Classical Indian Traditions,* University of California Press, Berkeley, 1980.

Kanai Lal *: Buddhism in India : A Historical Survey,* Buddhist World Press, 2009.

Kenneth W.: *The Path of the Buddha,* Ronald Press, New York, 1974.

Michael H.: *The Shambhala Dictionary of Buddhism and Zen,* Shambhala, Boston, 1991.

Murcott, Susan: *The First Buddhist Women,* Parallax Press, Berkeley, 1991.

Nyanaponika Thera: *The Heart of Buddhist Meditation,* Samuel Weiser, New York, 1973.

Pal, Pratapaditya: *Light of Asia: Buddha Sakyamuni in Asian Art,* County Museum of Art, Los Angeles, 1984.

Prothero, Stephen R.: *The White Buddhist: The Asian Odyssey of Henry Steele Olcott,* Indiana University Press, Bloomington, 1996.

Pye, Michael: *Skilful Means: A concept in Mahayana Buddhism,* Duckworth, London, 1978.

Rabten, Geshe : *The Preliminary Practices of Tibetan Buddhism,* Burton, WA: Tusum Ling Publ., 1974.

Rawson, Philip: *The Art of Southeast Asia,* Praeger, New York, 1967.

Ray, Reginald A.: *Buddhist Saints in India: A Study in Buddhist Values and Orientations,* Oxford University Press, Oxford, 1994.

Reedy, Chandra L. : *Himalayan Bronzes: Technology, Style, and Choices,* London: Associated University Presses, 1997.

Robert C.: *Theravada Buddhism in Southeast Asia,* University of Michigan Press, Ann Arbor, 1973.

Roger Warner: *Angkor: The Hidden Glories,* Houghton Mifflin, Boston, 1990.

Shaw, Miranda: *Passionate Enlightenment: Women in Tantric Buddhism,* Princeton University Press, Princeton, 1994.

Singer, Jane Casey : *Tibetan Art: Towards a Definition of Style,* London: Laurence King/Alan Marcuson, 1997.

Sopa, Geshe Lhundub : *Cutting through Appearances: Practice and Theory of Tibetan Buddhism,* Ithaca, NY: Snow Lion, 1989.

Stcherbatsky, Theodore: *The Central Conception of Buddhism and the Meaning of the Word "Dharma",* Royal Asiatic Society, London, 1923.

Stephan V. : *The Cult of Tara: Magic and Ritual in Tibet.* Berkeley, CA: University of California Press, 1973.

Tsomo, Karma Lekshe: *Sisters in Solitude: Two Traditions of Buddhist Monastic Ethics for Women,* State University of New York Press, Albany, 1996.

Wagle, Narendra: *Society at the Time of Buddha,* Humanities Press, New York, 1967.

Warder, A. K.: *Outline of Indian Philosophy,* Motilal Banarsidass, Delhi, 1971.

Weidner, Marsha: *Latter Days of the Law: Images of Chinese Buddhism, 850-1850,* University of Hawai'i Press, Honolulu, 1994.

Welch, Holmes : *The Buddhist Revival in China,* Cambridge, MA: Harvard University Press, 1968.

Zürcher, Erik: *Buddhism, Its Origin and Spread in Words, Maps, and Pictures,* E. J. Brill, Leiden, 1959.

# Index

**T**



**V**



**W**



**Y**



**Z**



❑❑❑